RETURN TO REASON

RETURN TO REASON

Stephen Toulmin

HARVARD UNIVERSITY PRESS

CAMBRIDGE, MASSACHUSETTS

LONDON, ENGLAND   2001

Library of Congress Cataloging-in-Publication Data

Toulmin, Stephen Edelston.
Return to reason / Stephen Toulmin.
p. cm.
Includes bibliographical references and index.
ISBN 0-674-00495-7 (alk. paper)
1. Reasoning. I. Title.
BC177.T596 2001
128'.33—dc21   00-047186

Contents

Preface

I T IS A PLEASURE to recognize the debt I owe to Isaiah Berlin, who unwittingly set me off on the inquiries of which this book is a belated fruit. In 1948 he invited me—as a young research fellow of King's College, Cambridge—to spend time at our sister college, New College, Oxford, where he was the Philosophy Tutor; there he told me in terms that I never forgot that, for Anglo-American philosophers, the History of Ideas was a *non*-subject. Since that time he has shown that a historical grasp of social, political, and scientific ideas is indispensable if we are to make sense, either of Modernity in general, or of Modern Philosophy in particular.

Isaiah's insights remained with me during the years when I was working in the history and philosophy of science, and underlie my concerns in the present book. This work extends into the social, economic, and practical realms the critique of theory to which I was led by a Wittgensteinian approach to the physical or biological sciences, and by the historical reinterpretation of the seventeenth-century Scientific Revolution that is the core of my book *Cosmopolis*. To sum up the central themes of the present book, let me quote a radio talk on "Political Judgement," which Isaiah gave for the BBC Third Programme on June 19, 1957. The idea that political science rests on laws and experiments like those of physics, he said, "was the notion, either concealed or open, of both Hobbes and Spinoza, each in his own fashion—and of their followers—a notion that grew more powerful in the eighteenth and nineteenth centuries, when the natural sciences acquired enormous prestige, and attempts were made to maintain that anything not capable of being reduced to a natural science could not properly be called knowledge at all."[1] Quite the reverse, he continued:

"The arts of life—not least of politics—as well as some among the human studies turn out to possess their own special methods and techniques, their own criteria of success and failure . . . Bad judgement here consists not in failing to apply the methods of natural science, but, on the contrary, in over-applying them . . . To be rational in any sphere, to apply good judgement in it, is to apply those methods which have turned out to work best in it . . . [To demand anything else] is mere irrationalism."[2]

      In the fifty years since my visit to Oxford, I have incurred plenty of other debts—more than I can redeem here. Aside from Ludwig Wittgenstein's classes and R. G. Collingwood's writings, I was directed to questions about practical wisdom by the urgent concerns of my friends in the fields of Medicine—especially Mark Siegler and Christine Cassell—in Engineering—notably Albert Danielsson in Stockholm and Yoichi Arai in Tokyo—and in Action Research—particularly Björn Gustavsen and his colleagues at the Swedish National Institute for Working Life. In all of these areas, I recognize an intellectual kinship with Hans van Beinum in Sweden, Claude Faucheux in France, and Richard Ennals of Kingston University in England, as well as the benefit of continuing exchanges with my colleagues and co-authors, Allan Janik, Albert Jonsen, and Richard Rieke. Parts of this book have been published previously in a different form: the chapter on Method, for instance, revisits an essay in the book *Beyond Theory*, from the John Benjamins series, *Dialogues on Work and Innovation*.

Working with the National Commission for the Protection of Human Research Subjects in Bethesda, Maryland, taught me a lot about case methods in Medicine and Ethics, and led me to reread Aristotle's *Nicomachean Ethics* in a new, clinical light. This reading was reinforced by reflection on the essays of William Gass. A dispute with Harry Johnson in the 1960s about the justification of government science policy, in Edward Shils's journal *Minerva*, led me to despair over current economic theory; but later I regained enough confidence to revive my criticism of the methods of economic theory, with the help first of BDO Groningen, for which I lectured in 1995, next of Kenneth Mischel, Joseph Heilbronner, and colleagues at a symposium held at Baruch College, New York, and chiefly from my daughter Camilla, of the International Institute for Environment and Development, who does what she can to rescue me from my worst confusions about applied economics and the work of nongovernmental organizations.

For several years, I have been meeting with Ton Meijknecht of the Delft Institute of Technology to discuss the moral problems facing engineers and technologists in their professional life; his deep questions about the standards involved in these disciplines are a constant challenge. In revising this book, I had constructive comments from Steve Fuller, Nancey Murphy, and notably Steve Shapin, who urged me—not wholly successfully—to soften my criticism of the risks of the disciplinary rigor that shapes the departmental life of our universities.

Academics who criticize the Academy, of course, put themselves at risk. Few people are as helpful to us as the students we encounter in our colleges or universities, whose graduate work we oversee: here, let me mention Nancy Baker, Jim Block, Daniel Herwitz, Mike Hickey, Robert Nelsen, Lisa Raphals, and above all Richard Schmitt, who has been a continual source of useful references. At the last moment, too, my good friend Jack Bemporad saved me from some foolish errors.

Institutionally, I have in recent years received important support from the Henry R. Luce Foundation and the National Endowment for the Humanities, which chose me as Jefferson Lecturer for 1997; also from Clare Hall, Cambridge, and the Tanner Trustees, as well as more colleagues than I can enumerate at the University of Chicago, Northwestern University, and the University of Southern California. Without the help of Morty Schapiro and his fellow Deans in the College of Letters, Arts, and Sciences at U.S.C., little of what I do here would have been achieved.

Gerald Holton made possible my move to the United States in the 1960s, and our like-mindedness has always been an encouragement. Marx Wartofsky and Robert Cohen, with their Boston Colloquium for the Philosophy of Science—always the wild card in an over-formal scene—have provided friendly and collegial support to all those of us who were willing to cross academic boundaries in the pursuit of a broadly-based understanding of the varied enterprises of science. Their friendships are something the rest of us never forget.

Joyce Seltzer, my editor at the Free Press and later at Harvard University Press, knows how far she is responsible for what merits this book—like *Cosmopolis*—may prove to have: at every stage in its conception and development her keen intelligence and tact have helped me to write a book that technical readers should take to heart, yet non-technical ones can enjoy. Not least, Holly Hebert of WordsWorth at Los Feliz, Los Angeles, took on the work of producing a publishable text: her enthusiastic response to this task made me feel that I had succeeded in doing what we had all aimed to do.

They will get it straight one day at the Sorbonne.
We shall return at twilight from the lecture,
Pleased that the irrational is rational.

Wallace Stevens, *Notes toward a Supreme Fiction*,
X, ll. 16–18

I

Introduction: Rationality and Certainty

Intellectuals in the year 2000—philosophers or social scientists, literary critics or economists—have inherited a family of problems about the idea of Rationality and its relations to those of necessity and certainty. But they tend to ignore the more practical, complementary idea of Reasonableness, or the possibility of living, as in pre-modern times, without any absolute necessities or certainties.

I N THE TWENTIETH CENTURY, scholars in the universities of Europe, North America, and their zone of influence have been preoccupied with the concept of *rationality*: preoccupied, at times, to the point of obsession. This is true in academic philosophy, the behavioral and social sciences, and even—more recently—across the whole spectrum of academic fields, from the physical sciences at one pole to the humanities at the other. As a result, subjects like comparative literature, linguistics, and aesthetics have refocused on methodological questions about the legitimacy of ideas and ways of thought whose validity they had previously taken for granted.

Eighty or ninety years ago, scholars and critics, as much as natural scientists, shared a common confidence in their established procedures. The term "scientific method" embraced, for them, all the methods of observation, deduction, generalization, and the rest that had been found appropriate to the problems and issues preoccupying those subjects. How little of that confidence remains today! Among some humanists, the phrase "scientific method" is even pronounced with a sarcastic or ironic tone; and one even hears it argued that the concept of rationality itself is no more than a by-product of Western or Eurocentric ways of thinking. From its earlier dominance, through a period of doubts and difficulties between the two world wars, to the downright skepticism of contemporary debate, the claims of rationality have been progressively challenged, to the point of being sidelined.

In focusing attention on *rationality*, however, whether to praise it or to challenge it, academic writers have neglected to analyze the complementary concept of *reasonableness*. In the World Academy (it seems) the term "rationality" can amount to anything, only if it amounts to everything: otherwise, it will amount to nothing, and the claims made on its behalf will become absurd. Only in the last few years, in this respect, has the tide turned. In medical ethics, ecology, and other practical fields, the years since the 1960s have seen a revived interest in questions about values that for a while had come to appear foreign even to philosophy. This turning of the tide points to a future in which the rational demands of scientific technique will be balanced by attention to the demands of the human situations in which intellectual or practical skills can reasonably be put to use. ✓

For now, however, the spotlight remains on the intellectual validity of Rationality itself: the human values of Reasonableness are expected to justify themselves in the Court of Rationality. The question has not yet been generally accepted in the Academy—let alone any answer agreed upon—whether the twin concepts of "rationality" and "reasonableness" are not interdependent ideas, of comparable authority and philosophical interest. Indeed, it is not always recognized that the two ideas can be distinguished. Some European languages use only one word for both concepts. In German, for instance, a single word (*Vernünftigkeit*) serves as a translation of both English words; you may hear the word *Rationalität* uttered in seminars devoted to the discussion of Anglo-American philosophy, but it does not have any lexicographical standing except as a technical barbarism.[1]

How do these two concepts differ from, and relate to, each other? And how did we reach a point at which they came to be at cross-purposes with each other? On its face, this is a historical problem, to be answered in historical terms. Yet on what level, and in what kind of terms? In his noted book *A History of Civilizations*, Fernand Braudel has distinguished three different levels of narrative and analysis. On the day-to-day level of *events*, the traditional historian "hovers from one event to the next like a chroni-

2

cler of old or a reporter [but] too often leaves us unsatisfied, unable to judge or to understand." On a second level of *episodes*, which typically last "ten, twenty or fifty years," facts are grouped, interpreted, or explained as forming (say) the French Revolution, the rise of Romanticism, or the First World War. These may still include "events of long duration," but they are "stripped of superfluous detail" and so given explanatory force.

Still, there is another, much longer term perspective:

> At this level, the movement of history is slow and covers vast
> reaches of time: to cross it requires seven-league boots. On this
> scale, the French Revolution is no more than a moment, how-
> ever essential, in the long history of the revolutionary, liberal
> and violent destiny of the West. Voltaire, likewise, is only a
> stage in the evolution of free thought.

On this final level—what Braudel calls *la longue durée*—civilizations are distinct from the accidents and vicissitudes that mark their development. Any historian who embarks on this kind of analysis launches himself into "blue-water cruising on the high seas of time, rather than prudent coastal navigation never losing sight of land." This adventure is only to be undertaken circumspectly. To this day, professional historians do not agree on whether Arnold Toynbee's *Study of History* successfully avoided the same weaknesses and risks as those of Braudel, or whether, like Oswald Spengler's *Decline of the West*, it was uncritically over-enthusiastic. If we are to be put out onto the ocean here, we will not go too far beyond the horizon, but will remain, like Braudel, within the reach of the coastal lights by which we can check our navigation.[2]

The sudden loss of confidence in our traditional ideas about rationality in the last twenty or thirty years is marked enough, and widespread enough, to constitute (in Braudel's terms) an episode, not just a collection of contemporary events: many writers today refer to it as the End of Modernity. Dagmar Barnouw, for instance, has referred to this change as the development of a "post-culture":

> The 20th century has been the age of the aftermath:
> post-modern equals post-war, post-holocaust, post-colonial,
> post-gender, post-history, and, most important for the cultural
> critic's enterprise, post-'master narrative.'[3]

To write about the change in such terms is at once to relate it to the historical development we know as Modernity itself: as to that, the question is still arguable whether Modernity is part of the long march of human destiny, or "only a stage in the evolution of free thought." Here I shall be primarily concerned with the relations between changes in our twentieth-century ways of thinking and the longer-term episode of Modernity, from the late sixteenth century to the present day. But I shall also look, from time to time, at some "deep water" questions, with a time scale closer to three thousand years. How far, then, do the leading themes of Modern Thought and Practice harmonize with the longer-term histories of philosophy and human self-understanding generally? And in what ways have European thought and action over the last four hundred years been at odds with that longer journey?

Looking at the phases which our confidence in rationality and scientific method has passed through during the twentieth century, we can identify several stages. Trust in the procedures of intellectual inquiry went hand in hand with a view of language and meaning as embodied in "propositions" that represent "facts" in the world. Colloquially, this idea is captured in the everyday statement, "The cat is on the mat," which reports a situation that we can instantly visualize; technically, it is captured by Ludwig Wittgenstein's statement, *Wir machen uns Bilder der Tatsachen* ("We create representations of facts for ourselves").[4] Seen from this point of view, language is an enterprise in which, among other things, we fashion representations of situations, or states-of-affairs, and rational inquiry helps us find the truth about these situations by examining the relations between such observations and the hypotheses to which investigation leads us.

The key word in that sentence is "relations"; and the stages through which the idea of rationality has passed reflect changes in our assumptions about those relations. For the Vienna Circle philosophers of the 1920s and 1930s, and the logical empiricists who continued their work in the United States after World War II, they were *logical* relations in a narrowly formal sense of the term. Scientists advanced their speculations as hypotheses, and these could be accepted as established truths if and only if they were supported by sufficient evidence. Both hypotheses and evidence were presented in propositions, and the task for philosophers was one of "inductive

4

logic": analyzing the formal links between hypotheses on the one hand, and reports of evidence on the other. Very varied accounts were given of the formal relations required to show that a hypothesis was rationally adequate; the terms "verification," "falsification," and "corroboration" (inter alia) were used to mark the differences between these accounts.[5]

The formal relation between evidence and hypotheses was, however, only one of the central issues for the new Inductive Logic. In addition, there were questions about the relations between the propositions within any scientific theory. As to that, there was little disagreement among the Viennese philosophers of science or their post-war successors. Initially, they all took it for granted that scientific theories can be formulated as axiomatic systems, on the model of Euclid's *Elements of Geometry*, with statements of principle serving as axioms, and factual observations being interpreted as deductions from those principles in the given situation. Logicians thus had the authority both to judge the validity of theoretical systems and to measure their evidential support; and the solutions to both sets of problems were to be given in the formal Euclidean style.

One aim of the present book (let me say right away) is to show the error of both these views. Despite Newton's reliance on a Euclidean model in his mathematical theory of dynamics, Euclid's geometry was never a good model for scientific theories in general; nor can one give a good general account of the relations among observations and theories by treating them as formal relationships between different propositions. On the contrary, we can establish formal relations between observations and the hypotheses they support only after those observations are massaged into theoretical terms. As for the cult of axiomatics, which was popular among American social and behavioral scientists up to the 1950s, this was ill-adapted to the needs of such disciplines, and they are now learning to cultivate their links with the Biological Sciences rather than with Newtonian Physics alone.

The major break with this approach—what is widely referred to as the "positivist" approach—came with the success of Thomas Kuhn's widely admired book, *The Structure of Scientific Revolutions*. Not that Kuhn was by any means the first to present a serious critique of the positivist philosophy of science. The Polish pathologist Ludvik Fleck and Wittgenstein's pupil W. H. Watson both presented strongly worded alternatives in the years before the Second World War, but there was little audience for their criticisms until the 1950s. Even so, Kuhn's attack on the standard approach did not go very far. His book would have best been called *Revolutions in the Structure of Science*. He did not seek to undercut the Euclidean assumption that theories should have a logical structure; he argued only that they are from time to time subject to drastic reconstructions, after which they take on different axiomatic structures. (The modesty of his argument became clear in the second edition of his book, where he explained that he had only meant to underline the fact that there are no purely deductive relations between pre- and post-revolutionary theories: after all, he added, is this not the difference between "deduction" and "induction"?)[6]

It took a second step to break more effectively with the positivist approach to the natural sciences. This came with the philosophers' growing realization that changes in our basic scientific concepts involve more than changes in the logical structures of theories. During much of the 1960s, the central issue under discussion was the problem of conceptual change. How can we offer a "rational" account of this process, if we give up the formal methods of Viennese inductive logic? The underlying motto was Hilaire Belloc's maxim, "always to keep hold of Nurse / for fear of meeting something worse": formal logic gave philosophers of science the reassurance that irrationalism might yet be avoided, though many, even R. G. Collingwood, concluded that on a deep level conceptual changes must be explained in *causal*, not *rational*, terms. (Being ahead of the game, Collingwood advanced powerful arguments to this effect in his *Essay on Metaphysics* before the Second World War, and was attacked for being a Marxist!)[7]

As a result of fresh interactions between philosophers and historians of science in the 1960s, another stream joined with this one. So long as George Sarton at Harvard ruled over academic History of Science in the United States, collaborating with philosophers was taboo. This separation of the disciplines suited those logicians who were anxious to defend the historical immutability of Reason and Rationality. They were only too happy to follow Gottlob Frege's injunctions to avoid the "historicist" fallacy: it took a level head to keep the conceptual change debate in the middle of the road between formal logic and historical relativism.[8]

At this point, the argument was already on the verge of the skepticism I noted at the outset. Perhaps it was always an illusion to believe that people from different cultures can understand one another's scientific theories any more than can people from different historical periods. If that were so, is it even clear that people from the same culture at the same time are capable of reaching intellectual consensus? In this way the idea of rationality became as open to idiosyncrasy as those of justice or morality. (Alasdair MacIntyre's book title, *Whose Justice, What Rationality?*, says it all.)[9]

This is my reading of the historical phases by which the rationality debate reached definitive form in the years from the 1920s to the 1990s. My aim in the chapters that follow will be to steer a middle way, and to show how the idea of Reasonableness lets us keep on an even keel. Yet one preliminary question must be addressed: what kind of evidence or testimony can we rely on in these chapters? Here let me forestall the objection that I am falling into a foreseeable trap, of substituting autobiographical recollections for an analysis of the changes involved in eighty years of intellectual history. Such a criticism misses the point. By now, the challenges to the concept of rationality are so extreme that a theoretical analysis of the period will carry "rational" conviction for only a small cadre of readers. The only way to proceed, therefore, is to go behind all the rival theoretical positions and present a narrative with a personal perspective. Yet what can such a personal narrative do for us? Will not my personal background and standpoint inevitably slant it? So how can I claim to be throwing light on the history of twentieth-century thought "as it really happened"?

This objection can be undercut at the outset in philosophical terms. The view that each of us has of the events through which we have lived is inevitably *incomplete*, but that is not the same as being *slanted*: that is, biased to the point of actual distortion. So the claim that there is no way to avoid bias or distortion—that a man can never appreciate a woman's point of view, a Christian a Buddhist's, an Albanian a Serb's—elevates a practical problem to the level of an outright impossibility. Instead, we may state the point in anthropological terms: if the following account relies, as it sometimes will, on my memory of events and changes, it does so for ethnographic, not egotistical, reasons. I shall treat myself here as a "native informant" whose testimony is sufficiently reliable for present purposes, even if it is not supported by the costly data collection and analysis that some sociologists would prefer. Let the resulting narrative stand on its own, for what it is. Others will tell the same story differently, and these differences may be illuminating; but, under the circumstances, a vast amount of statistically backed documentation would at best increase the bulk of the argument, without adding to its weight. If the general outlines of the story are sound, that is all that our present purposes demand.

It remains to make explicit the angle from which my story is told; this will answer the question that reentered intellectual debate in the 1960s, "Where are you coming from?" It was no accident that the question of alternative perspectives emerged out of the world of colloquial conversations and personal exchanges of opinion, not in the formal realm of the Academy: in academic debates, we are always challenged to frame our arguments in terms appropriate to one discipline or one forum of argument rather than another, not in general nondisciplinary terms or in ways open to a lay public. Like individuals, academic disciplines have their chosen perspectives, and this selectivity may have the effect of needlessly limiting our chosen arguments.

Very well then: I shall not adopt the standpoint of any one particular discipline. When my friend Marx Wartofsky wrote an essay on my work, he said—out of affection, rather than as a criticism—"Toulmin is an odd duck"; and this description was wryly apt.[10] Long before entering the professional world of philosophy or social science, I was exposed to two influences whose effects were too powerful to ignore. On the one hand, I came to academic philosophy at a time when its arguments were unusually *ahistorical*. The most influential philosopher active at Cambridge in 1945 was Wittgenstein, and his only known comment on History is the solipsistic question, "What is History to me? Mine is the first and only World."[11] Like his colleagues C. D. Broad and R. B. Braithwaite, Wittgenstein's predecessor in the Chair of Philosophy, G. E. Moore, displayed a little more knowledge of his forerunners' views than Ludwig Wittgenstein himself, but he too gave no sign of believing that the soundness of philosophical arguments depended at all on the situation in which they were presented. On the contrary, Moore attacked John Stuart Mill's discussion of the relations between the "desirable" and the "desired" in a way that treated it as a matter of rival dictionary definitions, and completely ignored the role that Mill's *Utilitarianism* had played in nineteenth-century British social history.[12]

By contrast, I was born into a family where History was a matter for dinner table conversation. If my father had come of age after instead of before the First World War, he would himself have been an economic historian;

as it was, before I went to Cambridge, he introduced me to the varieties of History, from Arnold Toynbee's *Study of History* to J. L. Motley's *Rise of the Dutch Republic*. With this background, it was a relief, later on, to discover the books of R. G. Collingwood, who was a philosopher and historian at the same time. (Collingwood was the "odd duck" in 1930s Oxford.) Most significant of all was the fact that my family lived in the shadow of the Nobel Peace Laureate Norman Angell, with whom my father worked before the First World War, and we continued to see N. A. throughout the 1920s and 1930s. (If any book could have prevented the outbreak of the 1914–1918 War, it would have been Angell's *The Great Illusion*, published in 1910, which argued that such a war would leave all the great powers of Europe equally as losers.)

On the other hand, my own interests took me in the direction of theoretical physics, notably cosmology, rather than academic philosophy. As a teenager in the mid-1930s I would sit in bed reading books with titles like *The Restless Universe* or *The Infinite Universe*: the idea of a single theory that could grasp the whole World of Nature had for me a charm that was as much aesthetic as intellectual, and the question how to tell if any particular theory was "correct" did not for the time being strike me as urgent.[13] In the 1930s the idea of a *chaotic* Universe was not yet taken seriously. Physicists still took it for granted that the World of Nature operated "regularly"; and, as the Greeks supposed, the heavens formed a *cosmos*—well ordered or "cosmetic."[14] Cosmological speculation also appeared intellectually "pure" and unaffected by technological concerns or commitments. Theoretical physics in the 1930s was still—as the seventeenth-century founders of modern science had called it—"natural philosophy"; engineering and manufacture, in which scientific ideas were applied to human needs and problems, were seen as separate and largely inferior activities.

I was not alone in this intellectual snobbery. A sharp distinction between the pure and applied sciences was a feature of scientific culture right up to the Second World War. In January 1939, the Irish Marxist crystallographer John Desmond Bernal published his book *The Social Function of Science*, and his colleagues rejected it as politically radical: though Bernal's arguments quoted the works of Francis Bacon from the early seventeenth century, he was pilloried by Michael Polanyi and John Baker as an enemy of democracy, and they set up a Society for Freedom in Science to defend scientists against any need to rely on government or industry to finance their research.[15]

Then, in 1942, I was posted to a government research establishment working on radar for the Royal Air Force, where my clumsiness soon taught me that I would never be a successful experimentalist. So, in 1946, I followed my inclinations and went to study at Cambridge during Wittgenstein's last years as Professor. I found myself in a dilemma. All the books and papers I was given to read on the philosophy of science seemed to have been written by mathematicians *manqués*: they were concerned only with the formal consistency or logical coherence of theoretical arguments in physics, and they paid little attention to the question whether such arguments were practically applicable to the world that we live in and seek to understand. By contrast, my experience of physicists-at-work had taught me this: that such formal arguments must, at least, be seen by members of the scientific community as having a bearing on the world that we deal with. From the outset I was pulled in two ways, between philosophers, who framed any claim to knowledge in propositional form—as made up of statements whose meaning was evident on their faces—and working scientists, who left the practical bases of knowledge unstated, and thought them none the worse for that.

When I went to Oxford University to lecture on the philosophy of science in 1949, I was struck by a related dilemma. A few philosophy teachers at Oxford had developed a sensitive feeling for intellectual history and the history of ideas; but they too had the same experience of being pulled in two directions. Collingwood died in 1943, still with a sense of being an outsider among Oxford philosophers. Stuart Hampshire wrote fine essays on the history of moral ideas in Sainte-Beuve and others, but in a style quite at odds with that in which he wrote about moral philosophy. Isaiah Berlin's own lectures on political philosophy are at last fully appreciated in the 1990s, for their blend of historical depth and philosophical perception; but he himself had continued to live with an active doubt about whether he was really a "philosopher" at all![16]

       That, then, is where I was coming from as I wrote my first three books. *Reason in Ethics* was my doctoral thesis at Cambridge; it entered the world in 1949 and was continuously in print for thirty-seven years. (When I worked with Albert Jonsen on our book about case reasoning in ethics in the mid-1980s, I was amazed to find that Benjamin Nelson's article on "Casuistry" for the *Encyclopedia Britannica* linked *Reason in Ethics* with John Austin's famous essay, "A Plea for Excuses," as prefiguring a revival of interest in such reasoning.) Next, in 1953, I published a slim book entitled *The Philosophy of Science*, which compared the explanatory power of scientific theories—especially physics—with maps for finding a way around Nature, rather than formal axiom systems of propositions. Finally, in 1958, I set out to broaden my position from ethics and physics to reasoning procedures generally, in *The Uses of Argument*. Peter Strawson brushed this book aside in the BBC's weekly, *The Listener*, while one of my colleagues at Leeds called it "Toulmin's anti-logic book." Later, I was sorry to discover that the book had wounded my *Doktorvater* at Cambridge, Richard Braithwaite, since he read it as an attack on his own basic positions.

At the end of the dispute, the central issue remained what it had been at the start: Are the *meanings* philosophers set out to analyze embodied in isolated verbal propositions, or is language intelligible only as having a meaning within the larger framework of actions and institutions? As it was, *The Uses of Argument* went on selling, despite being condemned by British philosophers. It took time to find that scholars in the field of Communication read it as a theory of "argumentation": that is, language as working in human situations, not by way of "desituated" propositions, divorced from the larger patterns of human life.[17]

In this situation, there began the series of critiques that, over the next forty years, demolished the confidence in Rationality with which philosophers and scientists had begun the twentieth century. The year 1958 saw the appearance not just of *The Uses of Argument*, but of Peter Winch's book, *The Idea of a Social Science*. Three years later, Kuhn's *Structure of Scientific Revolutions* put into general circulation the idea that our criteria of rationality change from one stage in the history of a science to the next. In the 1970s this critique was extended from history into sociology and anthropology: this development is summarized in the essays collected by Martin Hollis and Steven Lukes in 1982, under the title of *Rationality and Relativism*. Two years later the critique became more radical, at the hands of Alasdair MacIntyre and Jean-François Lyotard. Lyotard's essay on "The Post-Modern Condition" rejected the notion that philosophers can aim at an all-embracing "master narrative" about the nature of things. Now the eddies began. By 1992, Bruno Latour had denied that the episode of Modernity had ever depended on such an all-embracing narrative. "We were never really Modern," he declared: indeed, before the twentieth century we never really mounted any serious claim to being modern. Finally, the Danish writer Bent Flyvbjerg's *Rationality and Power* shows how, to this day, differences of "clout" affect the ability of competing arguments to carry weight in politically loaded situations.[18]

All in all, a skepticism that at first rested on doubts about the historical permanence of criteria of rationality widened to become—in effect—universal. From now on, permanent validity must be set aside as illusory, and our idea of rationality related to specific functions of the human reason. For students of rhetoric and argumentation, such skepticism toward the claim that rationality has a permanent validity is a commonplace. For philosophers in search of formal proofs, by contrast, this skepticism is catastrophic. For me personally, the outcome of forty years of philosophical critique was thus a new vision of—so to speak—the *rhetoric* of philosophy.

The rhetoric of philosophy? Reflecting on that phrase, I hesitate. The initial attack on my *Uses of Argument*, as an "anti-logic" book, assumed that Rhetoric and Logic were inescapably at odds. Logic is the formal demonstration of truths; Rhetoric is the deceptive peddling of falsehoods. Yet those years of critique were not without an effect. For many years, the University of Pittsburgh's Center for Philosophy of Science was the Vatican of the subject, protecting and preserving its formal principles against the mirages of its rivals. But in November 1992, the Pittsburgh Center organized a symposium on the relation of Reason to Rhetoric in the physical sciences themselves. After all, it turned out, my own position in *The Uses of Argument* still had merit, and the Cambridge University Press tells me—as I write—that, for all the objections from philosophers, the book remains in print, after a life of more than forty years.

Up to a point, then, Bruno Latour is right: the intellectual program of Modernity, with its assumptions about the universal and permanent character of Rationality, achieved full expression only in the twentieth century. Still, the current imbalance between our ideas of "rationality" and "reasonableness" sprang from seeds planted as early as the seventeenth century. Intellectually and institutionally alike, we can understand the current transition in our theoretical and practical lives only by taking such a longer-term historical perspective. Then we can see to what extent the changes going on today are *undoing* things that were originally done in the 1630s and after, and represent a recovery of commitments that sixteenth-century humanists took for granted. Nor is this imbalance a feature of intellectual history alone, or of institutional history alone: any redressing of the imbalance requires us to correct both over-intellectualized ideas and over-bureaucratized institutions at the same time.

In some ways, this is already happening. Philosophy and social science are sharing the experience of music. Little now remains of the twelve-tone music of Berg and Webern, which seemed in the 1920s and 1930s to be laying down the road into the musical future. Only the "conservative revolutionary" Arnold Schoenberg went on arguing that twelve-tone music had all along been just another step on the highway marked out from Palestrina to Bach, and on to Haydn and Mozart, Beethoven and Brahms.[19] As in music, so in philosophy and the human sciences, the price of intellectualism has been too great, and we are now having to work our way back to broader modes of self-expression.

Seventeenth-century natural scientists (we shall see) dreamed of uniting the ideas of rationality, necessity, and certainty into a single mathematical package, and the effect of that dream was to inflict on Human Reason a wound that remained unhealed for three hundred years—a wound from which we are only recently beginning to recover. The chief task of this book is to show what is needed if we are to treat that injury, and reestablish the proper balance between Theory and Practice, Logic and Rhetoric, Rationality and Reasonableness.

2

How Reason Lost Its Balance

Before Galileo, Descartes, and Hobbes, human adaptability and mathematical rigor were regarded as twin aspects of the human reason. From the 1620s on, this balance was upset, as the prestige of mathematical proofs led philosophers to disown non-formal kinds of human argumentation.

T HE SPECULATIVE PURSUIT of knowledge has played a central part in human culture for 2,500 years and more. From early on, the word "philosophy" referred to the systematic and methodical treatment of any subject. In this sense, it covered the whole range of inquiries that lent themselves to systematic investigation and debate, regardless of whether the twentieth century would classify them as Science and Technology or not. This spectrum reached from geometry and astronomy at one pole to autobiography and historical narrative at the other. Along the way, it embraced the study of bodies in motion; organic functions and development; law and ethics, whether in individual relations or political institutions; the patterns of change in general; aesthetics, rhetoric, and oral or written literature; the choices involved in piecing together a well-lived life;[1] even the place of those lives in the workings of Nature, not least in cosmology. From the start, speculation about these matters ranged all the way from mathematicians such as Euclid, Galileo, Riemann, and Gödel, to writers of literary essays and personal reflections such as Marcus Aurelius and Boethius, Montaigne and Santayana.

In all these human activities "reasons" play a central part. They may be occasioned by particular events, the specific aims of individual actions, the goals of social policy, the factors responsible for successes or failures, the biological and physical causes of effects or phenomena, the striking features of an art object, the style or delivery of a speech, and a dozen other things. And, for more than two thousand years, all such activities were given equal consideration. No field of investigation or speculation was dismissed as intrinsically unphilosophical. A few, like astrology, might prove to be ineffective, but that was another matter.

From the mid-seventeenth century on, however, an imbalance began to develop. Certain methods of inquiry and subjects were seen as philosophically serious or "rational" in a way that others were not. As a result, authority came to attach particularly to scientific and technical inquiries that put those methods to use. Instead of a free-for-all of ideas and speculations—a competition for attention across all realms of inquiry—there was a hierarchy of prestige, so that investigations and activities were ordered with an eye to certain intellectual demands. Beside the *rationality* of astronomy and geometry, the *reasonableness* of narratives came to seem a soft-centered notion, lacking a solid basis in philosophical theory, let alone substantive scientific support. Issues of formal consistency and deductive proof thus came to have a special prestige, and achieved a kind of *certainty* that other kinds of opinions could never claim. So, as time went on, academic philosophers came to see literary authors like Michel de Montaigne—an essayist who had little use for "disciplines" and put equally little reliance on formal logic—as not being philosophers at all, let alone scientists.

It had not always been so. In mapping the reach of philosophy and human reason, the contrast between the reasonable and the rational is only one of half a dozen differences in our methods of inquiry. The contrast between the reasonableness of narratives and the rigor of formal proofs, between autobiography and geometry, is the contrast between the "soundness" of substantive *argumentation*, which has the body and force needed to carry conviction, and the "validity" of formal *arguments*, whose conclusions are determined by the starting points from which they are deduced. There is a parallel contrast between our local knowledge of the patterns we find in concrete events, and the universal, abstract understanding embodied in purely theoretical points of view. The substance of everyday experience refers always to a "where and when": a "here and now" or a "there and then." General theoretical abstractions, by contrast, claim to apply *always and everywhere*, and so—as Tom Nagel points out—hold good *nowhere-in-particular*.

We need first to look more carefully at the contrast between *formal arguments* and *substantive argumentation*, and the relations between them, beginning with some samples of each kind. These must, if possible, be clear type examples, which can serve as templates in judging whether other examples are "purely formal" or "truly substantial"; if possible, too, they should be neither sophomorically simple nor excessively technical.

Consider, for a start, the eighteenth-century story of the Count and the Abbé:

> Two old ladies are receiving visitors, and the first to arrive is a
> bigwig, who happens to be a Count. The three of them discuss
> the Confessional, and the Count remarks, "Well, Mesdames, I
> can tell you this much—I was the Abbé's first penitent." He
> soon leaves, and the Abbé himself comes in. The conversation
> goes on and, under pressure, the Abbé clears his throat and
> says, "Without violating my duty of secrecy, Mesdames, let me
> simply tell you this: My first penitent was a murderer."

We have only to hear this story to jump to the conclusion: "The Count was a murderer"; and truly, if we take the two statements at face value—"The Count was the Abbé's first penitent" and "The Abbé's first penitent was a murderer"—they lead as they stand, by a *formal argument*, to the conclusion: "The Count was a murderer."

Yet the same story can be parsed, instead, as a piece of *substantive argumentation*. What guarantee have we that either the Count or the Abbé is telling the truth? The ladies are not likely to challenge them, so either or both of them may be grandstanding. Leaving open the possibility of such doubts, we may qualify our conclusion and say: "It looks as though the Count may, quite possibly, be a murderer." This change situates the formal argument in a human situation, so that it becomes a component in a substantive exchange of views. If we jump to a premature conclusion, we put both statements in a single mouth or mind, and the inference that the Count is *necessarily* a murderer overshoots the mark. Because the statements came from different mouths, the exchange has a different significance, which is apparent only if we have attributed each of the statements to its proper speaker. Once we "resituate" the formal argument, what conclusion we see as soundly or solidly based will depend on our assessments of the parties to the exchange. (At this point the distinction I noted earlier, between "situation" and "context," begins to show its importance.)[2]

This example is a straightforward *syllogism*—Greek for "arguing together"—though it is an especially simple one, as neither statement is a generalization of the form "All A's are B's." For a more representative example, we may look to mathematics. There, we must take care not to oversimplify the argument. The multiplication table may be formally in order, but the task of explaining the formal relations between the "numerals" is either too naive or too sophisticated to explore here. (Bertrand Russell and Giuseppe Peano spent years working on a formally rigorous analysis of those relations.) So let us look instead at another example, which at any rate is a mathematical argument that gives us a sense of discovery, and can bring us some genuine insight.

This example is the famous proof that the square root of 2—usually written as $\sqrt{2}$—is an *irrational* number, which cannot be expressed as a fraction x/y, in which both x and y are whole numbers. (Contrast $\sqrt{4}$, which is equal to the fraction in which $x = 2$ and $y = 1$.) This proof starts by assuming that the square root of 2 is expressed as a fraction in which the numerator and denominator are both whole numbers, and shows that this assumption leads inevitably to a contradiction. Here is how it does so:

> If the square root of 2 is rational, it can be written as p/q,
> where p and q are whole numbers and have no common factor.
> If p is even, then q must be odd, or they would have 2 as a
> common factor. If p is odd, q may be either even or odd, but
> they must have no common factor, whether 2 or otherwise.
>
> If p is even, $p/2$ is a whole number: call this r. Now p-squared
> $= 4 \times r$-squared, while (by definition) p-squared $= 2 \times$
> q-squared, so that q-squared $= 2 \times r$-squared, and q must be
> even. This contradicts what we noted before.
>
> If p is odd, p-squared $= 2 \times r$-squared, so p must be even.
> Whether p is odd or even, we thus end in a contradiction. In
> short, our assumption that the square root of 2 could be the

ratio of two whole numbers leads to contradictions, and is impossible for logical reasons.[3]

Can we treat this example as a case of substantive argumentation, as we did with the tale of the Count and the Abbé? This time, we cannot take that step, for this part of mathematics has been cut off by an act of abstraction from all empirical considerations of what is the case here and now, not there and then. Its arguments preserve their *purity*—to repeat—by defining mathematical concepts so as to apply, not just to particular times and places, but either everywhere and always, or else nowhere and at no given time.

This reply also helps to explain the first reaction we have on reading such a proof: not one of discovery, but a feeling that we have been surprised and tricked. If we do feel this, we are not the first to do so. When our school teachers taught us about square roots and whole numbers, there was no way to know in advance what ramifications those ideas would have. Yet no step in this proof refers to empirical facts: the steps just explore the formal implications of the initial ideas. Platonist mathematicians like G. H. Hardy saw such discoveries as reporting Universal Truths about a World of Ideal Entities; we may see them, rather, as dealing with abstractions that have no direct contact with the World of Real Things. This tension, or ambiguity, will recur throughout our inquiries, whenever the relationship of concepts to objects, or permanent abstract ideas to temporary particular things and states of affairs, moves into the center of the picture.

In any case, surprise at the unforeseen power of mathematical proof was itself one of the historical origins of the philosophical tradition. Plato was fascinated by every new illustration of this intellectual power. When Theaetetus demonstrated that there can be only five convex regular solids, Plato was delighted at the new resources this proof gave natural philosophers and, in his *Timaeus*, proposed these figures as shapes for atoms of different kinds of substance: the four-sided tetrahedron for Fire, the six-sided cube for Earth, the eight-sided octahedron for Air, the twelve-sided dodecahedron for Water, and the twenty-sided eicosahedron for the entire Cosmos, considered as being composed of its own special material.[4] No one could have foretold that the idea of "convex regular solids" would prove to have such ramifications. For Plato, however, this discovery was a standing demonstration that mathematical discoveries can be not just intellectual tricks but sources of genuine theoretical surprise.

Plato is also a source for our other type example, the Trial of Socrates. In this case, the issue to focus on is not so much the formal relations among the different statements presented to a jury of 1,500 Athenian citizens, as it is the situation in which charges were laid against Socrates in the first place, and the way in which the situation gave them plausibility. The central charge (to summarize) was that Socrates had led the talented youths of Athens astray, thus undermining the political condition of the Commonwealth; and, in retrospect, we may be reminded of those twentieth-century states in which a *Führer, Duce,* or other authoritarian leader—together with his class-based clique of supporters—discouraged all attempts to teach young citizens from influential families to think about matters of policy for themselves. In the event, of course, Socrates explained that teaching his students to think for themselves was his exact purpose, and he submitted to the death penalty rather than abandon his loyalty to the ideals for which, in his view, Athens stood.[5]

If we describe the argumentation at the trial only in these terms, however, we may encourage people to see this second example as involving persuasion alone, and so fail to consider the relative merits of the arguments presented for and against the accused. This is what perpetuates the hostility toward Rhetoric that many philosophers display, and lends color to the libelous description of Rhetoric as "dishonest persuasion" in contrast to the "formal proofs" of Logic. So we need to recognize a third, intermediate approach to the analysis of substantive arguments, combining the strengths of these rival views. This was the subject of my book *The Uses of Argument,* and the hostility it met with from many of my professional colleagues shows how much investment analytical philosophers still had, in those days, in keeping the study of argumentation—sometimes called "informal" logic—out of the realm of Philosophy proper.

In studying this third approach, the first thing to comment on is the *formal necessity* that attaches to the conclusions of arguments in pure mathematics. Substantive arguments are historically situated and rely on the evidence of experience: the best they can claim to do is to put a conclusion "beyond a reasonable doubt" and establish the "strongest possible presumption" on its behalf. True, we use the language of certainty or necessity in talking of substantive arguments, too; but in day-to-day matters of eth-

ics and experimental physics "certainty" and "necessity" are not the rigorously formal concepts exemplified, for instance, in the case of the square
root of 2. How, then, can we read *Athens vs. Socrates* as a substantive rather
than a formally necessary argument? In such a case, what considerations
can ever come close in their rational force to those that we encounter in
mathematics? Summarizing the Athenian prosecutor's case against Socrates, for example, we can think of him as saying:

> Experience shows that bright, educated young men who begin
> to think for themselves are more likely than dim, uneducated
> ones to engage in activities that undermine, rather than
> strengthening, the political state of the Commonwealth. So,
> given that Socrates was teaching his students to think for
> themselves, there is a strong case for concluding that he is
> Guilty as charged.

Two things about this argument mark it off from an argument in pure
mathematics. For a start, whether experience really shows what is here
claimed is scarcely beyond doubt: the testimony of any relevant experience is presumably open to more than one interpretation. (Are not many
disruptive Fascist thugs dim and uneducated?) Second, there is more than
one view about what undermines or strengthens the Commonwealth:
whereas the mathematical ideas of "a square root" and "a whole number"
(by contrast) are carefully defined to avoid all ambiguities, "the political
state of the Commonwealth" is not so unambiguous an idea.

Expanding this argument, to make all its different elements explicit, we
may start by asking what historical events the prosecutor might point to as
supporting his reading of the relevant experience: these we may refer to as
the *data* of his argument. Next, there are the general rules or *warrants* he
cites to justify his interpretation of those historical data: these, too, are less
generally accepted here than in mathematics. Third, there is the strength
and character of the support that—in his view—these data and warrants
provide, as expressed in the *qualifier*, "a strong [rather than a possible or a
conclusive] case," or (say) "a compelling presumption" in favor of a Guilty
verdict. Finally, the substantive conclusion is the *claim* that Socrates is
Guilty as charged. Still, whatever we may do to tidy up this case so that it
resembles a proof in pure mathematics in its form, there are three inescapable differences between strict formal inquiries and strong substantive in-

vestigations: the fact that all historical evidence is dated; the scope for rival interpretations of any given data; and the room for ambiguities in the concepts employed.[6]

This analysis, of course, leaves open all questions about both the intellectual force and the relevance of the data and warrants cited, and also the extent to which the argument, as actually presented, drew its power to convince from the situation in which the case was tried. In a political case like the Trial of Socrates, these two kinds of consideration are not as distinct and separable as they are in a mathematical case. Here, if anywhere, it becomes clearer to what extent Rhetoric and Logic—the situational and the intellectual—are inseparable in practice.

Before leaving these three ways to analyze human argumentation, let me add two asides. First, I am using the words *situation* and *situational* in place of the more familiar words *context* and *contextual*. It is misleading to suggest that the situation in which an argument takes place is a larger "text" within which the argument is a "subtext." Of course, a text can derive its meaning from the larger text from which it is taken. A couplet may be part of a complete poem, a chapter may describe a single episode within a novel, and so on. But situations can influence actions even before being described in human language, so the action and the situation are not related in the way that a shorter text is related to the longer text from which it comes. Politics cast a cloud of mistrust over Socrates before the first word of the Trial was uttered.

Second, the relation between these parallel ways of analyzing arguments bears a close similarity to that which is our primary concern in this whole discussion: the relation between acting rationally or irrationally, on the one hand, and reasonably or unreasonably, on the other. If we concentrate our attention exclusively on the propositions that figure in an argument, while ignoring the situation in which it is presented, we can be described as viewing the argument from the strict standpoint of Rationality. If we focus exclusively on the devices that make an argument persuasive, by contrast, the best that can be said about a case is that we present it as reasonably as we can: only if we can balance concern for the substance of an argument with a style that is convincing but not too pressing can we be credited with a Reasonableness that combines intellectual force in content with a moderation of manner. Rationality goes with focusing narrowly on matters of content, Reasonableness with a feeling for the dozen ways in which a situation may modify both the content and the style of arguments.

Widening our attention, a capacity for Rationality also tends to be inborn rather than acquired; and the same is true of the tendency to act "irrationally." A phobia toward snakes, for instance, means that a glimpse of a snake—even the picture of a snake—may provoke an instant and uncontrollable reaction: of freezing, fainting, or screaming. Such a reaction we typically describe as *irrational*, certainly not as *unreasonable*. Conversely, a habit of acting in ways that needlessly offend your friends, or regularly arguing in sloppy and unfounded terms, typically results from not having learned to pay reasonable attention to your own conduct: this is an acquired failing, not a mark of inborn irrationality. Yet a rigid contrast can rarely be insisted on; and it is a measure of the difficulty of preserving the Balance of Reason that the war of Logic against Rhetoric continued for so long after 1600.

The switch from philosophical egalitarianism to the scientific hierarchy that began in the seventeenth century did not at first exclude entirely from philosophy those essayists who set out to illuminate key features of our lives rather than trying to prove theoretical truths, and who invited us to share reflections rather than checking deductions. This change took place only gradually over three or four centuries. Before 1620, indeed, one of the most widely admired philosophers was the pioneer essayist, Michel de Montaigne. Though his views were quite unlike those of Bertrand Russell, Montaigne had—especially in the France of the 1580s and 1590s—the kind of reputation in educated circles that Russell had in early twentieth-century Britain. He set out, above all, to write about aspects of daily experience that all human beings can recognize. Like his successor, Francis Bacon, Montaigne wrote everyday, colloquial essays about Friendship, Books, Tragedy, Suicide, Sexuality, and—finally—Experience in general. His position was not a theoretical one, and he was deeply suspicious of writers who relied on abstract theories to undermine the truth of our common experience.[7]

Montaigne himself was more a lawyer than a scientist, and he was disinclined to put much trust even in physicians: like a late twentieth-century believer in alternative medicine, he relied, first of all, on the wisdom of his own body to take care of accidental injuries and medical misadventures, and restore him to health. As in George Bernard Shaw's play, *The Doctor's Dilemma*, Montaigne regarded physicians as ax-grinders, who were misled by their personal investment in (say) homeopathy or metallic remedies into peddling them as universal remedies.[8] Like Socrates, too, he did not trust any single system of natural philosophy, knowing too well how the pre-Socratic philosophers told alternative stories about the World of Nature, without ever arriving at a well-grounded choice among them.[9] This skepticism about Theory attracted a following in the late sixteenth century not just in France, but in other countries as well; and it was a challenge to younger thinkers and writers, who viewed the world differently, but recognized the need to meet Montaigne's challenge. The two most distinguished mathematical philosophers of early seventeenth-century France—René Descartes and Blaise Pascal—were both deeply familiar with the *Essais*, and looked for formal arguments to counter the things they considered most corrosive in Montaigne's position. Still, their writings did not display any sign of doubt that Montaigne was a true philosopher, even if a misguided one; rather, they shaped their own arguments in terms designed to undermine the skeptical, or even cynical, risks and doubts to which, in their view, Montaigne exposed his readers.[10]

Among modern-day English-speaking academics, Montaigne is regarded as a figure in Literature rather than in serious Philosophy. But that is not at all how he was seen in his own time. It is anachronistic to think of European thought as having developed quite discontinuously, with the seventeenth century's exact science rapidly displacing sixteenth-century humanism; nor was the reputation of these humanists as philosophers entirely forgotten. In the late nineteenth century, for instance, Montaigne was admired by Emerson in America and by Nietzsche in Germany. But in the twentieth century, notably in America, academic philosophy became a narrowly technical subject concerned with abstract theories, and the concrete concerns of autobiographical authors like Montaigne were generally ignored as being intrinsically unphilosophical. Theory acquired the dominant role, and Practice came to be spoken of as merely a way of applying Theory. Even in clinical medicine, where a fresh concern with practical, concrete, and particular issues has arisen beginning in the 1960s, prestige still tends to attach to academic studies that focus on abstract, universal theories. Thus we see such a distinguished writer as

George Santayana following Montaigne into the realm of philosophical non-persons.[11]

If philosophers had so little to say after the mid-seventeenth century about the contrast between rationality and reasonableness, historians of philosophy have not done much better. If they had paid attention for a moment to the fact that Immanuel Kant did not use different words for the Pure and Practical aspects of Reason, they would surely have raised their eyebrows and asked why this was so. Surely there must be some colloquial German term for the "reasonable," as distinct from the "rational," functions of the Human Reason? At first I was inclined to conclude that there is no such term, and that *Vernunft* and *vernünftig* cover the "pure" and "practical" (*rein* and *praktisch*) aspects of Reason equally. The Dutch use the word *redelijk* to mark the "reasonable" off from the "rational" clearly, but Germans seemed to use *vernünftig* and *verständig* almost interchangeably. So the question arises, "Why did not Kant call the topic of his Second Critique 'praktische *Verstand*'—understanding, not reasoning—rather than praktische *Vernunft?*" By the time he gets to the *Critique of Judgment,* he is uneasy about the point. Kant finally conceded that judgment (*Urteilskraft*) is distinct from abstract deductive reasoning (*Vernunft*); but the point remained obscure, and historians have done little to clarify it. For me, however, an even more tantalizing question is: "How would Kant's ideas about the *pure* Reason have changed, if he had written the Third Critique first, and so paid more attention to the role of *practical judgment* in the physical sciences?" In that case, he might have addressed many of the central questions of the present book at least two hundred years ago.[12]

One topic above all captures the core difference between the rival views of Reason. The analysis of theoretical arguments in terms of abstract concepts, and the insistence on explanations in terms of universal laws—with formal, general, timeless, context-free, and value-neutral arguments—is nowadays the business of Logic; the study of factual narratives about particular objects or situations, in the form of substantive, timely, local, situation-dependent, and ethically loaded argumentation, is at its best a matter for Rhetoric. Academic philosophers and serious-minded theorists in any field are concerned only with the first: the contrast between convincing and unconvincing, neatly phrased and clumsily argued argumentation is left to literary students of elocution or style. For much of the last three hundred years, and most of the twentieth century, scholars treated these investigations not merely as *distinct*, but as *separate*. Analytical philosophers and scientific theorists need not—indeed, must not—be distracted by rhetorical or stylistic issues; studies of literary style or forensic technique, for their part, had nothing to teach philosophers or scientists.

If there is anything solid to this distinction between logical analysis and rhetorical power, genuine reasoning and mere persuasion, however, how realistically or universally can it be applied? Consider all the "theories" we appeal to in one situation or another: how far are these framed in ways that are indifferent to who is presenting them to whom, where and when they are invoked, how they are presented, and so on—in a word, how they are "embodied" in human lives? Given the varied kinds of facts we observe and report in one situation or another, again, how far can these be described in terms of context-free and timeless concepts? Presumably, a world might exist in which the relationship between language and reality let anything we say about the-world-as-we-find-it be articulated in "disembedded" terms; equally, a world might exist in which all our theoretical language could be read in strictly ahistorical and context-neutral ways. In that world, the contrast between Rhetoric and Logic—between the substantive appraisal of argumentation and the formal analysis of arguments—could indeed be treated as absolute, and the two resulting kinds of knowledge could be kept separate.

Still, any assumption that the World-as-we-know-it is wholly or even mainly of that kind proves on examination implausible. Certainly, the Classical Greek philosophers who coined terms for Logic and Rhetoric never relied on such an assumption. Nor do speakers of modern Greek: they use both sets of terms more or less interchangeably, with at most a difference of emphasis. In the streets of Athens, for instance, the words *logos* and *logikos* are by no means restricted to formal, demonstrative proofs: they cover the whole spectrum of reasoning and thought.[13]

The point is worth underlining. The word *logos* came from the verb *legein*, which at first meant to gather, choose, and/or pick out objects for use, or situations to remark on: stones with which to build a wall, problems to discuss, or people to be your companions. Here as elsewhere, one primary use of language was in the service of inventory: counting things or telling them over. One basic meaning of the word *logos* was thus a computation, or monetary account. (In Greek restaurants, one learns the phrase *logariazmo parakalo* for "the check, please.") Similarly, the adjectival form *logikos* meant only that a thought was expressed in speech, suited for prose, or based on an appeal to a reason—whether concrete or abstract, logical or dialectical, practical or intellectual—and, in due course, these words expanded to cover any of the uses of speech or language: a history or narrative, a speech in court or a fable, a piece of common talk or a rumor, the plot of a story or the subject of a painting. Yet the same was equally true of the family of terms with the root *rhetos*, along with affiliated terms like *rhetoreia* (oratory), *rhetorizein* (to practice oratory), *rhetorikos* (oratorical, or skilled in speaking), and so on. If the two families of Greek words differed subtly in use, the *logos* family leaned more toward matters of content, the *rhetos* family more toward the speaker; still, in most respects their meanings overlapped in ways that would be inconceivable if they had been seen as both distinct and separate.[14]

Conversely, creatures or situations incapable of using language, incapable of being described in language, contrary to our expectations, or unfit to a purpose, could be referred to using terms from either family: they were unaccountable or inexpressible, unutterable or unspeakable, irrational or shameful. In arithmetic, for instance, magnitudes or quantities that do not lend themselves to reckoning in simple integers or fractions had two names: the "irrational" magnitudes that mathematicians call *surds* in English, the Greeks called either *aloga* or *arrheta*. (The square root of 2 is one of these.) As we move from the *logos* family to the *rhetos* family and back, the emphasis of the former may be on the groundedness or groundlessness of an opinion, the latter on its amazing or disgraceful character, but there is no sharp separation between the two families. Both belong in the same overall picture.

In a word, all kinds of speech and language are more or less *situated* or *embedded* in their occasion of use, and, if abstracted from that occasion, they can in theory be more or less "desituated" or "disembedded." Some familiar uses of language are more, some less situated or desituated; none of them are written or spoken alone. Take a test case: that of "proofs" in mathematics. Mathematicians have always set out to minimize the historical or cultural relativity of their statements, but they cannot even carry this program through to its logical conclusion. As Imre Lakatos showed in his elegant essay, *Proofs and Refutations*, the ideas of mathematical "valid-ity" and "rigor" have had their own histories: there are changes of para-digm in mathematics as much as in the natural sciences. So we can ask, an-swer, interpret, or understand questions about the validity of a proof by Diophantus in Antiquity or by Gauss in the early 1800s, only by referring to its given date. The dream of a perfectly or self-evidently "valid" theory or proof thus remains an unrealizable one.

Rather than Logic and Rhetoric being rivals, offering competing recipes for judging the merits or defects in our reasoning, the considerations they focus on are complementary. Formal validity is one thing. If the state-ments making up our *arguments* are intellectually inconsistent or claim "necessity" for inferences that later prove self-contradictory, we must ask ourselves whether they were meaningful in the first place. Substantive soundness is something quite different. Once we understand what is at is-sue in any piece of *argumention*, we can ask what data its claims rest on, how solidly those data support it, and how far the resulting claims carry conviction; but only a consistent, meaningfully stated argument can have substantive strengths or weaknesses. (Not that its formal consistency guar-antees its substantive strength.) Conversely, a conclusion presented with substantive argumentation may be beyond doubt or may be wholly un-grounded. But the strength or weakness of an argument takes its intelligi-bility for granted: it in no way guarantees its formal rigor or consistency. As it stands, the world of formal validity, meaningfulness, and consistency barely overlaps the world of substantive evidence, testimony, or convic-tion, and the statements we advance as "logical reasons" for our conclu-sions are only the abstract skeletons of "reasoning" that may or may not, here and now, succeed in convincing its audience.

In our time, as in Classical Greece, the tasks of Reason thus fall along a spectrum. The general concepts in which we articulate our ideas and be-liefs have formal implications, and it is the task of theoretical analysis to sort out and elucidate them. But, by itself, such a theoretical analysis does not tell us in what situations—how, where, or when—everyday life and practice exemplify those ideas. By contrast, the objects or situations we have occasion to notice and investigate are exposed to cultural variations and historical changes, and it is the business of empirical inquiry to ex-plore and throw light on those vicissitudes. But, by themselves, inquiries on an empirical level do nothing to indicate what theories we can best appeal to in order to explain those vicissitudes. So matters stood in Classical Greece two and a half millennia ago, and so they still stood four hundred years ago in the intellectual and practical world of sixteenth-century humanism. Our first question here must therefore be, "Why did our ideas change after the year 1600, and what led our modes of thought to move off in such a different new direction?"

In addition, however, the seventeenth century saw the birth of the Modern Dream of a purely formal language, which did all the things that everyday, colloquial language could do, but "perfectly"; and the complementary Dream, of a formal theory whose intellectual merits outweighed all the products of everyday experience. What lay behind this shift in our views of Language and Rationality, and lent a pervasive charm to the dream of formal theories and exact languages? That is the other question we must put on our historical agenda.

3

The Invention of Disciplines

The invention of disciplines, a change that began in the seventeenth century, involved both intellectual and institutional factors. Intellectually, Descartes's use of geometry as the model for knowledge provided its slogans; institutionally, the division of labor into professions and disciplines gave it wings. But the change did not happen quickly, and it has reached its peak only in the twentieth century.

FROM CLASSICAL ANTIQUITY to the mid-sixteenth century, philosophers, theologians, and writers on human affairs—knowledge, experience, reasoning, and the rest—respected the multiple ways of thinking and acting that make up what I here call the Balance of Reason. True, all the four main philosophical schools of late Antiquity had supporters in the Middle Ages and after. Some scholars developed themes and styles of thought originating in Plato and his successors. Others followed the more eclectic example of Aristotle, and in time the debate was joined by the therapeutic attitudes of Epicurus and Lucretius on one side, and the Stoics on the other. But the schools rarely claimed any monopoly for their viewpoints, so a real Balance was maintained. Not until 1600 A.D. was there any widespread tendency to insist on the superiority of theoretical abstraction and logical deduction, at the expense of directly human modes of analysis. Along with this rivalry there emerged the contrast—now so much clearer—between C. P. Snow's "Two Cultures" of the Natural Sciences and the Humanities.[1]

The years from 1500 on also saw a revolution in communication as deep as the one we have lived through in the late twentieth century. The methods of thought we know as the Two Cultures diverged because they put Gutenberg's movable type to different uses, each with its own philosophical concerns. In 1500 it at last became economical to distribute written texts in print, rather than as manuscripts. Before then, the worlds of learning and public service had been closed to all but a few of the lay public, and they had little access to the manuscripts that were composed and distributed mainly among ecclesiastics. Once printed books became readily available, there was a revival of the older tradition of *literae humaniores*, which developed into what we call the Humanities. Medieval scholars, for example, had talked about the theory of human nature in abstract terms, but print showed readers the complexity and diversity of human experience. In place of earlier theories of Sin and Grace, it gave them rich narratives about concrete human circumstances. Aquinas was all very fine, but figures like Don Quixote and Gargantua were irresistible.

You did not have to approve of or condemn such characters: rather, they were mirrors in which to reflect your own experience. Like today's filmmakers, the sixteenth-century humanists, from Erasmus and Thomas More to Montaigne and Shakespeare, gave you the full kaleidoscope of life. As such, they conveyed a sense of personal individuality. No one could mistake Hamlet for Sancho Panza, or Pantagruel for Othello: what counted were the differences among people, not the generalities they shared.

Consider, for instance, the English storyteller Victor Pritchett, who died in March of 1997 at the age of 96. In an appreciation of his work quoted in the *New York Times*, Eudora Welty seized on this theme of individuality:

> The characters that fill [his stories]—erratic, unsure, unsafe,
> devious, stubborn, restless and desirous, absurd and passionate,
> all peculiar unto themselves—hold a claim on us that cannot
> be denied. They demand and get our rapt attention, for in the
> revelation of their lives, the secrets of our own lives come
> into view. How much the eccentric has to tell us of what is
> central.[2]

What an "unscientific" thought Eudora Welty offers us: that the eccentric can be used to explain the central, rather than the other way around! No wonder the Humanities had so little to contribute to the creation of the

Exact Sciences. As late as 1580, Montaigne still questioned whether any universal theories about Nature were possible at all—let alone mathematical theories, such as Newton's would be: given the uncertainties, ambiguities, and disagreements in our experience, that ambition struck Montaigne as presumptuous.

The other main product of the new lay culture made possible by printed materials had a different origin and historical development. Events that appear tragic from a humanitarian point of view gave opportunities and motives for creative new activities in the natural sciences. Not that this difference was immediately obvious. The investigations we know as Natural Science were still referred to as Natural Philosophy—a name that reflected the continuities between earlier philosophers and their seventeenth-century followers. Even the phrase "sciences of nature" came into general use only in the eighteenth century, and the term "exact sciences" took its familiar form even later. Still, the work of Galileo Galilei set an example that transformed the theory of "locomotion"—or change of place—into the first of these "exact" sciences. Since Galileo's "kinematics" took a strictly mathematical form, made up of formal deductions that achieved a certain logical necessity, his new method seemed to provide a way of overcoming the uncertainties, ambiguities, and disagreements that people had tolerated—and even relished—in the Humanities.

Why was this important in the long run? For Galileo, the theory of locomotion was an attack on theoretical issues left unresolved by scholars in sixth-century Alexandria and Byzantium like Philoponos and Simplicius, as passed on by the Islamic scholars of later centuries, and reformulated in fourteenth-century Oxford and Paris by Buridan, Oresme, and the advocates of "impetus" theory. But it was Galileo's work, from the late sixteenth century up to his death in 1642, that created the first consistent mathematical theory of motion, and so gave substance to his famous description of Nature as a Book written in symbols capable of being deciphered only by people who had a grasp of mathematics.[3]

This point of view was music to the ears of younger scholars with a yearning for certainty and consensus. From 1618 on, the last and most ruthless of Europe's religious wars engulfed much of central and western Europe. King Henri IV of France had tried to set an example of religious toleration, treating his Protestant and Catholic subjects as equal citizens, but this had led a fanatic to assassinate him in 1610; from then on, the political situation in Europe went downhill, and between 1618 and 1648 central Europe was largely laid waste. In thirty years of war, one-third of Germany's population was killed, and half its cities were destroyed. (Playwrights from Grimmelshausen to Brecht have depicted these horrors.) In a Europe split by war, the sixteenth-century humanists' modesty about the human intellect, and their taste for diversity and ambiguity, seemed like luxuries.[4]

The seeming certainty of Galileo's mathematical methods had a natural appeal, and they soon took hold. In theory and practice alike—philosophy and jurisprudence, as much as the training of infantry—Skill gave way to Technique, Artisanry to Artisanship. Caught up in the war, René Descartes looked for a rational alternative to rival theological systems that had lost their conviction: ideally, for an intellectual system free of the uncertainties, ambiguities, and disagreements that Montaigne regarded as unavoidable. Having read the works of Galileo, Descartes took as his goal a universal system of physics expressed in mathematical form. So began the series of scientific inquiries, driven by what John Dewey much later called "the quest for certainty," that culminated in Isaac Newton's *Mathematical Principles of Natural Philosophy*, published in 1687.

These two products of the new print culture—first the Humanities, later the Exact Sciences—embodied different ideas of philosophy, and different ideals of Human Reason. Humanists saw arguments as personal or social disagreements that Rhetoric had a role in resolving, while the mathematical natural philosophers (or Exact Scientists) interpreted them as formal inferences that Rhetoric could only distort. In the Humanities, the term "Reason" referred to reasonable practices; in Natural Philosophy, to rational theories and deductions. The humanists recalled the variety we are familiar with in day-to-day experience: in real life, generalizations are hazardous, and certitude is too much to insist on. Exact scientists sought rather to put everything in theoretical order: formal certainty was their goal. So emerged that tension between Rationality and Reasonableness—the demand for correct answers to questions of Theory, and respect for honest disagreements about matters of Practice—that has remained a challenge up to our own times.

So much for the *intellectual* origin of the new Imbalance of Reason. Galileo and Descartes's rational ideals emphasized the rigor of theoretical arguments, and accepted the need for technical terminology based on abstractions, even if this limited the relevance of their theories to day-to-day experience. From the standpoint of daily life, abstract ideas were often stratospheric, though this seemed a small price to pay for the certainty they claimed to provide. But in the long run their *institutional* origins were of equal importance to the development of natural sciences as disciplines. The flowing together of these two sets of issues—intellectual and institutional—is our immediate topic.

Before 1600, the countries of Western Europe were, globally speaking, a minor promontory at the northwestern extremity of the Eurasian continent. In World History, as emphasized by that great scholar of Islam, Marshall Hodgson, the Chinese and Islamic world-cultures were economically more productive than Europe, which had spent a long time shaking off the Dark Ages after the end of the Roman Empire (700–1100 A.D.) and, later, the effects of the fourteenth-century plagues. Medieval Europeans made good use of technical innovations modeled on examples from Central Asia and the Middle East—the stirrup and the horse collar, in particular—and these made possible improvements in social organization and agricultural productivity. But only after 1600 A.D. was there, as Hodgson puts it, a "general cultural transformation [that] had far reaching effects, not only among Europeans but also in the world at large":

> By about 1800, the Occidental people (together with the Russians) found themselves in a position to dominate, overwhelming most of the rest of the world—and, in particular, to dominate the lands of Islamdom. The same generation that saw the Industrial and French Revolutions saw a third and almost equally unprecedented event: the establishment of European world hegemony.

So the seventeenth and eighteenth centuries saw in Europe the development of "a decisively higher level of *social power* than was to be found elsewhere":

> Individual Europeans might be less intelligent, less courageous, less loyal than individuals elsewhere; but, when educated and organized in society, the Europeans were able to think and act

far more effectively, as members of a group, than could members of any other societies.[5]

Coming from an admiring student of Islamic culture, these are notable claims, but they are not without foundation, and the seventeenth and eighteenth century invention of disciplines can serve as a case study of Hodgson's thesis. Furthermore, the period of European dominance is turning out to have been remarkably short, as the social and economic success of Singapore (for example) reminds us; and some contemporary commentators think it likely that the first city with a hundred million inhabitants will grow up around the Pearl River Delta, and incorporate both Hong Kong and Canton.

We are tempted to see scientific ideas as the creation of solitary individuals working on their own: a Newton, a Darwin or an Einstein seems to have been successful because he could innovate from a standpoint outside that of his contemporaries. Still, what these geniuses *succeeded at* was solving problems that were already the concern of a community of scholars or scientists. In that respect, they were already operating within "disciplines"; and, as Steven Shapin underlines in his book, A *Social History of Truth*, the rise of natural science in seventeenth-century Europe was facilitated by social conditions that encouraged the collective pursuit of scientific truths.[6] The seventeenth century's intellectual innovators in fact came from groups of people, mainly men, among whom the social relations were so easy and trusting that they could unhesitatingly "take each other's word" for the truth of the observations they reported.

In our commercially minded times, we have learned to distrust the noisy claims of advertisers and promoters: we would never dream of taking such claims at their face value, or rely on their correctness in shaping our World View. The development of a community such as Shapin describes, of people who shared a scientific trust, was a new thing, and had new results. Of course, this novelty also influenced their idea of scientific "truth," and we have inherited that idea; but what made the development of this conception possible at all was the formation of communities that shared—as Aristotle put it—the highest form of friendship or relationship (*philia*): the *philia* that unites people whose interest lies not in profiting from one another's situations, but in enjoying together shared good things.[7]

34

Such scientific friendships could, however, be productive only within a framework provided by larger institutions. Here, an important example was set by the work of Prince Maurits van Nassau, the son of William the Silent, who had led the movement to liberate the United Provinces of the Netherlands from their sixteenth-century colonial masters in Madrid. Maurits is also notable for having set up a Military Academy whose staff developed systematic methods of training; they taught standardized procedures as a drill, which students had to perform step by step, in one and only one correct way. The traditions of Maurits's Academy are preserved in the Dutch officers' training academy at Breda, though the institution itself is seen rather as a precursor of the present-day Technological University at Delft. (The Mauritshaus in the Hague, which houses some of Rembrandt's finest paintings, was the home of his younger relative, Count Johan Maurits van Nassau-Siegen.)

Drills are, of course, an integral part of what we ourselves call *discipline* in military affairs; but they were by no means universal in the armies of other centuries and cultures. The armies of the Ottoman Empire were known for the gallantry of individual members, but they were not organized in the ways we take for granted today. (Ottoman soldiers did not march in step, for instance, but ambled along independently.)[8] The idea that an army consisted of a multitude of individuals organized to work together in time—not a *turba* or rabble—was argued in the 1590s in Justus Lipsius's treatise *de Militia Romana*. Lipsius defined the word *disciplina* as referring to the rules governing the professional conduct of soldiers. He himself—his name is a Latinized version of the Flemish name Joest Lips—was a leading classical scholar in the last years of the sixteenth century, widely known for his exposition of classical Stoicism. His account of the Roman army relied largely on a Greek history of the Roman Empire by Polybius, who became a close friend and protégé of the Roman commander Scipio Africanus.[9]

Maurits's Academy was known to all parties in the Europe of the 1610s and 1620s. (The reputation of Breda was such that Voltaire chose it for the birthplace of Cunégonde, the heroine of *Candide*.) The Academy drew scholars and soldiers from both Protestant and Catholic countries: the Catholic Descartes, having given up law school after one year of studies, spent some time at Breda before leaving to join the Duke of Bavaria's staff. Like Galileo and Descartes, Maurits admired the consensus achieved in mathematics: if religious ideas had been discussed with the same neutrality and impartiality—he thought—what miseries Europe might have escaped! Maurits himself was a Calvinist, but in his eyes religion was not a killing matter. Even on his deathbed he refused to speak as a partisan: when a Protestant minister attending him invited him to make a formal declaration of his beliefs, Maurits is said to have pointed to a colleague at his bedside and responded,

> I believe that 2 and 2 make 4, and 4 and 4 make 8. This
> gentleman will tell you the other details of our beliefs.

The virtue of mathematics, that is to say, lay for him not in helping support one religious position against another, but in setting an example of the inner coherence appropriate to any rational body of knowledge.[10]

Is there really one-and-only-one way to carry out the duties of military discipline? Or might different armies employ alternative sets of procedures? This question occurred to Polybius in writing about the Roman Army. The disciplined nature of their procedures was well shown, in his view, by the way Roman Legions set up their camps. Once the decision to camp had been taken, a position for the consul's tent was chosen. Everything else followed in a rule-governed way: the same design, pattern, and layout were followed exactly, whatever the natural features of the territory were. If this required more labor than was strictly necessary, that was no objection: the key demand was that the location of every building in the camp relative to the consul's tent must be known precisely in advance, so as to guarantee free movement around the camp. In this respect, all the steps needed to set up a camp were done either "rightly" or "wrongly"; and the overall result conformed, or failed to conform, precisely to established rules. As we ourselves would say, the entire activity of camp-building was, for the Romans, a strictly "rational" matter.

Polybius himself had been born in Greece and taken forcibly to Rome in 167 B.C., as a hostage for the good behavior of his native Achaea; and he realized that a Greek army would face the task of setting up a camp with different priorities, and so adopt an opposite approach to that of the Romans. The Greeks thought above all of the security they would achieve by taking advantage of the natural strengths of a position: they begrudged the extra work involved in the Roman ways of entrenching, and they saw man-made defenses as inferior to those provided by the natural features of a campsite. As a result, they would choose any kind of shape to fit the lay of the land, and sometimes placed different parts of the army in unsuitable places, so that everyone was uncertain about his own position in the camp. For the Greeks, that is, the "rationality" of a camp layout was not enough by itself: everything depended on how it could best be adapted to a particular location. A Greek military camp could be better or worse, more or less successful in execution, but there was nothing precisely "right" or "wrong" about it. For the Greeks, the requirements of *rigor*—exactness, precision, and predictability—were always weighed against other priorities.[11]

Consider a very different case: the practice of garden design in seventeenth-century France and eighteenth-century Britain. Crossing the Loire Valley in the late 1940s on a trip back to England from the Midi, I noticed that my guidebook recommended a château with a "two-star" garden. Lured by this mark of distinction, I went out of my way to visit this prodigy, and was—perhaps unfairly—amused by what I saw. To be sure, a visit to this garden was worth a detour, as the guidebook implied, but not for just the reasons its authors had in mind. Within a stone wall, a square area some 70 or 80 feet each way had been cleared to form a gravel parterre. In the center there were four square beds—two by two—planted with low clipped hedges with leaves of contrasting colors: Black and Red / Red and Black. Finally, the box hedging was planted in the center of each segment in the four shapes of Spade and Heart, Diamond and Club. That was all.[12]

Why did I find this garden problematic? Why was my reaction one of amusement? Coming from England, I had a lot of expectations about what constituted excellence in a garden, and by English standards this "two-star" garden was less a Beauty than a Folly. To qualify for a mark of excellence, in my view—whether one, two, or three stars—it would be more reasonable to apply the ideas of the nineteenth-century English landscape gardener Lancelot Brown, who used to gaze over the fields surrounding any client's country house, looking to see where and in what respects the prospect they offered showed—as he put it—"capability of improvement." For Capability Brown, as he is still known, the task of the landscape gardener was not to impose on a garden a pattern to which it did not lend itself, but to take things as he found them, and at most "improve" them.

This contrast in ideas of garden design, between the strategy of abolishing the existing patterns of Nature and replacing them by a plan worked out in advance—*a priori*, so to speak—and the strategy of taking Nature as one finds it and improving it as the occasion permitted, stuck in my mind from the 1940s on, as a distinctive contrast between French and English gardens, not to mention much else. This impression was reinforced when I visited Versailles, and found that the area of wild garden allowed to grow up in one corner of that carefully tailored design was still referred to as Marie Antoinette's *jardin anglais*. Conversely, when I compared Le Nôtre's Versailles with Blenheim Park outside Oxford, whose estate was Capability Brown's crowning achievement for Winston Churchill's ancestor, the Duke of Marlborough, the same contrast came to mind. By Le Nôtre's standards, the Blenheim estate was not a "rational" piece of garden design, but a stretch of Nature permitted to run wild. Evidently, this contrast was worth pursuing.

At this stage I saw this matter of garden design as only one aspect of a larger issue: the systematically different ways in which the French and English traditions understood the ideas of reason, rationality, and reasonableness. Something in the contrast between Le Nôtre and Lancelot Brown echoed, for instance, the differences between the ideas of Descartes and those of John Locke. Was this an accident of history and culture, or a piece of enthusiastic self-deception on my part? A hint of a direction in which to pursue this question came soon after. To my surprise, I found an intriguing account of the history of electrical theories by Pierre Duhem, the French writer on thermodynamics and the history of science. In a chapter of his book, *The Aim and Structure of Physical Theory*, Duhem contrasted the respective intellectual strategies of physicists in early nineteenth-century France and late nineteenth-century England, and the parallel with attitudes to garden design was striking.[13]

A new treatise on electricity by Oliver Lodge had recently been published, whose style offended Duhem's sensibility. He himself came from the land of Poisson, Ampère, and Biot, who had used Euclid's axiomatic styles of theorizing. Oliver Lodge based much of his argument on analogies with material objects and mechanical models, and this Duhem saw as a mark of intellectual frailty, in the author or his intended audience. (To his sorrow, it was a frailty that other English physicists shared, notably James Clerk Maxwell.) Duhem looked in Lodge's book for formal arguments; in their place, he found cogwheels that engaged each other, or tubes filled with water that expanded or contracted: "We thought we were entering the tranquil and neatly ordered abode of Reason [he comments] but we find ourselves in a factory."

If Duhem had left matters at that, we could speak of this as a historical accident, but he introduced this criticism with an intriguing argument, pointing out other contrasts between French and English habits of life and thought. Take the contrast in philosophy between René Descartes and Francis Bacon: on one side soaring reflection, on the other pedestrian observation. Take the contrast in poetic style and vision between Racine and Shakespeare: on one side a noble embodiment of superhuman ideals, on the other plausible presentations of an all-too-human reality. Or take the contrast in juridical argument between the Code Napoléon, at the heart of French law, and the part played in Anglo-American jurisprudence by cases and precedents: on the one hand, clear and distinct definitions of any legal idea; on the other hand, pragmatic refusal to frame formal definitions, to avoid prejudicing future decisions. In a similar way in all these cases, French insistence on geometrical exactitude faced English commitment to pragmatic flexibility.

In their attitudes to garden design and electrical theory, then, the English and the French chose up the same sides as they did in legal procedure, dramatic characterization, and epistemology. With these instances in mind, we can quickly think of others. Indeed, the hunt for parallels can turn into a highbrow parlor game: take, for instance, the contrast in style between the polished precision and regularity of Nadia Boulanger's music and the rough and episodic spontaneity of Ralph Vaughan Williams.

True, the difference of styles in garden design between France and England might illustrate almost too vividly the rival views of the relation between Reason and Nature. This was not just a debate between the French and the English: a similar argument had already been vigorous in Antiquity. Its initial focus, however, had not been Nature viewed as vegetation or landscape, plants or trees. Up to the year 1800, the English were as ready as anybody to see untended landscape as "horrid and impolite." In that sense Nature was an object of admiration only after the eighteenth century, as an element in Romanticism. Still, the features of the Loire Valley garden that struck me so forcibly in the 1940s helped pose a general question that is not obviously one about rival cultures: "Is the primary task of

Human Reason to find formal solutions to abstract problems, and impose these solutions on the raw material of the world, as we experience it?", we may ask, "Or is its primary task to get acquainted with the world of experience in all its concrete detail, stating our problems and resolving them later, in the light of that experience?"

A gravel parterre, planted in imitation of playing cards, is a model of the first view: there was no way to guess what plants and contours occupied the terrain before the new design flattened it. The other view is captured in an estate improved by Capability Brown, with its tidied-up contours, artfully placed hillocks, and rechanneled brooks: we can easily see past the final product, and reconstruct the natural precursor that was "improved on" by Mr. Brown's work. Is the path of wisdom to compromise with Nature, and make the best of things as they are? Or must we clear the ground, reject Nature, and start from scratch? A revolutionary geometrical rationalism confronts a pedestrian, craftsman-like reformism: theoretical prescriptions challenge the finger on the pulse.

This is not meant as a general contrast between two countries, any more than the contrast between the Roman and Greek ways of setting up military camps; rather, it is a matter of priorities. This is evident if we pay attention to the parallel difference between the formal designs of large French aristocratic estates, and the pragmatic shapes of their peasant neighbors' smaller gardens. This matter had as much to do with the differences between upper-class life in France and Britain as it did with inherent cultural tendencies. Given the demands of life at court, the centralization of French society left the nobility little time for agricultural activities. By contrast, the English nobility spent only a few weeks every year in London: their lives were largely focused on the country pursuits of farming, gardening, fox-hunting, and the like. Such contrasts in their modes of life meant that, when it came to laying out their gardens, their priorities were equally different.

We have yet to examine two crucial points about disciplines. Are these two examples accidents of history or by-products of national character? Do they tell us any more about military traditions or garden designs than that the Romans did this and the Greeks did that, or the French this and the English that? These points (we saw) are not limited to military affairs or garden design, as distinct from (say) scientific theory. How we think and act embodies traditions that show an onlooker who we are, and where we came from; but that is only the beginning of a much longer story.

What profits, then, did disciplines yield, in either theoretical or practical respects? And what constraints did the new disciplined methods impose as the price of those gains? The full advantages of such discipline took time to make themselves felt; but, if Marshall Hodgson is right, they led to the great increase in social and technical power about which he writes in comparing world cultures. Yet how did they do this? What gave these modes of organization such an advantage over their forerunners and rivals? Once again, we need a twofold answer: in part intellectual, in part institutional. What fueled this expansion was not just the replacement of craft activities by disciplines; it also required a separation of different specialized activities, each with its own set of drills and techniques. In a phrase that became familiar in the writings of Adam Smith and the economists, the key was a *division of labor*. So, as time went on, all the enterprises involved gave rise to more narrowly focused sub-enterprises, each with its own cadre of specialists, and this specialization was responsible for much of the productivity of the new procedures.

Still, the constraints that disciplinary practices place on human activities were just as important, and here the division of labor and specialization are again a central thing to bear in mind. To reap these benefits, it was not necessary for participants in the activities to understand their significance: on the contrary, these fruits might be increased by narrowing the range of skills that participants were required to master. The benefits might be increased still further by requiring those involved to focus *exclusively* on the things they knew best and did best. In the short run, that is, intellectual or practical blinders might enhance the "comparative advantage" of those who were ready to wear them. A new focus of attention forced itself on people: there was no value in wasting time and energy on irrelevant activities. (This encouraged what Anthony Flew christened the Specialist Fallacy: a belief that the words "I am only *paid* to know about these things" mean the same as "I am paid to know *only* about these things.") Thus, the very advantages of disciplinary specialization carried with them the risk that rigor might degenerate into rigidity; while the attention to experience that the humanists had insisted on called, rather, for the openness and breadth of approach that such rigidity was liable to undermine.

The advantages were undeniable. They might demand selective attention to the technical aspects of life and language, and conformity to drills; but, if the necessary price was to set aside "all other things" for the purposes of an activity, so be it. The question was—and still is—how a balance between rigidity and openness, between a discipline's core values and the varied situations to which it applies, is struck and maintained. Problems begin when people forget what limits they accepted in mastering the systematic procedures of their disciplines. Once forgetfulness sets in, the ground is prepared for misunderstandings and cross-purposes: the selective attention called for in a disciplined activity is elevated to the status of being "the one and only right way" of performing the tasks in question, and the possibility of approaching them from a different standpoint, or with different priorities, is ignored or, we may say, "bracketed off."

This need not happen, but does so often enough. Greek soldiers preparing a camp paid attention to the natural features of a site: the strengths of that position were a relevant consideration in their work. Roman soldiers with the same task paid little attention to those features: for them the plan of a camp was determined in advance. If they took their own priorities as absolute, and did not recognize other options, each group of military engineers could view the other's techniques with scorn. Similarly, Capability Brown might, but need not, dismiss Le Nôtre as ignorant or misguided—different folks, different strokes. So there was something excessive in the tone Pierre Duhem used to berate Oliver Lodge: implying that the demands of Euclidean theory have an overriding importance for anyone who wants to make a serious contribution to physics. To Duhem, the intellectual priorities in scientific theory were not open to debate, let alone contestation. On one side there was The Way—that is, the Euclidean way; on the other there was the childishness and error of those who do not have the intellectual strength needed to handle exact and complex mathematical argumentation. Duhem did not recognize that, at his stage in the history of physics, alternative standpoints might call for different strategies, and yet be equally capable of making constructive contributions to the larger tasks of the physical sciences.

In mastering any discipline, we learn what things to pay attention to and what to set aside, for the purposes of our particular activity or argument. "Bracketing off" does no harm, if it leaves open the possibility of other, alternative procedures: selective attention is one thing, blinders are another. If we set alternative procedures aside without realizing it, however, we may put ourselves in a false position, from which we cannot take advantage of alternatives as they arise: military history is full of examples. Cross-purposes are possible also between activities that a moment's thought will remind us have different purposes and priorities. This is so where the languages of two enterprises overlap, as they do in (say) criminal law and psychiatry. Why did one man strike another with such violence that he died, and can an understanding of his childhood traumas lead us to forgive his offense? Taken by themselves, the professional procedures of criminal law and psychiatry do not resolve this tangle of issues, but lead us into even deeper waters. To insist on viewing them exclusively from either a judicial or a psychiatric point of view, and to dismiss other standpoints as foolishness, puts blinders on us whose only effect is to reinforce earlier misunderstandings.

Historically, the effects of disciplinarity and professionalization were not evident quickly. Descartes's insistence on the Euclidean model of knowledge planted some seeds in natural science between 1600 and 1650; in other fields, they took longer to germinate. If we are particularly aware of the problem of over-specialization now, that is no accident. As Max Weber taught us, these problems go with an increasingly bureaucratic social practice and organization. Some people therefore argue today that an over-emphasis on disciplinary expertise is, in part, a product of the bureaucratization of knowledge in the Academy.

All the same, between 1650 and 1900 there was still plenty of slack in academic and practical activities alike. When Denis Diderot and Jean d'Alembert created the great French *Encyclopédie*, beginning in the mid-1740s, the fact that one of them was a literary man, the other an expert mathematician, caused no difficulties. Quite the contrary: their pages display detailed pictures of carpentry tools and farm machinery alongside expert analyses of Newtonian physics, without any sense of intellectual incoherence.[14] A century later, the poet Alfred Tennyson could still become a Fellow of the Royal Society, and take part in serious discussions with a Darwin or a Maxwell; but, as discipline-based professions came to take up more and more space in academic institutions, amateurs were squeezed out, and the subjects of academic inquiry were increasingly confined to topics with a clear place in a known discipline. Just as problems that do not fall within one or another department in the bureaucracy may scarcely be regarded as "problems" at all, issues that do not fall within the scope of a recognized discipline are scarcely seen to qualify as "academic" at all.

Disciplines—in particular professionalized ones—are, of course, parts of the larger enterprises whose goals they serve. Their central tasks do not come down out of the blue, nor are they self-explanatory; rather, they are generated within a larger historical situation. When Maurits van Nassau established his Military Academy at Breda, the tasks he took on were one response to the Religious Wars: the need to develop systems of military drill for the recently liberated Netherlands or other well-organized countries. Another response was his ambition to maintain a non-partisan or "ideologically neutral" attitude toward the issues that were tearing Europe apart. What reason was there to think such a neutral attitude could be maintained? As his dying confession shows, the consensus of mathematicians in many countries was evidence of that possibility. The belief that mathematics was the possession of all humanity, which Descartes found in Galileo, harmonized with Maurits's pragmatic thinking, so that a visit to Breda reinforced Descartes's own previous convictions.

Not only was mathematics potentially the property of all humanity: it was also a vehicle for arguments whose necessity and certainty evaded Montaigne's skepticism. Properly pursued, this approach should stand on its own feet, and outflank all theological controversies. The necessity of inferences and the certainty of conclusions in mathematics, however, reflected at most the inner consistency of formal systems. Assume the validity of an axiom system, and we can infer all the theorems that (in this sense) "follow necessarily" from the axioms by steps that (in this sense) achieve "certainty." But what such axiomatic arguments show about everyday experience, or about the objects of the everyday world, is another matter. Without further guarantees that these proofs are relevant to the behavior of familiar objects, we cannot feel any psychological certitude of their relevance to everyday, practical knowledge.

Still, Maurits's mathematics was a splendid intellectual instrument in situations that involved much doctrinal controversy but little practical certitude. Descartes's *Discourse on Method* expounded this view so convincingly that later generations forgot the distinction between theoretical certainty and practical certitude, and treated mathematical inference as the Royal Road to Truth: from this point on, there was a straight road by way of Newton, Leibniz, and Euler, to Kant and beyond. So, for a century and a half, "the philosophies of knowledge and nature"—epistemology and physics—were in step with one another.

Descartes took his project for natural philosophy as far as he could in a four-volume *Principles of Philosophy,* published in 1644. It was successfully and strikingly completed forty years later, in Newton's *Mathematical Principles of Natural Philosophy,* which is still known as "the" *Principia.* Newton's careful arguments show that he understood the need to distinguish the formal rigor of mathematical proofs from the practical relevance of the empirical examples he used to put astronomical flesh on a mathematical skeleton; but this need to accept the limitations on the empirical relevance of purely mathematical arguments was not universally welcomed. Leibniz saw this aspect of Newton's theory, too, as a mark of intellectual frailty, for the same reasons that later led Duhem to challenge the intellectual methods of Maxwell and Lodge.[15]

As we shall find in all our present inquiries, the bureaucratization of learning has created as many problems as it solves; and one of the things unfortunately "bracketed off" from consideration in the human disciplines is Ethics. Even Max Weber made a case for handling social problems in a "value-neutral" way, if we were to speak of social knowledge as "scientific" at all. Why must Ethics be bracketed off in the academic social sciences? This was not inevitable; and, if we suppose that it was, we again risk clinging to blinders that cut off a broader view. Despite the attitude of value neutrality entrenched in the social sciences, however, the idea of Values is, in practice, as little open to question in Europe or America today as was the idea of God in medieval times. We may disagree about cases, but we understand claims about the value of saving life, or building happy families, or respecting personal autonomy: all these claims have clearly recognizable meanings.

If we look at the concepts and theories of the human sciences—whether concerned with individual behavior, or with institutions and social relations—however, we find weight put on the need to confine ourselves to "facts" and steer clear of "values" because these (it is said) may introduce a damaging bias into our inquiries. In the Academy, human scientists as much as natural scientists are expected to treat the contrast between facts and values not just as a distinction, but as a downright separation. Yet how can we do factual work in our scientific theorizing, while recognizing "values" in all our practical activities and relations? That is a central issue here, and we shall begin by examining one of the crucial situations in which the founders of the human sciences convinced themselves of the need to frame their inquiries in value-neutral terms: namely, the influence of physical theory on the evolution of ideas in Economics. This will provide clues to the wider tasks we must tackle in reconciling the demands of Thought and Practice, and rescuing our everyday understanding of values from their current ostracism in the behavioral and social sciences.

4

Economics, or the Physics That Never Was

The major outcome of seventeenth-century physics was Newton's work, which gave modern human scientists ideas for an agenda. Yet a misunderstanding of Newton's achievement led them to aim at a kind of prediction that Poincaré discredited in the 1880s, even in Physics. The classic example is Economics. From Adam Smith on, its success as theory was striking, but its excessive rigor weakened its claim to practical relevance.

W E MAY START FROM a problem that arises the moment we leave the Natural Sciences for the would-be Science of Humanity. The question is: "Why was Newtonian dynamics seen as the type example of a Serious Science, to be emulated by economists, sociologists, and psychologists no less than physiologists and biochemists? Why were social scientists so keen to be the 'Newtons' of social theory?" Surely, we may think, the activities of human beings are unlike the motions of planets, or of rigid spheres rolling down inclined planes: surely they are far more like the activities of living creatures. Planets and rolling balls are not aware of the attention that observing scientists are paying them; but it is hard—and of little use—to eliminate this awareness from studies of human conduct and institutions. So why did theory-building in the human sciences so often rely on implausible analogies with physics, rather than on biological models? No work of natural science had more influence on the human scientists' idea of "theory" than Newton's *Principia*—at least as this idea was interpreted in the Academy—yet no work (I argue) has been more deeply misunderstood.

The chief reason for which Newton's physics was seen as the model for a truly "hard" science was its supposed success as an instrument of prediction and control. Yet those who hold it up as an example for the human sciences have not studied carefully enough the conditions under which it can play this role *even within physics*. Around 1800, Laplace had dreamed of an Omnipotent Calculator who, given the positions and velocities of all atoms in the Universe at the Creation, might use Newton's equations to compute the entire subsequent history of Nature. From the outset (it now turns out) this was only a fantasy; and if we ask how far it reflected the original claims for theoretical Physics, we shall find that the human sciences, not least theoretical Economics, based their programs not on a realistic account of the actual methods of Physics, but on their vision of a Physics that Never Was.

How can this claim be backed up? Let us focus on one of the chief features of Newton's dynamics that led Leibniz to dismiss the *Principia* as impossible: namely, the puzzle mathematicians call the Three-Body Problem. The mathematicians' hope was that, if they devised a way of representing the motions of all the planets in the Solar System in a single algebraic equation, they could prove that it was an *inherently stable* system, whose structure guaranteed its permanence—at least until the Creator chose to close it down. Faced with a challenge from Leibniz, Newton and his followers attempted, from 1715 up to the late nineteenth century, to formulate the required equation. In a monograph by Henri Poincaré, published in 1889, all the best resources of mathematics were deployed to resolve this problem, but without success. Now, more than a century later, this monograph—instead of rescuing the Solar System from the threat of instability—has become one of the starting points for Chaos Theory.[1]

Notice my phrase "rescuing the Solar System from the threat of instability": it refers to an assumption that went without saying from the seventeenth century up to the first years of the twentieth. From Grotius and Descartes on, the ideals of rational intelligibility and intellectual order current in Europe emphasized regularity, uniformity, and above all stability. From this standpoint, the merit of the *Principia* was to have shown that the Solar System was a prime example—a *paradeigma*, in Greek—of "an intrinsically stable dynamical system." The mathematical and experimental natural philosophers who took their lead from Galileo, Kepler, and Descartes relied on Newton's supposed success to argue that taking Euclid's *Elements of Geometry* as their model for a new Physics—or in

Hobbes's case a political theory—was not a dream born of Platonist theo-rizing alone, but a realistic program for scientific research.

In the 1630s, Descartes's *Discourse* had argued in philosophical terms that Euclid's *Geometry* should be seen as the model for "theories" in all ar-eas of inquiry. Fifty years later, Newton showed that a geometrical model was not just formally rigorous, but empirically powerful as well, since it ap-parently resolved all the intellectual problems that had plagued European thinkers since the publication of Copernicus's *de Revolutionibus* in 1543.[2] If this could be done in Astronomy, was it not possible in other fields? For the next two hundred years and more, this challenge engaged the imagina-tions of talented mathematicians and scholars. This was what recom-mended a Newtonian model of hard science to European intellectuals, and its fiercest opponent was Newton's old enemy, Leibniz.

What exactly, then, "went without saying" in planetary theory in New-ton's last years? And what continued to go without saying in natural phi-losophy and the social sciences for much longer—even, for some, until af-ter the two world wars? At the heart of this approach lay a belief that the Solar System is the exemplar of a "rationally intelligible" system in Nature, but we must take care just how we state this belief. What was at issue was not just the *geometrical* move from a Ptolemaic to a Copernican picture of the Solar System: rather, it was the *dynamic stability* of the whole System. As Newton declared in a Scholium to the second edition of the *Principia*, the Stability of the Sun and Planets is our visible assurance that the World of Nature demonstrates the Creator's Rationality. This belief did not de-pend on accepting a Copernican view of the Heavens: it was consistent with any account of the geometry or dynamics of the Solar System. Tycho Brahe, whose astronomical theory was neither Ptolemaic nor Copernican, took the stability of the Solar System for granted quite as confidently as Copernicus and Galileo had done; nor did it matter whether one appealed to Descartes's "vortices" or Newton's "universal gravitation" to explain its physical operation. Above all, it was compatible with any theory about *how far* and *in just what respects* the system was stable, and so "rationally in-telligible."

At this point, we need to look more carefully at the things Leibniz found unacceptable in Newton's theory. Some of them were minor queries, such as how to define *vis viva*. (Was it equivalent, in twentieth-century terms, to "momentum" or "kinetic energy"?) More important, there began here a bifurcation in Physics and Philosophy that lasted for 150 years, not just in Physics, but in the human sciences too—most surprisingly, in economic theory. The issue that divided Leibniz and Newton was the question, "Can the Creator's Rationality, as displayed in the design of the Solar System, be mathematically *proved?*" Newton was content to show that the regularities Kepler had found in the planetary orbits can be accounted for by appeal to his inverse-square Law of Universal Gravitation: in this (he argued) they displayed a kind of pattern we might expect a mathematically-minded Creator to prefer. Leibniz was not ready to accept a merely empirical demonstration. He would accept only a formal proof that the planetary system *must* display the regularities that we in fact observe; and by that measure (he argued) Newton had failed. When Newton's amanuensis, Samuel Clarke, replied, "Evidently, this is how God *chose* to create it," that sharpened the antagonism. To show what God chose *in fact* was not enough: you must also show that it was *right and just* that He chose as He did. For Leibniz, Newton's theory was incomplete, because it included no Theodicy: no demonstration that the way things are in God's World is *for the best*. Thus he provided a model for Dr. Pangloss, the character in Voltaire's *Candide* who continues to argue that "Everything is for the Best in the Best of all Possible Worlds," even after the catastrophic Lisbon Earthquake of 1755.[3]

In this respect, the Three-Body Problem became—in Leibniz's eyes—a fatal blow to the Newtonians' hope of giving a convincing proof of God's Rationality. The precise source of the trouble was this. The equations that Newton used to explain the elliptical form of the planetary orbits, and their relative speeds of motion around their orbits—both of them facts established by Kepler's observations—were oversimplified. In fact, these theorems proved only that the Law of Gravitation accounts for the motion of *one planet at a time* around a more massive center of attraction, such as the Sun. With this simplification, the equations of motion for a single planet are easily solved, and we get general theoretical equations of the same form as Kepler's observed regularities. Once we introduce into the picture a third body—say, a second planet—the equations are, however, no longer algebraically soluble. The best a Newtonian could do was to compute the third body's influence arithmetically, from moment to moment, as a "perturbation" of the simplified orbit, and such arithmetical dodges—while empirically useful—struck Leibniz as pragmatic dodges, not as convincing proofs of God's Wisdom.

How are we to react to this discovery? In practical terms, we may be happy to improve our methods of computation bit by bit, so that the arithmetical match between the results of theoretical computations and the record of the astronomers' planetary observations becomes more and more exact. That was the eighteenth-century observers' agenda: to reduce the perturbations bit by bit in ways that culminated, in 1804, in the final volumes of Laplace's *Système du Monde*. Laplace himself merely showed that refined Newtonian calculations could reduce these perturbations to such a low level that all the motions were as close an approximation to what the theory implied as could be observed in practice; and he rejected Newton's hint that God was free to intervene in the Solar System from time to time, to remove all irregularities and restore the System's stability. (As he reportedly said, "Je n'avais pas besoin de cette hypothèse.") Leibniz could never have taken this step: for him, a correct theory must yield general algebraic solutions for any set of bodies, however complex—not merely two bodies at a time. Once it was clear that Newton's *Principia* provided no such solutions, he dismissed it as metaphysically flawed; and, indeed, his writings provide little evidence that he ever read much past the first thirty pages of the *Principia*.

Leibniz died in 1715; Newton lived on until 1727. After Leibniz's death, right up to the late nineteenth century, the division in the philosophy of physics persisted. Starting with Leibniz himself and continuing up to Pierre Duhem—by way of the German physicist Euler, and Laplace in his more metaphysical moments—there was the Continental tradition of *rationalism*. Starting with Newton and continuing to Maxwell and Rutherford—by way of Dalton, Herschel, and Laplace in his more practical moments—there was a British tradition of *empiricism*. Empiricists saw all regular phenomena as marks of God's Rational Order; Rationalists still looked for mathematical theories with the full rigor of Euclid's *Elements*. Only Immanuel Kant kept to the sidelines in natural philosophy, as he did in epistemology and metaphysics, and took neither part. In the *General History of Nature and Theory of the Heavens* (1755) his intellectual imagination reached out beyond the Newtonian limits, sketching out a comprehensive cosmology in evolutionary terms, of a kind barely glimpsed by his predecessors.[4]

Working physicists in Britain took the empiricist line: it was enough to balance the books by improving the match between calculations and observations. So, after 1810, the Three-Body Problem tended to fade into the background, being treated as a metaphysical, not a scientific issue. By the 1860s, the tide was turning. Lyell's *Principles of Geology* was preoccupied with the Earth's history, and the debate over Darwin's *Origin of Species* made it more urgent to adopt again a historical view of Nature—cosmology and all. Meanwhile, the Scale of the Universe in both Space and Time proved to be vaster than was earlier assumed, and so provoked the anxiety evident in Tennyson's poem, *In Memoriam*.[5] Soon, this debate became a main focus of religious and intellectual discussion, which defined the background against which we can usefully set Poincaré's monograph, "Sur le problème des trois corps et les équations de la dynamique."

The monograph appeared as a special supplement to *Acta Mathematica*, the leading journal of the time in pure mathematics. From 1882 on, its editor was Professor Göran Mittag-Loeffler of Uppsala, assisted by an editorial board that included two of Europe's finest mathematicians: Karl Wilhelm Theodor Weierstrass from Germany and Charles Hermite from France. (Poincaré was Hermite's most talented pupil.) From the start, *Acta Mathematica* concentrated on "pure mathematics," as that discipline was then understood. All the most eminent mathematicians published in it, including Georg Cantor, Heinrich Hertz, and David Hilbert, and in 1885 King Oscar II of Sweden lent his patronage to a competition for the best essay on a subject in pure mathematics.[6]

In announcing the competition, Weierstrass, Hermite, and Mittag-Loeffler chose four areas for special attention. Three of the problem areas lay in theory of functions, or other subjects still recognized today as belonging to "pure" mathematics; but the first topic was *la stabilité de nôtre système planétaire*—that is, the stability of "our" planetary system. As a problem in pure mathematics, this topic was framed in oddly singular terms: not as having to do with the general "stability conditions" for *any* planetary system but, quite explicitly, with *our particular* Planetary System. Shortly before his death in 1859—as the editors explained—the

French mathematician Dirichlet claimed to have a proof of this stability; but he never explained his proof, and entrants to the competition were invited to reconstruct it. They were asked to send anonymous entries to Sweden, each marked with an epigraph, with their names sent separately in sealed envelopes with the same epigraph, so that the entries could be judged in a wholly unbiased manner. Twelve entries arrived, and five of them tackled the stability problem. Two prizes were awarded, one for a monograph that bore the epigraph, *Nunquam praescriptos transibunt sidera fines*—"Never do the heavenly bodies transgress their prescribed bounds." This was Poincaré's meticulous reanalysis of the Three-Body Problem, in twenty-three chapters and 270 pages.[7]

Poincaré's epigraph recalls the antiquity of a belief in celestial stability, but the choice was also ironic. The questions "Do planetary motions have *any* 'prescribed limits'?" and "Can one *prove* that the planetary system must in fact be stable?" were just the points at issue. By the time one reaches the last page of Poincaré's monograph, the resources of nineteenth-century mathematics have been exhausted, and there is no more prospect in 1889 than there was in 1715 of finding general methods to solve the equations of motion for two or more planets going around the Sun at the same time.

Another result of the analysis was philosophically still more damaging. It showed that, when many objects move freely under their gravitational attraction, critical collisions (*chocs*) may take place, whose outcomes are radically unpredictable. Instead of Laplace's dream of a world whose history is computable in Newtonian terms, a picture emerges of a world in which—aside from the artificially simplified case of the Sun and a single planet—complete predictability is out of the question. So the world of physical determinism that had been a nightmare for nineteenth-century thinkers gave way to what we now call the World of Chaos. True, Poincaré did not immediately appreciate the full effects of his work. In the 1880s, his painstaking analysis only reinforced the Three-Body Problem. It provided no new way to solve equations of motion for three bodies or more: without a radically new kind of mathematics, there was no prospect of overcoming the problem. Later in the 1890s, Poincaré wrote a three-volume book entitled *New Methods in Celestial Mechanics*, which went halfway toward a break with classical ideas; but it was only in his philosophical essays, from 1902 on, that he touched on the issues of chaos and complexity that are preoccupying scientists today.[8]

Poincaré's interest in the Three-Body Problem was never purely personal. Questions in many-body dynamics still fascinated mathematicians, from Sweden to Italy, Germany to North America: such questions cropped up in *Acta Mathematica* through the 1880s and 1890s and up to 1906. Nor was this only a technical issue: the year 1906 also saw the publication of H. G. Wells's novel, *In the Days of the Comet,* in which the Earth faces annihilation by a massive comet, and humans are moved to reorder their affairs. Indeed, in our own time the dynamics of our planetary system are still a matter of public concern. In 1994 we saw "by far the most spectacular event in the Solar System ever witnessed by the human race": a collision with the planet Jupiter of fragments of "Comet Shoemaker-Levy 9," while in March 1998 astronomers temporarily forecast the impact on the Earth—in October 2028—of an asteroid violent enough to provoke a catastrophe for humanity as grave as that which seemingly destroyed the dinosaurs, and transformed the living population of the Earth.[9]

Far from the standard pattern for any hard science being Euclidean, then, as social scientists assumed from the early nineteenth century on, working physics never exemplified that exact form. When social scientists took Newtonian dynamics as the example of a Serious Science, they hoped to win three prizes at the same time: developing (a) an abstract theory with a rigorously valid axiom system, (b) deductions of the nature of human institutions from its universal principles, and (c) scientific explanations of the character of particular social institutions. Yet this triple prize was never a realistic possibility: it had never been achieved even in planetary astronomy. Were Mercury, Venus, and Mars (as Newton assumed) "physical objects moving freely through empty space, and acted on by a single inverse-square force of attraction"? Or was interplanetary space full of "subtle fluids," as the Cartesians argued, so that the planets' movements would not continue unless they were forcibly swept around the Sun in "vortices"? For forty years after 1687, the evidence was not sufficient to justify that choice, and no formal link existed between the mathematicians' axiom-systems and the empirical observations of the astronomers.

Initially, they had simply to choose a set of priorities, and develop a program for theoretical physics in the light of that choice: that was the underlying reason for the dispute between the Rationalists, from Leibniz to Duhem, and the Empiricists, from Newton to Rutherford. Only after Newton's death were British physicists free to assume that the space between the planets is in fact empty, so they could continue arguing with empirical confidence, even if not with strict logical rigor. Meanwhile, the theological implications of Newton's theory gave rise to grave problems: as to that, Leibniz was right all along. For most of the eighteenth century, anyone who had pursued the matter as keenly as it deserved could have made the strong case for chaos theory, radical unpredictability, and non-linear mathematics that was in fact presented only after the mid-twentieth century. Failing that, the model that for so long held center stage as "the ideal form of theory for any would-be Science" remained that of a Physics that Never Was.

How did the debate about Cosmic Stability affect the development of the human sciences? Was the ambition of the eighteenth-century social theorists to be the Newtons of the human sciences any more than rhetoric or self-delusion? If we are to map the influence of these ideas on human thought and practice, we must look more closely at the people who laid a foundation for the social sciences: in particular, the creators of mathematical economics, who tried hardest to model their work on what they understood of mathematical physics. Of all human scientists, the ones most confident of the rigor of their methods and the superior validity of their results are those economists who rely on abstract and universal mathematical systems. The formality of their theoretical arguments gives them an air of logicality; the generality of their concepts makes them appear universal. As a result, the ideas of "neoclassical equilibrium analysis" have had unequaled prestige in the academic social sciences.

There are two ways to write a history of economic theory. We can start from where we are now, and look back at those earlier writers who already used mathematical methods of analysis like those familiar today. In this way, we establish an honor roll of the *precursors* of modern Economics. This is a recipe for surprise and disappointment: surprise at the foresight of a few imaginative individuals, disappointment that their example took so long to follow up. Alternatively, we can begin at the other end, and ask what personal projects each of these creative individuals was originally engaged in, and how their excursions into Economics contributed to those larger projects. Depending on which of these two roads we take, we will end with a different story about the birth of economic theory. In the first account, its creation was delayed by the failure of successive researchers to pursue lines of argument already sketched by their creative precursors. In the second, theoretical Economics as we know it is the result of abstractions that were available only in the twentieth century, while the work of the supposed precursors reflects intellectual ideas and ambitions that were connected with Economics only marginally or accidentally.

Until recently, histories of economic theory chose the first road, constructing an account of the successive writers whose work contributed to the mathematical analysis of economic transactions and phenomena. When J. A. Schumpeter died in 1950, he left unfinished a massive *History of Economic Analysis,* which gives an excellent picture of the mid-twentieth-century view of Economics: notably, a thorough history of equilibrium analysis in economic theory. In this account, he pays special attention to Adam Smith (1723–1790) and Antoine Augustin Cournot (1801–1877), William Stanley Jevons (1835–1882) and Léon Walras (1834–1910). Each of these writers had his own reasons for being interested in the links between economics and physics: particularly, the parallels between the role of equilibrium analysis in the history of economics, and that of planetary stability in the history of physics.[10]

To begin with Adam Smith: Smith was an economist *among other things.* All his biographers remark on the unusual scope of his work, which ranges from the theory of the moral sentiments to the uses of rhetoric, the wealth of nations, and the history of planetary astronomy. His versatility they attribute in part to the range of academic discussion and education in the eighteenth-century Scottish Enlightenment, in part to the variety of his personal interests, and the breadth of reading he accumulated during a long bachelor life. Yet for many years his personal project was evidently to develop a comprehensive vision of the universe—one might even call it a cosmology—of which he fully completed only the history of astronomy: he seems to have abandoned the project only when he saw that it was too vast to finish in a single lifetime. The essay on astronomy stands as testimony to his ideas about the proper method for an intellectual system, but he never pursued the parallels between physics and economics into more substantive fields. After Adam Smith, the empirical tradition in British economics paralleled that which we saw earlier in physics linking the ideas of Newton to those of Rutherford. From Adam

Smith and David Ricardo to Alfred Marshall, British thinkers similarly focused on particular economic phenomena, rather than on universal abstract analysis.[11]

In Continental Europe, similarly, the precursors of twentieth-century Economics formed a *rationalist* tradition similar to that which we saw in Natural Philosophy, from Leibniz in the early eighteenth century to Duhem at the close of the nineteenth. At times, the analogy between "rationalist cosmology" and "rational economics" was even stronger. Cournot's use of mathematics in his *Recherches sur les principes mathématiques de la théorie des richesses* (1838) was elementary: it contributed little to our grasp of real-life transactions. For most of his career, indeed, Cournot was less interested in economics than in broader issues of cosmology. To see the place of economics on his agenda, it is revealing to look at his *Traité de l'enchaînement des idées fondamentales dans les sciences et dans l'histoire* (1861). In the 707 pages of this major work, fewer than thirty are devoted to topics in economics.[12]

The rationalist aim of Cournot's cosmology is clear from his intellectual evolution, as reported in his *Memoirs*. He came from a conservative Royalist family, and did not at first go to University; instead he spent four years in a law office beginning in 1820. These he later came to regard as largely wasted. Still, he read widely at this time, and four authors particularly attracted him: Bernard de Fontenelle's *La pluralité des mondes*, Laplace's *Système du monde*, the *Port Royal Logic*, and the *Leibniz-Clarke Correspondence* in the French translation by Desmareaux. This last defined the rival, empiricist and rationalist methodologies for physics, and Cournot's loyalties were clear. In his *Considérations sur la marche des idées* (1872), he insists that the writers who added most constructively to the development of Newtonian astronomy in the eighteenth century were not empirical-minded physicists in Britain, but Continental mathematicians like Euler and Clairault, d'Alembert and the Bernouillis.

The final pages of Cournot's late *Revue sommaire des doctrines économiques* (1877) are pure epistemology. They discuss the proper method for any theory of human transactions in terms that exactly parallel the theory of planetary astronomy. In both fields (he concludes), we may distinguish the general laws that define the "essential" form of given phenomena from the perturbations that arise from the "accidental" influence of intervening agents. So, at the end of Cournot's life, astronomical theory had for him an undiminished charm as a model for the analysis of economic trans-actions. Both fields were in his view co-equal parts of the larger discipline that he himself refers to as "rational mechanics."

Jevons, too, is often discussed in terms that exaggerate the centrality of Economics to his thought. Looking back from the twenty-first century, we may see him as a precursor of our economic theories, but that is not where his thinking began or ended. He was at first a logician and a natural scien-tist, and he took a job in the mid-1850s in Sydney, Australia, as an assayer. Once there, he developed an interest in the social sciences. Invited to speak at the annual meeting of the British Association for the Advance-ment of Science in 1862, he set out a "brief account of a general mathe-matical theory of political economy" which was later expanded into a book, *The Theory of Political Economy* (1871), but his work on Economics was mostly published only after he died. Far from economics being the sub-ject of central importance for Jevons himself, his whole *oeuvre* belies that impression. He was increasingly concerned with the analytical power of Logic in scientific theories of all kinds. When he brought these general ideas together in his 600-page *Principles of Science* (1874), he did not de-vote a single page to Economics: the very word "economics" is not in the index. Excursions into mathematical economics were, for him, one more way of making wider methodological points.[13]

The most intriguing figure among these precursors of economic theory is Léon Walras, a French scholar who, to his frustration, never held a univer-sity position in his native country, but spent his career in Lausanne, Swit-zerland, where one of his colleagues was Vilfredo Pareto. As an economist, Walras was more single-minded than either Cournot or Jevons, but, like them, he was preoccupied with questions of method: notably, with paral-lels between the phenomenon of "equilibrium" in planetary theory and economic affairs. In the last ten years of his life, from 1900 to 1910, Walras was anxious to put these parallels on a formal basis, by showing that the relevant equations had identical forms in both subjects. He wrote to Henri Poincaré, hoping to win the mathematician's approval for his comparisons between the laws of economic equilibrium and those which (as he as-sumed) ensured the stability of the planetary system: his last paper was, in fact, called *Économique et Mécanique*. By this time, however, Poincaré himself no longer believed that the planetary orbits were essentially stable, let alone that Newtonian dynamics guaranteed that stability, so he was too embarrassed to answer Walras's pressing letters candidly, and the letter that Walras printed as an annex to his last paper reads in retrospect more like a delicate brush-off than an endorsement.[14]

Even after the hope of finding guarantees for the stability of the planetary system had faded among mathematical astronomers, then, they remained alive among economic theorists. To this day, indeed, the idea of theory that many economists rely on is one they find in formal parallels between their theoretical systems and those of Newton's *Principia*: the debate in Economics has been slow to change its themes. A footnote to Schumpeter's *History* points, however, to the beginning of a shift in this point of view.[15] There, he comments on the work of Alfred Marshall (1842–1924), who in 1885 had set up at Cambridge a Department of Economics independent of Sidgwick's Faculty of Moral Sciences, or Philosophy:

> The truth that economic theory is nothing but an engine of
> analysis [Schumpeter explains] was little understood all along,
> and the theorists themselves, then as now, obscured it by
> dilettantic excursions into the realm of practical questions. But
> it was emphasized by Marshall who, in his inaugural lecture at
> Cambridge, coined the famous phrase that economic theory is
> not universal truth, but "machinery of universal application in
> the discovery of a certain class of truths."

Two phrases shine out from this footnote: first, Schumpeter's judgment on economists' attempts to apply economic theory to practical issues as dilettantic, and second, Marshall's claim that, even if economic analysis abandons all pretensions to universal truth, it still has universal application. For Marshall, in other words, concepts like "equilibrium" remain of general relevance, even if we stop reading them as accounts of human reality.

In the twenty-first century, public life and policy are dominated by applications of economic theory to practical questions. So we must ask, both how such applications can escape Schumpeter's charge of dilettantism, and to what extent Alfred Marshall's claim that "the machinery of economic analysis" is "of universal application" still holds good. One way to answer these questions is to look at some situations in which economic analysis has either been applied more or less straightforwardly and helpfully, or else seems to have been wrong-headed or even disastrous in its results. Too often (we shall find) any assumption that the standard methods of economic analysis are applicable similarly to all situations introduces distortions that we can escape only by "de-universalizing" them, and limiting their application to well-recognized and carefully analyzed conditions.

Two contrasting vignettes will illustrate the difficulties that face us, and the ways in which they can best be overcome. The first of these has to do with the Island of Bali.[16]

"I have an anthropologist friend with a Dutch wife, and they do field work on Bali. His main focus of research has been the system of water temples whose priests—by tradition—controlled the schedule for allocating irrigation water to the rice fields of different communes or individual farmers. For some 800 years, these temples were a feature of Balinese society; but when the Indonesian Islands came together politically, neither the Dutch colonial administration nor the central government of Indonesia recognized that water temples had any underlying economic significance: rather, they saw them as religious, and so cultural, monuments.

"In the late 1960s and early 1970s, the National Government of Indonesia decided to introduce to Bali, on a massive scale, new strains of so-called 'miracle rice' developed at the International Rice Institute in the Philippines. So, my friend points out,

> Balinese farmers were forbidden to plant native varieties of
> rice: instead, double cropping or triple cropping of IR 36 [or
> similar varieties] was mandated. Farmers were instructed to
> abandon the traditional cropping patterns and plant
> high-yielding varieties as often as possible.

"Along with this policy, the Asian Development Bank supported an engineering project on the basis of a report from economic consultants in Milan, Italy and Seoul, South Korea. From a purely technical and economic point of view, this engineering project was a strictly 'rational' recipe to increase rice production, and help to make Indonesia self-sufficient in rice, which was the prime aim of the policy.

"What happened? For two or three years the policy succeeded as forecast. The rice crop soared, and farmers put money in the bank. But, as the 1980s went along, the local authorities began to record explosions of insect pests, and infestation by funguses both old and new. Before long, the farmers of Bali were afflicted with all the Biblical plagues of Egypt:

> By the mid-1980s, Balinese farmers had become locked into a struggle to stay one step ahead of the next pest, by planting the latest resistant variety of Green Revolution rice. Despite the cash profits from the new rice, many farmers began to press for a return to the older system of scheduling by the water temples, in the hope of cutting down the pest populations. Foreign consultants at the irrigation project, however, interpreted any proposal to return control of irrigation to the water temples as a product of religious conservatism and resistance to change. The answer to pests [they retorted] was pesticide, not the prayers of the priests. As one frustrated American irrigation engineer declared, 'These people don't need a high priest, they need a hydrologist!'

"Until the situation reached crisis point, the experts at the Asian Development Bank found it hard to admit that the traditional irrigation schedules operated by water temples had been *functional*: that what had worked was not the prayers of the priests, so much as the centuries of experience embodied in the schedules. As the experts saw matters, the water temples—as religious institutions—*must be* economically irrelevant; and this was a hard lesson for them to learn."

This story must not be misunderstood. I tell it, not from any dislike for technology or economics—I am not a machine breaker—but to make a different point. Professionals who are committed to particular disciplines, technical or economic, too easily assume that economic and technical issues can be *abstracted from* the situation in which they are put to use, and so can be defined in purely disciplinary terms. They assume, for instance, that economists and engineers can know in advance what things are (or are not) relevant to their policy decisions. If Engineering and Economics are truly scientific (they will argue) their principles must be universal, and, in that case, the views of theoretical analysts in Milan or Seoul may be not *less* but *more* clear-sighted than the beliefs of lay people on the ground, in Bali itself.

The Indonesian Government's policy decision to replace the traditional schedules by uncoordinated multiple cropping, based on the Asian Development Bank's 1979 report, had two unhappy side effects. First, it threatened the material infrastructure of Balinese culture: waterways and practices developed through the history of the island that succeeded in minimizing the exposure of native crops to insects, diseases, drought, flood, and other natural enemies. In addition, it undermined the people's respect for the institutions that grew up around those waterways and practices: what we might call the "moral infrastructure" of local society. Subsequently, beginning in the 1990s, the economy of Bali has been deeply affected by its transformation into an international tourist destination; but it has been possible to redeem the damage done to its agriculture in part by striking a compromise between the older water temple schedules, and the demands for water by the new varieties of Green Revolution rice.

A second vignette will show how a recognition of the need to redefine the current methods of economic analysis can lead to the development of new procedures that had no such adverse side effects. This time, we leave Bali for Bangladesh.[17]

"The key figure in this story is a young graduate student from Bangladesh who took a doctorate in Economics at Vanderbilt University in Nashville, Tennessee. There, he was taught—among other things—the economic principles of Banking and Finance, in a form supposed to apply in the same way in all countries. Returning home to a teaching position in Chittagong, he ran into difficulties. In class, he handed on the 'laws of the market' as he was taught them in the United States, but every day after class he walked home and found that the transactions going on there, in the local real-life market, were hard to square with the theoretical principles of the market he had just been teaching.

"His name is Muhammad Yunus, and in recent years he has become an international figure. What is most striking about his achievement is the simple fact that, confronting this divergence between the established teachings of economics and the lives he saw his fellow-Bangladeshis living in his native country, he could not rest, but was determined to find a way of understanding its origins, and turning this knowledge to the advantage of the people among whom he found himself living."

This encounter stimulated Muhammad Yunus to embark on the inquiries that led finally, in the late 1970s, to the establishment of the

Grameen Bank, which has been the prototype for a banking system of a new kind. His initial research made it clear to him that what stood in the way of his neighbors' escaping poverty was the impossibility of raising loans through the existing banking system in their own names. The only way they could support any kind of productive activity was to resort to the local middlemen or money lenders, who charged usurious rates of interest on their loans. A quick survey among the neighbors revealed that forty-two families remained trapped in poverty, by the need to borrow—between them—a total of some twenty-seven dollars. What made them ineligible for regular banking loans was their inability to offer anything in return, as collateral, in the usual sense of that term. Meanwhile, rich Bangladeshis could (Yunus found) get loans through the government-supported Bangladesh Industrial Development Bank, thanks to their collateral, even when their rate of repayment was barely above 10 percent.[18]

Two linked problems had to be solved: one theoretical, the other procedural. As a matter of theory, the idea of "collateral" had to be rethought in a way that would permit its application to people who owned nothing material, such as a house, a car, or even a sewing machine. Meanwhile, as a matter of procedure, banking practices needed to be revised in ways that gave practical meaning to this revised concept of collateral. Yunus's innovation (which had precedents in other times and cultures) was to set up small groups among the poor in the villages of Bangladesh, who collectively agreed to guarantee the repayment of an initial small loan to their poorest member, on the understanding that this would in turn qualify the other members of the group for loans.

This social experiment made it possible to put flesh on the idea of "social" rather than a "material" collateral, which could justify a willing bank in making loans even to the poorest customers. By now, indeed, Muhammad Yunus's Grameen Bank operates in some fifty thousand Bangladeshi villages, and makes loans to local groups, chiefly composed of poor women, who maintain a repayment rate of approximately 97 percent—in sharp contrast to those official organizations that do not complain about a repayment rate of only 10 percent. If the concept of "transparency" has attracted attention in the last five or ten years, this is not least because of the success of the Grameen experiment; by now, such "microcredit" schemes are operating successfully in more than fifty countries around the globe, and even in the United States.[19]

What do these two vignettes have in common? Both record episodes in which the accepted methods of economic analysis were applied in situations that they did not easily fit, and had to be modified to rectify the damage they might otherwise inflict. In the first case, the need for these refinements was recognized only after the damage had been done, by the eventual admission that "religious" institutions might, after all, be functional, instead of being—as "cultural" institutions—economically neutral. In the second case, the inadequacy of the existing views was recognized at the outset, and further damage was avoided by redefining the concept of collateral, which was an obstacle to effective procedures all along. In both cases, it proved, reliance on pure economic theory was empirically empty without full consideration of the social, cultural, and historical conditions of its application, and what forced itself on people's attention in the end was the need to consider those social, cultural, and historical conditions explicitly. In real life, that is to say, economic analysis could yield a just and fruitful human outcome, only when all these conditions were taken into account.

Muhammad Yunus understood the culture of his homeland well enough to see that it was no good equating the local economic transactions in the suburbs of Chittagong with the idealized "market" of economic theory. But the lack of material collateral, of kinds familiar in developed economies, must not be a reason for further penalizing the poor: rather, it was a call to extend the application of the term *collateral* to fit the social conditions better. Universal economic theories have too often led economists to overlook "non-economic" factors, like the Bali water temples. So, in both situations, it was necessary to rethink both the language of economic theory and the actual practices of economic activity, if you were to match the actual situations on the ground.

These discoveries are not in themselves a reason to mount a more general attack on Economics, or on the individuals engaged in the existing institutions. True, there are times when Muhammad Yunus's account of his experiences with the Grameen experiment comes close to unleashing such a broadside:

I was in the process of discovering the World's basic banking principle, namely that, "the more you have, the more you get." And conversely that "if you don't have it, you don't get it." Why have economists remained silent when banks insisted on the ridiculous and extremely harmful generalization that the poor are not creditworthy? . . . A university should not be an island where academics attain higher and higher levels of knowledge without sharing any of this knowledge with its neighbors.

Yunus's attitude has been basically constructive, however, and he has never broken either with the Academy or with the discipline of Economics, understood in a liberal sense:

To me, in order to qualify as a social science, an academic discipline must create an analytical framework which will enable and encourage human beings to explore their unlimited potential, not start with the assumption that their capacity is given and limited, and that their life-long roles are fixed . . .

If Economics [as it stands] were a social science, economists would have discovered what a powerful socio-economic weapon credit is . . . If we can re-design economics as a genuine social science, we will be firmly on our way to creating a poverty-free world.[20]

Without abandoning the legitimate claims of Economics to be a genuine social science, these two episodes support Schumpeter's description of excursions by economic theorists into the practical realm as "dilettantic." The question is not whether we can afford to ignore Economics in the formation of policy, on a national, local, or corporate level; it is only, "How can Economics best be put to use, in dealing with practical issues of government or business decision-making?"

Here, both the history of Economics and the practical experience of politicians and business executives point in the same direction. The general belief of expert economists that the "data" to be considered in such decisions can be purely "factual," and so free from ethical and political assumptions, blinds them to the full range of factors they should take into account. The crucial questions do not turn on ensuring the formal correctness and consistency of our calculations; they depend rather on collecting all the relevant social, historical, cultural, and even personal information about the people involved, and their actual needs. In this respect, a traditional reliance on Euclidean and Newtonian models of theory continues to focus attention on "doing your sums right" and conceals the equally important task of making sure that you are "doing the right sums": in other words, doing calculations that are directly relevant to the practical situation in question.

A final brief vignette will complete this story. It has to do with an American cultural anthropologist who went to work in Japan. Why did he go there, and what did he do when he got there? He went because the Nissan Car Company hired him to lead their strategic planning unit, and advise them about ways of breaking into the U.S. car market. That's the whole story. Theory aside, someone at Nissan understood that all economic problems are *in practice* cultural and social problems, too, and long-term planning that fails to take this into account is liable to be shortsighted and unproductive. On that assumption, they saw that it would be helpful to have the profile of their prospective American buyers drawn up by a real live cultural anthropologist.

This message does not, of course, affect Economics alone: similar traditions in the other human sciences have led to similar misunderstandings and errors of practical judgment. When our present inquiries turn in a more constructive direction, we shall reconsider the distinction between disciplines whose interest is in better explanations, and disciplines that are concerned above all with practical decisions and actions, and we shall return to these economic examples to illustrate, also, the differences between "theoretical" and "clinical" approaches to our problems. But, for the moment, we should examine just how deeply rooted the Rationalist tradition in Western thought and practice has become since the seventeenth century, and how it has shaped the development of our ideas about many other matters besides those of Physics and Economics.

5

The Dreams of Rationalism

The rise of the exact sciences brought with it three rational dreams, which expressed the new scientists' hopes for "rationality": a Universal Method, a Perfect Language, and a Unitary System of Nature. Leibniz, for instance, believed that a perfect language would need no interpretation; but, as so often, this belief turned out to face insuperable obstacles.

LOOKING BACK at the twentieth century, historians will speak of it as the Century of Representation: a time when, in all fields of art, thought, literature, and science, people considered, or reconsidered, the place of language in human life, and the basis on which our reliance on it rests. A few earlier writers around 1790, such as Hamann, had made tentative moves toward a general critique of communication and representation. But the subject won general attention only in the late nineteenth century, when it was the focus of debate in Vienna about a dozen fields. In the last decades of Habsburg rule, artists and scientists acted like bicyclists: they pedaled with confidence just so long as no one asked how they did it; but, once they were asked how they avoided upsetting the machine, they lost their balance. Methods of representation and communication that had served well previously were challenged: more self-conscious techniques were needed, to avoid assumptions that were seemingly taken for granted in earlier language and literature, the fine arts and the sciences.[1]

The resulting critique of representation and language went through several phases, and brought to the surface one issue about which philosophers and psycholinguists have been deeply divided. To put it as a question: "Are natural languages *in general* adapted to human tasks, or are they essentially defective media for representing experience or communicating exact thoughts?" On this issue, there was a conflict between two parties: those who saw natural languages as riddled with shortcomings and unsuitable as a vehicle for knowledge, and those, like Wittgenstein, who claimed that "All propositions of our colloquial language are logically fully in order, *just as they are.*"[2]

This conflict was partly generational. The idea that everyday means of expression, communication, and representation are radically defective was a *fin de siècle* idea; by the 1950s, when Russell revived it in his later books on philosophy, it seemed quite out of date. Similarly, after the cultural landslides of the 1960s, all the radical means of artistic, musical, and scientific expression that had been thought to define the Main Road to the Future in the 1920s and 1930s—nonrepresentational painting, twelve-tone music, or the tensor calculus—lost their credentials. In the process, a dozen cultural products that had been discredited in the 1920s, not least the music of Anton Bruckner and Gustav Mahler, were once again high fashion.

By now, the turn-of-the-century attack on natural language by Gottlob Frege and Bertrand Russell is a historical curiosity. It is no longer clear what they saw wrong in natural languages. Certainly, they were not calling for practical reforms in specific sectors of language, in (for example) Law, Medicine, or Science: these things are routinely improved in day-to-day professional work; and even colloquial speech takes on new features, as the drives for verbal compression and syntactical simplification take effect. Such practical changes were neither radical nor general enough to demand a profound epistemological or metaphysical critique: being confined to professional usage, and local application, they were instead judged pragmatically.

The issue is not what the early twentieth-century philosophers *said*, but what they *meant*—recalling that (as Wittgenstein used to say) "What philosophers 'mean' is *always* right!" Frege and Russell saw natural language as a fancy dress that veiled from onlookers the true "logical forms" of statements, and this view kept its force in Russell's later works. Russell's first mentor, F. H. Bradley, had denied that everyday concepts capture Reality with a capital "R": all they can present is Appearance. Though he claimed to have broken with Bradley in 1903, the Russell of 1950, too, called everyday language a rough and ready instrument, incapable of expressing Truth with an uppercase "T."[3]

Both Russell and Bradley thought of a Language as a mirror that reproduced and reflected the structure of Reality and Truth. Neither of them was happy to find that everyday language works in *timely* ways, lacking the timelessness of "eternal objects." Yet why should anyone expect language to work in eternal ways? Wasn't that an excessive demand? About that, a much older story can be told, in which Russell and Frege are no longer the main characters. In the *Cratylus*, Plato asks if we cannot free the "meanings" of human language from convention and make them clearly "right" or "lifelike." Surely, meanings exist *in the world*, waiting for us to recognize them, and find a means to express them.[4] (Fire c r a c k l e s; water r u s h e s; yet onomatopoeia is only a crude expressive technique.) The Dream of Eternal Meanings, whose shadows flicker on the wall of Plato's Cave, thus haunted the philosophy of language from its beginning.

A warning—philosophical dreams are soap bubbles. Taken at face value, they may deceive us; but if handled roughly they vanish. Either way, their latent meanings are more revealing than their surface sense, and a single dream can telescope several latent meanings. In dealing with such powerful dreams, therefore, we should step back and ask, "Why did this dream affect people when and where it did? What did they hope or fear at that time? What was *at stake* in 1900 that found expression in the dream?"

The Dream of an Exact Language was also powerful in seventeenth-century Europe. It was shared by scientists and philosophers in many countries, not least the founders of the Royal Society of London. From Francis Bacon to John Wilkins or George Delgarno, from 1605 to 1641 and 1657, ideas were developed that became common form after the Restoration of the Stuart monarchy in 1661: for example, John Wilkins's *Essay toward a Real Character, and a Philosophical Language*, published by the Royal Society in 1667. Still, as a scholar of Europe-wide reputation, the most significant figure in this movement was Johann Amos Comenius, the "admirable Moravian" who acknowledged a debt to the mystic, Jakob Boehme, but allowed a draft of his system of "real characters" to circulate in his treatise, *The Way of Light*, as early as 1641.[5]

Not without reason, however, we associate the *characteristica universalis* with Gottfried Wilhelm, Freiherr von Leibniz, who lived from 1646 to 1715. Leibniz gives us the best clues to the *kinds* of things at stake for those who dreamt this Dream. As a boy [he says], he had already conceived of a "universal system of characters" that would serve to "express all our thoughts."[6] Such a system, he declared,

> will constitute a new language which can be written and spoken. This language will be very difficult to construct, but very easy to learn. It will be quickly accepted by everybody on account of its great utility and its surprising facility, and it will serve wonderfully in communication among various peoples.

Is Leibniz here anticipating Esperanto, Volapuk, or other such artificial languages? In part, perhaps, but there is more to it. His new language uses a symbolism that will supposedly let us express *thoughts* (he says) "as definitely and exactly as arithmetic expresses *numbers* or geometrical analysis expresses *lines*." Such a language, Leibniz concludes, will not only have perspicuous meanings, so that people from different cultures can *talk* together with shared understandings; it will also embody and codify all the valid modes of argument, so that different peoples can *reason* together without fear of confusion or error—and this will make his language "the greatest instrument of reason."

Throughout his long life, Leibniz continued to pursue his project for a Universal Language which had Meaning and Rationality built in from the start. It took him in a dozen directions: to Chinese ideograms, the infinitesimal calculus, and the divinatory techniques of the *I Ching*. Why did he pursue the project so assiduously? And why was the project to develop a perfectly exact language a crucial issue for other seventeenth-century scientists, too? Both questions deserve serious historical answers.

Leibniz never worked on mathematics or metaphysics for their sake alone: they were always for him a means to an end. He had a lifelong theological mission, as an *ecumenist*. In his time, people did not find mathematics and theology as separate as they are today; after 1600, indeed, all the countries of Europe faced the problem of devising ways in which a single nation could accommodate citizens with several religious beliefs. As Richard Ashcraft shows, the intellectual and political conditions for religious toleration are a central topic in all of John Locke's writings; but for Leibniz the issue was even more urgent.

He was born in 1646, as the Thirty Years' War was coming to its exhausted close in the Peace of Westphalia. From 1618 on, Central Europe was the locus of theologically rationalized brutality unparalleled in Lebanon, Yugoslavia, or Iran. All across Germany, prosperous cities were destroyed, while 30 to 40 percent of the country's population were slaughtered to the greater glory of a Calvinist, Lutheran, or Catholic God. Leibniz dreamed of creating the intellectual and practical conditions for renewed dialogue among theologians from different camps, and gave much thought to the rational criteria relevant to that debate. This is no wonder: with the ruined Germany of the 1650s and 1660s as a backdrop, there was a special *actualité* to his dream of a *characteristica universalis* that was to "serve wonderfully in communication among various peoples." For thirty years he corresponded with colleagues on both sides of the theological gulf, even exchanging letters with the French historian Bishop Bossuet, whom he was anxious to enlist as an ally in the work of reconciliation. But (as it turned out) Bossuet was interested only in finding out on what terms the heretic, Gottfried Wilhelm Leibniz, might be converted to Roman Catholicism. So their exchange was aborted, and with it Leibniz's last hope of an effective Ecumenical Conference.[7]

If Leibniz had persuaded the theologians to sit down together, what would they have discussed? The task was to find shared elements in all their rival bodies of doctrine, and to define a minimum system of indispensable beliefs that all Christian believers could see as based on Sufficient Reason. In this project, a "universal language" would serve not only as the "instrument of Reason," but also as a way to heal the wounded body of Europe. For the rest of the seventeenth century, a *characteristica universalis* might bind together the ideas that *odium theologicum* had severed earlier in the century.

It was a noble dream, but a dream nonetheless. It rested on two assumptions that were unfounded and unrealizable: (1) that the characters of a perfect language could express *all our thoughts* without any need for conventional agreements on their meanings; and (2) that by substituting this language for the natural languages of their own nations, Europeans might free themselves from the communication breakdowns that had fueled, *inter alia*, the theological debates that had been used to legitimate the Religious Wars.

At an early stage, then, Leibniz's project for a *characteristica universalis* gave rise to novel questions about the role of representation in language. Are ideograms better than alphabets as a way of "representing" linguistic meanings? (The differences between the alphabetic Indo-European and ideographic Asian languages are still creating problems for us today.) How does our mental or physiological equipment "represent" those meanings? These questions require us to look, first, at the idea of *representation* itself.

One preliminary remark: this topic can be more subtly discussed in regard to German than English. In different contexts, the words "represent" and "representation" need to be translated by different German words, which the English language does not differentiate. At times, we have to use the German verb *darstellen* and the noun *Darstellung;* at others, the verb *vorstellen* and the noun *Vorstellung;* at yet others, the unrelated pair *vertreten* and *Vertretung;* while, recently, my travels through the German dictionary turned up a word I had not met before—*verkoerpern*. These different words have distinct overtones in German and suggest different ideas about what it is for one thing to "represent" another: to stand in for it, resemble it, or serve as a sign of it. Furthermore, the term "represent" is at home in a wide range of subjects, covering both the Humanities and the Sciences—Natural and Social—in addition to reappearing in the realm of practical politics. Much political theory today is devoted to the conditions for any system of government to be "representative": in *The Concept of Representation*, for instance, Hanna Pitkin inquires to what extent the make-up of a legislative assembly (say) must "resemble" the make-up of the electorate it "represents"; and that question teasingly parallels questions that Nelson Goodman deals with in his own philosophy of art.[8]

Meanwhile, "representation" has a part in Natural Science: in particular, in theories of perception and the philosophy of science. In neurophysiology, for instance, the model for thinking about perception scientifically was for a long time the *camera obscura*. The historical document for this discussion is Hermann von Helmholtz's *Physiological Optics,* but many of his questions carried further ideas that were implicit in the writings of Immanuel Kant, and even John Locke. If the image of an external scene formed on the retina of the eye is to be perceived in a "mental" realm in the depths of the brain, must that image be *inverted* in the process? Or, in terms closer to those of our own time: Do the patterns of excitation in the cortex copy the shapes of the images on our retinas? Is there an isomorphism between these images, patterns of excitation and the other elements in perception, as Piaget used to speculate? To leave everyday perception for theoretical physics: Do the forms of theory we use to explain physical phenomena mirror the forms of the physical phenomena, or is Nature a Black Box whose interior we cannot discuss? (Ludwig Boltzmann, Heinrich Hertz, and Ernst Mach provide rather different solutions of these problems.)[9]

At this point, we are close to the philosophical debate about language, perception, and the roots of *meaning*. Early attempts to develop a neurological theory of meaning were influenced by ideas about the relations between our percepts and the language we use to report them. The epigrams that come to mind—about "percepts without concepts" or "concepts without percepts"—are Kantian; but the underlying ideas can be traced back to Epicurus and Lucretius in Antiquity, while Hartley advanced the eighteenth-century theory that *vibratiuncles* carry the images of objects to our minds, as the counterparts of the *corpuscles* that are the fundamental units of material substance.

We noted earlier Plato's suggestion that onomatopoeia is a prototype of the ways in which language acquires meaning; but for present purposes it is convenient to start with Locke's position. This has to do with the relationship between *impressions* and *ideas:* the "impressions" that appear in the mind—via the *sensorium commune*—when we have sensory inputs about which we as yet have nothing to say, and the "ideas" generated by repeated exposure to similar impressions. Yet the puzzle remains: "How can meaningful 'ideas' be generated by the repeated impact of 'impressions' that are as yet meaningless? And how do particular words come to be linked to the resulting 'ideas'?"

If Locke's account had held water, it might have met Leibniz's need for a language intelligible to people in all cultures: repeated impressions generated ideas just because of their similarity, and this power should presumably work equally well for people in any country or community. Yet there was reason to doubt that different people had similar impressions, even in quite similar situations: this required a "pre-established harmony" for which Leibniz could find no independent reason, and he rejected Locke's theory as a solution to his problem. Nor could he accept Descartes's explanation of universal, innate ideas: these were to be independent of our sense impressions, and Descartes had to show how they acquired the *certainty* with which they presented themselves to reflective people in all cultures. In an unholy World, that appearance of certainty might have been illusory; so a perfectly Benevolent Creator must provide a Divine Guarantee of the adequacy of these ideas, and Leibniz could see no rational basis for this.

Thus, neither ideas alone, nor ideas produced by impressions, yielded an agreement about the origins of meaningful language. But this left open the third basic element in our linguistic activities, and the most plainly linguistic element—namely, "propositions." For seventeenth- and eighteenth-century believers, it was theologically unacceptable to regard Language as a human product: somehow or other, God's fashioning of Human Nature must have given us our inborn linguistic capacities. So an anthropocentric view can be found with real force only in the work of Ludwig Wittgenstein. In his *Tractatus*, the origin of meaning lies in the quasi-pictorial relationships we create between the *Satz*, or "proposition," and the *Tatsache*, or "state of affairs" that it represents. Wittgenstein uses for "represent" the term *darstellen*, which is also used for the relation between a map and the territory it maps, or between an art exhibition and the work of a painter.[10]

Wittgenstein's much-quoted statement in the *Tractatus* reads, *Wir machen uns Bilder der Tatsachen*. This is generally translated as "We picture facts *to* ourselves," but this fails to capture the constructive aspect of human action. So let me propose, instead, "We fashion *for* ourselves representations of states of affairs": this carries over into the language of Wittgenstein's *Philosophical Investigations*, which offer an explicit account of how new words are launched into the world, in the context of different activities and forms of life. Yet, we may ask, how far can we assume that people in different cultures, with different forms of life, end by sharing constellations of activity that require them to adopt the same patterns of thought and language as well? At times, I have known colleagues to insist that, as a cultural relativist, Wittgenstein could not explain how people from different cultures could possibly share the same concepts, while others insisted, to the contrary, that he was a "nativist" for whom—as for Descartes—these ideas and patterns of activity were already present at birth. Neither of these views was one that Leibniz would have found acceptable.[11]

Sadly, then, there is no way to do what Leibniz hoped to do: namely, equate the private "thoughts" of people in different cultures, language communities, or nations in a way that was evident to the reflective Reason, without any arbitrary assumptions. Nor, without some "providential harmony," was there any way of guaranteeing in advance that different peoples would spontaneously generate the same "thoughts" in the same situations. So creating a universal language was not only—as Leibniz had conceded—hard, but quite impossible. For it required people in all cultures to live their lives in ways similar enough to yield identical languages as end products. In other words, it assumed *from the outset* what the whole enterprise was intended to guarantee *as its final outcome*. Lacking prior agreement on meanings, posterior intelligibility could never be guaranteed.

To sum up this historical analysis: a common *method* of geometrical rigor, and a shared language in which to reason, constituted Leibniz's strategy for transcending the Babel of doctrine at the heart of the seventeenth-century religious conflict. But it was only one strategy among others. Such sixteenth-century humanists as Michel de Montaigne and Francis Bacon had had a real alternative. As a classical skeptic, Montaigne exhorted his readers to live with ambiguity and uncertainty—not to mention the plural beliefs we are familiar with from cultural anthropology. The empiricist Bacon discouraged people from trying to "prove" their beliefs at all certainly, since *certainty* was a mere Idol: rather they should explore the strengths and weaknesses of particular beliefs, using experiential instead of mathematical methods. Such undogmatic (or antidogmatic) methods of inquiry appealed to the heirs of Renaissance humanism; but after 1610 religious conflict got out of hand, and Montaigne's urbanity was no longer acceptable. By then—to recall a couplet from George Meredith—the intellectuals of Western Europe were "hot for certainty"; and, for the next thirty years, their most urgent questions received only "dusty answers."

Despite all objections, the charm of rationalism, which carried such conviction with seventeenth-century readers, was not just the formal elegance of mathematical arguments. They lived in times of turmoil. The emergence of nation-states led to the "establishment" of national religions, which deepened the task of religious toleration. Faced with Henri IV's insistence on mutual toleration, Conservative French Catholics had called, even before 1600, for *un roi, une loi, une foi*: persecuting Huguenots was a natural result, for how could loyal French citizens reject the religion of the French nation? In England, conversely, how could loyal Anglicans tolerate "Papists" who planned to hand the country over to foreign control? Thus, the corrosive seventeenth-century rhetoric of Papists and Heretics prefigured the rhetoric of Orthodox Serbs and Balkan Muslims, which was used in the 1990s to defend similar theologically based bloodshed.[12]

Am I claiming that, like seventeenth-century philosophy, Leibniz's Dream of an Exact Language sprang from the ideological deadlock of the Religious Wars? This is part of the story, but not the whole. Another factor is worth noticing. The turmoil that has led historians of early modern Europe from Mousnier on to speak of a "general crisis" was grave enough. But it occurred just as Copernicus's successors were questioning the larger cosmological scheme. For many people, this confluence of uncertainties—social, cosmological, and religious—was the last straw; but for the preachers it was a sign of cosmic decay, implying that God would plunge the World into Apocalypse in (say) 1657. So serious-minded European intellectuals had their reasons to reconstruct the World View on a more secure basis, and to see Descartes's philosophical project as having dual goals: its joint totems were Euclid and Galileo. As a physical theory, the *Principia Philosophiae* of Descartes deciphered the code of Material Nature; meanwhile, the *Meditations* served as one step toward the parallel goal of reestablishing grounds for certainty in the products of the Human Mind.

From 1690 to 1890, natural philosophers kept alive an unthinking confidence that, between them, Galilean mechanics and Euclidean geometry were the joint foundations of the Order of Nature and the Order of Mind. There might still be doubts about mental philosophy, but the basis of natural philosophy was laid with seeming certainty in 1687, and so remained for two hundred years. True, the Abbé Saccheri's failure to prove the "axiom of parallels" challenged Euclid's geometrical monopoly. But this was regarded as a purely formal difficulty: the new geometries of Lambert and Gauss, Riemann and Lobachevsky were irrelevant to planetary astronomy, let alone cosmology. The further challenge to Newtonian physics from Maxwell's electromagnetism, however, changed the situation radically, while the Three-Body Problem revived problems for a mathematical system of mechanics that had dated back to Newton's original arguments with Leibniz.

It was a multiple whammy. Max Planck's quantum theory of light absorption was followed in 1905 by Albert Einstein's paper on special relativity; so Newtonian physics, too, lost its intellectual monopoly, and the accepted World View was called in question. How did this affect the philosophical scene around the time of World War I? Frege wrote little about cosmology, but Russell from the start recognized that physics, epistemology, and logic were interdependent: he saw Einstein's work as a challenge, and wrote popular books on the new ideas, like *The ABC of Relativity*.[13] After 1919, with the rise of the Vienna Circle, the interdependence of Science and Philosophy was more obvious, and the name of Einstein kept recurring in the positivist debate. The crucial document was Russell and Whitehead's *Principia Mathematica*. So, inspired by Mach, the philosophy of science in this way tried to give back to natural philosophy the "objective certainty" it had lost with Kant.

The fortunes of cosmology and epistemology being once again linked in a debate about language, the story of twentieth-century philosophy—artificial languages and all—was launched on its familiar trajectory. In the twentieth century as in the seventeenth, this problem of language was still just the tip of the iceberg; and the dream of an exact language involved more than *intellectual* stakes. Today's problem has less to do with religious toleration than it does with cultural and racial diversity. How can Germans accept Turkish immigrant workers and their families as members of the *Bundesrepublik Deutschlands*? Can we reconcile a European "citizenship" with a dozen languages and several dozen cultures? What will save the Balkans from yet further disintegration? The task of transcending misunderstanding through new tools of "communication and reasoning among various peoples" is no less *actuel* today than it was for Leibniz in the 1670s.[14]

At the start of a new millennium, we do not need a *characteristica universalis* to replace colloquial English, *deutsche Sprache*, or *la langue française*—particularly in everyday life. In business dealings—as in air traffic control, or in conferences on artifical intelligence—Esperanto is dead; the only question is, "What will undermine the hegemony of English?" Yet on another level, Leibniz's project is still alive, in practical debates about worldwide computer links. Will PAL, NTSC, or SECAM become the international standard of TV transmission? What operating system will international computer networks use? Leibniz rightly saw Chinese as a special challenge: ideograms present software engineers with notorious problems. So, in practical terms, the people with the best claim to be the heirs of Leibniz are computer information engineers. Still, the bright aims of his program still face the same obstacles: what computers project across national boundaries is not just *universal* ideas and *error-free* reasoning, but equally cultural conflicts and international misunderstandings.

In 1677, the young Leibniz wrote about his plan in grandiose terms:

> I dare say that this is the highest effort of the human mind;
> and, when the project is accomplished, it will simply be up to
> humans to be happy, since they will have an instrument
> that exalts the reason no less than the telescope perfects our
> vision.[15]

We resonate to these ideals, but note that Leibniz's way of expressing them is confused. Now, just as much as three hundred years ago, no technical procedure can guarantee its own humane or rational use. It is one thing to *perfect* an instrument; it is another to ensure that it is *put to use* in just, virtuous, or even rationally discriminating ways. So the three chief Dreams of Rationalism turn out to be aspects of a single larger Dream. The Dream of a Rational Method, that of an Exact Language, and that of a Unified Science form a single project designed to purify the operations of the Human Reason by *desituating* them: that is, divorcing them from the compromising association of their cultural contexts.

Like Leibniz's exact language, then, the seventeenth-century Scientific Revolution was Janus-faced. The New Science was mathematical and experimental; but this left unclear just how the two leading features of this new Method—its mathematical structure and its basis in human experience—dovetailed together. This lack of clarity was initially an oversight, but it soon became deliberate. The rationalists only confirmed Pythagoras's feeling that a mathematical theory of sufficient power and elegance must have a practical application in human experience. Galileo declared that the Book of Nature is written in mathematical symbols, and thus a scientific cosmology was dependent on its decipherment. If philosophers could use mathematical methods to decipher the Book of Nature, they could read off the meanings of all natural phenomena, as we today may follow Michael Ventris and read (say) a text in Linear Minoan B.[16]

The success of Newtonian physics was thus a vote for *theoretical* cosmology, not for *practical* human dividends: the ideas of Newtonian theory were shaped by a concern for their intellectual coherence with a respectable picture of God's Material Creation, as obeying Divine laws. This view disregarded the sixteenth-century humanists' message, including Francis Bacon's vision of a *humanly fruitful* science. So they differed in spirit from the mathematical visions of Descartes and Newton, for whom Science paid theological, not technological, dividends. Only from the mid-nineteenth century did such practical-minded members of the scientific community as Rudolph Virchow revive Bacon's program for scientific technology. During the three hundred years after 1660, the natural sciences did not march along a Royal Road defined by a universal Rational Method. Instead they moved in a zigzag fashion, alternating the rationalist procedures of Galileo's mathematics with the empiricist methods of Baconian naturalism. Thus the rise of *ideas* in science was separated from a concern with its practical *fruits,* with scientists distinguishing the "pure" refinement of ideas from the "applied" exploitation of the technical possibilities they created. Under the hegemony of Newton, Bacon's practical program took a back seat: for many people, it was enough that scientists discovered the laws that govern natural phenomena, the better to glorify the God who created Nature in the first place. Using the understanding of Nature for material welfare, to reduce human pain and increase human comfort, was secondary to the spiritual and intellectual goals of Science.

As late as 1939, Bernal's book on *The Social Function of Science* (as we saw) had provoked reactions of horror in *bien-pensants* British scientists, who saw it as outrageous Marxist rhetoric. But after the destruction of Hiroshima the priorities of Science changed; these days, scientific research is financed in ways that balance off Newton's intellectual ideals against the technical aims of Francis Bacon. On the twenty-fifth anniversary of Bernal's book, indeed, many people remarked that the relations between science and government in Washington were more like those Bernal had advocated in 1939 than those that were current in Moscow, which were still governed by a traditional academic model.

Whether we rely on the eighteenth-century Sciences of Matter, the nineteenth-century Sciences of Energy, or the twentieth-century Sciences of Information, we still face two experiential tasks: to exemplify the abstract theoretical ideas of science in the concrete world of actual experience, and to use those universal calculations for the practical good of particular human beings. We can dream up all the theories we please, of communication and control, neurophysiological holography and artificial intelligence, deep grammar and brain function. But the further we move away from the Sciences of Matter and Energy, and toward the Sciences of Information, the more we must integrate *theoria* and *praxis,* and the fainter is the distinction between "pure" and "applied" science.

By now, the question "How should the new ideas of Science be utilized?" needs to be faced, even at the initial stage of conceiving possible new theories. So it is helpful to recall, at this point, why the threefold Dream of rationalist philosophy proved a Dream indeed. Some practical maxims will reflect this point:

> No formalism can interpret itself;
> No system can validate itself;
> No theory can exemplify itself;
> No representation can map itself;
> No language can predetermine its own meanings.

Similarly, no Science can decide which of its technologies are of real human value. If we are to face Bacon's issues about the uses of knowledge for human good head on, we must ignore the seventeenth-century ideal of intellectual exactitude, with its idolization of geometrical proof and "certainty," and recall the practical wisdom of sixteenth-century humanists, who hoped to recapture the modesty that had made it possible for them to live happily with uncertainty, ambiguity, and pluralism.

It is admirable to share Bacon's dreams in *The New Atlantis,* but let us be realistic about the obstacles to realizing those dreams—the most serious being the *epistemological* obstacles. The greater our interventions in the natural world, the less we can forecast or modify their effects, and the more significant will be their unintended outcomes. All the estimates of (say) the environmental impact of large-scale technological projects must be qualified by estimates of their intrinsic *un*certainty; and, before making collective political decisions about such projects, we need realistic estimates of the unplanned but calculable side-effects of their execution, so that our decisions have some claim to human wisdom. The story of the Aswan High Dam reminds us how the enthusiasm of engineers and politicians can override the human hesitations of scientists, and so generate technical disasters; the same risks are run today in the construction of the Three Gorges Dam on the Yangtze River.

Back in the 1960s Stevan Dedijer—a physicist who left Yugoslavia for Sweden to avoid being compelled to build a nuclear bomb for Tito—wrote about "the subversion of historical materialism by science." For historical reasons, Karl Marx and Friedrich Engels saw material production as the "base" of society, scientific ideas and the fine arts as "superstructure." A century later, it is not clear how to tell superstructure from base, and this very contrast is now problematic. In telling the story of twentieth-century life, we can hardly refer to the ideas of Norbert Wiener, Alan Turing, and John von Neumann as mere "superstructure." The output of the knowledge industry is not measured in tons of coal and iron ore, or in megawatt hours of energy transmitted from place to place. By now, the material products of the newer industries are far more dependent on their foundation in the mental activities of human beings than the reverse. The index of productivity in economically advanced countries is now the quality of their new ideas, not the quantity of material goods they fabricate.

One side-effect of this change has been a transformation in financial affairs. The economist Brian Arthur, writing about the phenomenon of increasing returns, and Bill Joy, the guru of Sun Microsystems, agree this far: that information technology is playing a major part in replacing the old economy of scarcities by a newer economy of abundance. If economic transactions are no longer limited by a universal law of diminishing returns, the classical business cycle may seem to have been suspended. Nor is this phenomenon confined to the highly developed parts of North America and Europe: with an educated intellectual class of Brahmins and others, India has a similar chance to develop a rich and livable economy. In our time, then, institutions adapt to needs defined by the technical capacities of our microprocessors; but the technical devices made possible by intellectual work on silicon architecture and computer software impose on the institutional responses understandings that go far beyond technical ingenuity. In computer technology and the like, intelligent action can only be judged against the situations in which it is exercised. As Aristotle knew, the role of Reason in fields like navigation and medicine is not shown in formal calculations, but in acting as the occasion demands with an eye to all the relevant factors of the action in question, including its unplanned side-effects.

We live at a time when the two branches of the Scientific Revolution—intellectual and technological—can at last be reconciled. We may take the intellectual imagination of Isaac Newton for granted, but in criticizing the practical uses of our understanding we equally need the humane wisdom of Francis Bacon. The dreams of seventeenth-century philosophy—infallible scientific method, perfectly exact language, and the rest—may still fascinate us and inspire powerful new theories. But the future depends just as much on our ability to recapture the values of the sixteenth-century humanists and maintain the fragile balance between the refinement of our practical skills and the human interests they serve.

6

Rethinking Method

One aspect of the standard view of "rationality" is the assumption that a single method can turn any field of inquiry into a "hard science" like physics. A more balanced view will allow any field of investigation to devise methods to match its problems, so that historical, clinical, and participatory disciplines are all free to go their own ways.

T O PICK UP AGAIN AN ISSUE I raised in the Introduction: at the heart of the current debate about Rationality lies a supposed link between rational thought or action and use of the procedures known to philosophers as "scientific method." This idea helped to prop up twentieth-century economists' belief that their theories were "scientific" in the same ways and for the same reasons as (they assumed) held good in the physical sciences. This is why I began by examining the supposed parallels between Economics and Physics on which that belief relied.

In its contemporary form, this argument is more coherent and single-minded than it was in the seventeenth century. Nonetheless, the belief that the ideas of rationality and method were tightly connected helped define the nature of that link from the start, and the standards imposed on scientific and philosophical arguments by the demand for a rational method were taken to be universal, not varying from place to place, from time to time, or from one subject matter to another. Again, the soundness of this method was taken to be self-evident and self-validating. Any reflective individual who—in Bishop Butler's phrase—"sat down in a cool hour" to consider its validity would see it without need for evidence or argument. Finally, the power this method of thought has over our reflections apparently compelled us to conform to it. In brief, a fully rational method would comprise universal, self-evident rules from which we deviated only at the risk of irrationality.

None of these assumptions was free of ambiguity, and throughout the subsequent debate they have been reinterpreted in significantly different ways. As to the *universality* of the method, the assumption that a "method" can ensure rational knowledge in all fields and cultures has been particularly challenged in the late twentieth century. Today's fashionable doubts turn on the question whether or not different peoples or communities have different systems of rules, with each claiming "universality" for its own rules. The *self-evidence* of the scientific method has also been open to doubt, since the very beginning of the debate. As for the idea that it is embodied in innate ideas that reflective humans cannot question, this means different things to different thinkers, and some have found the very notion of "innate ideas" frankly unintelligible.

In the last resort, Descartes was obliged to assume that God's Benevolence led Him to endow the human mind with these ideas; otherwise, some Demon could possibly disrupt the human reason in ways we could not detect. Leibniz dismissed this argument out of hand: the idea that rational modes of thought could be disrupted in this way was as offensive to him as Newton's suggestion that Nature was created by a capricious God. The necessity of these conclusions must be provable by arguments that anticipated Descartes's hesitations, and showed their incoherence in advance. (Those who find a belief in innate ideas bizarre or outdated may note that it resurfaced in the debate about Noam Chomsky's *Cartesian Linguistics*.) Finally, assuming that the procedures embodied in Scientific Method are also obligatory means that ignoring these procedures goes against our rational nature, and thus invites the philosophical charge of irrationalism.

It is useful to look back at the classical origins of the term *methodos*. This word referred to the pursuit of any goal, and made no particular reference to obligatory procedures. The type example given in Liddell and Scott's Greek lexicon is the phrase *numphes methodon*: "the pursuit of a nymph, or a young bride." The pursuit of knowledge was thus a special case of the broader idea of pursuits in general; and the idea of a pursuit that requires one to conform to a specific set of procedures is a further narrowing of the concept.[1]

A Wittgensteinian query is in order. Need the pursuit of human enterprises involve us in recognizing, or conforming to, any systematic set of rules *at all?* Do not misinterpret this reference to *rules*: scientific method is presented, not as a set of rules comparable to the Rules of Chess (which you ignore at risk of disqualification), but as a procedure for doing successful rather than ill-planned Science. There is no formal recipe for winning at Chess, and there is no reason why Science should be any different; this (as we shall see) is a point that Paul Feyerabend never tired of making. Rather, imaginative conception of new lines of investigation can take us far beyond the realm of rules.

The ease with which these ideas have become confused is illustrated by the story of Feyerabend's well-known book *Against Method.* In the 1960s and 1970s, Feyerabend acquired the reputation of a philosophical *enfant terrible,* and many readers understood him to be attacking Science itself, even to the point of advocating irrationalism in our pursuit of scientific knowledge. (His own phrase was "epistemological anarchism," which had quite different implications.) Though Feyerabend himself was certainly not hostile to science as an activity, his title was unfortunate. In the Greek sense, he was not opposed to *method,* only to the narrow conception of method that was regarded by some scientists—and even more by many philosophers of science—as the essential art of effective investigation.

As is clear to anyone who knows of Feyerabend's personal life and interests, he had a passion for Science, just as he did for opera and for the cinema. At one time, he was recognized as being a passable operatic baritone, and considered going on the stage professionally; for the rest of his life, too, he used to say that he would have preferred to be a film director rather than a philosopher. So, when he spoke of being "against method" in the sciences, all he wanted was to protect scientists from unreasonable constraints. There can no more be a set of fixed rules for making scientific discoveries than there can be for producing a great opera or a fine film. What was true of Verdi and Visconti was true equally of productive scientists: they must be allowed free rein, not criticized for a failure to conform to predetermined rules of composition.[2]

The perception of "rationality" associated with the popular idea of Scientific Method—as universal, self-validating, and compelling—has become increasingly implausible during the last thirty years, and this allows us to focus more directly on the resulting assumption that the pursuit of knowledge depends, not just on conformity to rules, but on acceptance of a *singular* set of rules and procedures appropriate for all peoples and all subject matters. So at this point let us take up again the alternative idea, that productive rational activities employ a *multiplicity* of procedures which depend on the multiple tasks we set ourselves in the course of all our different enterprises. Far from being fixed and universal, our procedures must vary with the different tasks that we are undertaking.

Six different claims are made about the nature of truly "hard" sciences. The first is the overall thesis, that a singular, universal "scientific method" governs all our enterprises. The second is that historical inquiries are essentially different from scientific ones, so that it is particularly difficult to bring a highly theoretical discipline like physical cosmology under the same set of rules as (say) traditional natural history. Then we must look at three related issues: the supposed objectivity of successful scientific discoveries, the need for scientists to be detached in their inquiries, and the temptation for them to handle professional matters in an elitist manner. Finally, we will look at a more political point: the need for those who deal with practical problems to be granted the same intellectual and social prestige as those who pursue the mathematical kinds of theoretical inquiries that attracted the "new philosophers" of the seventeenth century.[3]

We may begin with the idea of singularity itself. As we have seen, the preferred rational method for scientific inquiry, from the time of Galileo on, was that of mathematical physics in general, and planetary mechanics in particular. The methods attributed to physics were assumed to embrace—though in some cases indirectly—all other scientific and philosophical inquiries. From Galileo on, this idea rested on a theological basis, and involved questions of Faith. This dependence on theology was not without precedent: the historian R. G. Collingwood, for instance, argued that the idea of a single all-embracing theory of Nature occurred to human thinkers only with the rise of monotheistic religions. In the Homeric epics—the *Iliad* and the *Odyssey*—the struggles of the Greeks and the Trojans retained a polytheistic flavor. Different processes were interpreted as the work of different gods: Athena or Poseidon, for example. In literary terms, indeed, these epics often read like diplomatic discussions among rival powers, who call up different natural agencies to serve their interests. By contrast, a more familiar view of a unitary theory is to be found in Lucretius's long poem *On the Nature of Things;* but Lucretius's view was only one of the alternative pre-Galilean programs for a rational Science, and the scale tilted definitively in Galileo's favor only in the seventeenth century.

The realization of this dream took time. Leibniz was as firmly convinced of the need to move in this direction as Descartes or Newton, but had a clearer and more refined understanding than they did of the problems it involved. As a result, although he continued to advocate Unity as a general program, Leibniz saw the world as made up of multiple levels of units: not all of them had the same theoretical status as "particles" in Newton's dynamics. Instead, he recognized differences of complexity in the activities—even the perceptions—of different natural systems, and referred to them as so many distinct kinds of "monads" within his overall System of the World.

Even Descartes found it hard, in the last resort, to develop an all-embracing Natural Philosophy. Thoughts and Things (he believed) display different regularities, and must be governed by different laws: to the end of his life, he found the relations of thoughts to things something of a mystery. Of all the seventeenth-century philosophers, Hobbes was the one who struggled most determinedly to overcome this problem, while preserving the strong points of Descartes's philosophy. Thoughts and Things, in Hobbes's view, had more in common than Descartes ever conceded; and, in his own theoretical system, he assumed that, on a fundamental level, they both obeyed the same laws.

In the underlying European world-view, then, the value of a single all-embracing system of theories, into which phenomena of all kinds could eventually be fitted, was taken for granted right up until the twentieth century. Even after Euclid's and Newton's ideas were called in question, this view of scientific method remained the one to beat, and Russell's system of mathematical logic, published with Alfred North Whitehead in 1903 as *Principia Mathematica*, filled the niche for an abstract, fundamental theory left vacant by the loss of Euclidean geometry and Newtonian mechanics.

By the 1920s, it was clear that the accepted theories faced a great many unsolved smaller problems. From the mid-nineteenth century, there had been serious scientists who saw the idea of explaining natural phenomena in statistical rather than causal terms as a confession of failure. The physiologist Claude Bernard was one, and his hesitation to allow statistical explanations the same legitimacy as causal ones was also influential in physics.[4] Thus, the development of quantum mechanics led Albert Einstein to protest at the probabilistic nature of quantum-mechanical explanations.[5] But the full depth of our difficulties has been clear only in the last twenty years. We saw earlier how Henri Poincaré's reanalysis of the Three-Body Problem opened the door to possibilities that have come seriously into play in contemporary Chaos Theory; and, for better or for worse, a system of cosmology based on such ideas as these is quite as unlike the classical Newtonian World Picture as are (say) the new theoretical models for social and economic theory being developed at the Santa Fe Institute.

From 1500 on, plenty of scholars were more interested in History than in Physics, but their investigations played little part in the development of cosmology from Galileo to Newton. Even when their speculations about the history of nature overlapped into fields that we recognize as scientific, the questions they asked were ones that became central only after chemistry united with physics in the early 1800s. As the chief ideologue of the new physics, Descartes did not see that natural philosophers had much to learn from history. In retrospect he admitted that, in his youth, he had found poetry and history entrancing enough; but, once the focus of his interests moved into mathematics, he decided that these fields, though pleasing, lacked intellectual depth and seriousness. History he compared to foreign travel: it broadened the Mind, but could not deepen it. Intellectual depth could be achieved only in fields where knowledge was framed in mathematical terms.

In the seventeenth century, then, history was at odds with the natural sciences: in particular, it was detached from cosmology. Only with Kant's *General Natural History* (1755) do we find an attempt to frame a developmental account of Nature in terms adapted from Newtonian dynamics. Aside from that, scientific naturalists in the late seventeenth and early eighteenth centuries were concerned with the variety of living forms, on the one hand, and with early speculations about historical geology, on the other. Devout zoologists like John Ray took it for granted that God created the World with its species of plants and animals already fixed and distinct.

Indeed, Ray's book about the variety of species, as part of the Creator's Design for Nature, was actually called *The Wisdom of God.*

For their part, the historical interest of geologists was piqued by discoveries, in the course of mining and surveying, of buried fossils and valleys seemingly eroded by water. Around 1750, observant naturalists traveling in central France remarked on the prevalence of hexagonal basalt rocks, like those visible in the volcanic regions near Vesuvius. (Even the cathedral at Clermont Ferrand was built from this stone.) As a result, those observers who brought their experience in other countries to bear on the mountains to the west of the Rhone from whose foothills basalt had long been quarried recognized that their peaks had been the cones of volcanoes now extinct, whose topsoil had been covered with vegetation for so long that the inhabitants never recognized this origin. One basic assumption alone obstructed the volcanic hypothesis. Before the 1750s, and for many people long after, the new geology was generally interpreted biblically, as one part of the story of a World that had been created six thousand years ago, with basic forms unchanged down the centuries. Yet, if that were so—educated readers asked—how could these geological transformations have taken place as violently and quickly as Biblical literalism assumed, and why did we have no surviving reports or legends about their occurrence?[6]

Quite aside from Biblical issues, the question of organic evolution, already active well before Charles Darwin and Alfred Russell Wallace, faced methodological objections. As historical studies, theories of evolution did not possess the level of abstraction expected of cosmological theories. Unlike Newton's *rigid bodies* and *attractive forces*, their topics—populations of animals or plants—were rooted in particular places and times, and available to direct observation, so they could not display the kinds of "necessity" or "certainty" open to a theory of dynamics or universal gravitation. This problem was even more acute in the human sciences. There, one collects evidence of the ways in which people live together, whether by ethnographic study or the reports of participants, and judges the rationality and certainty of our generalizations in the light of those data. The room available for theorizing thus both influences, and is influenced by, the particular ways in which humans adapt to the practical problems of living together; and, as we have begun to see, culture and history become inescapable, while the particularity of cases determines the kinds and scopes of the rational procedures involved in studying them.

At this point we must look at three problems having to do more with the intellectual attitudes of scientists and humanists than with the World of Nature: the question of *objectivity*, the need for scientific *detachment*, and the *postures* that set scientists apart from their fellows or colleagues in the lay public. It is convenient here to consider these three problems together.[7]

In our picture of the physical world, the demand for scientific objectivity arises on two levels. On the empirical level, in (say) the design of scientific experiments, the task is to keep experimental results as free as possible from bias or distortion; on the interpretive level, the complementary task is to undercut scientists' outside interests, both in the investigation itself and in interpreting its results. Although in law, government, and other practical professions, similar issues had long carried weight, this emphasis on the importance of detachment and objectivity was new to natural philosophers. If "objectivity" meant lack of bias, there had been a longstanding demand that judges, rulers, and other professionals should deal with the situations that came before them for judgment in ways unaffected by their own political, economic, or family interests.

Initially, issues of objectivity were understood differently on these two levels. On the empirical level, the most "objective" mode of observation is that of a field ornithologist who stays in a "hide" in observation range of his birds, so that he can record their behavior without attracting their attention, let alone disturbing them. An effective hide enables one to observe birds through binoculars, without serious risk that their daily activities will be changed by the activities of the ornithologists themselves. The situation is similar in experimental design: the aim of scientists is to minimize the influence of their procedures on the processes they are investigating, and so ensure that the recorded phenomena are not mere artifacts of the experimental set-up and interactions.

Once again, in the twentieth century, this influence turned out to be uneliminable: on the smallest scale, quantum mechanics sets a limit to the efficacy of our precautions. Still, for most purposes and in most cases, people can find out if the equipment they are using is sufficiently shielded from (say) heat or magnetic fields, and can make sure that it is built in a way that does not distort the sequence of events, so freeing it from irrelevant side-effects. This can be done because—in physics, at least—the point of experimental design is to guarantee that experiments are *repeatable*. The arts of experimentation put experienced scientists in a position to notice when someone else's experiment is sloppy, unreliable, or incapable of yielding significant results. If they have reason to suspect such shortcomings, they can try repeating the experiment for themselves, and if on repetition they get different results from those first reported, something must be wrong with one or the other of the two experiments, and the report must stay in limbo until that difference is resolved.

So presented, the empirical demands of objectivity are less ambiguous in Physics than in the Humanities. Physical phenomena may repeat themselves more or less exactly, but it is rare for human situations to do so. When we repeat an experiment in Physics, we may be confident of the resulting phenomena turning out as before; but we can be far less confident that sufficiently similar human situations will yield just the same results. The individuals whose behavior we are studying may act differently a second time just because they are aware of having been observed on the first occasion; and other groups of human research subjects may act differently for any of a dozen reasons.

In empirical sociology, for instance, it is hard to devise ways of observing human behavior comparable with the ornithologists' use of hides. Something of the sort can be managed at a price. If we study traffic at the intersection of two streets from an observation post on a tall building, for example, we may record the movement of pedestrians across a street without their being aware of our scrutiny; but in general, in the human sciences, we can eliminate interactions between the Observer and the Observed only to a limited extent. Indeed, if behavioral scientists try too hard to maintain their detachment by preventing such interactions, they reject a source of valuable insights. (A psychiatrist who never asks questions of his patients will have little material to work with!) In the human sciences, any distorting factors have their sources elsewhere, such as in the way we formulate and interpret scientific issues. Critical philosophers from Frankfurt, like Jürgen Habermas, see language itself as putting blinders on social scientists, and destroying their ability to give unbiased reports.

In anthropology, the problem of interpretation is somewhat different. It is rare for more than one ethnographer to live among, and write about, the same people or culture. Historically, their reasons for refraining from checking each other's observations were initially ones of pure courtesy: ethnography was an enterprise for gentlemen-administrators who took their colleagues at their word regarding the accuracy of their reports. Yet, aside from these conventional hesitations, there are other reasons why replicability has less force in ethnography than in electromagnetism. The multiplicity of occasions makes human conduct kaleidoscopic and circumstantial, and demands for exact replication would require keeping human subjects isolated from external influences, whether in cages, prison cells, or Skinner boxes.

The appeal of radical behaviorism—in which experiments are designed to conform, as far as possible, to the extreme demands of the traditional model—lay in B. F. Skinner's claim that this was the only way to make experimental psychology a truly "hard" science. Yet this claim also created problems for experimental psychology itself. In the 1960s, for instance, Holz and Azrin, two of Skinner's most influential lieutenants, published a paper in which Skinner's standards were used to appraise existing studies of human verbalization as a kind of language use. The surprising outcome of their study is that only three papers met those standards: these were concerned, respectively, with stammering, the enunciation of sibilants, and the speech of psychotic patients in a mental ward. In short, it turned out, you could make the study of human verbal behavior truly scientific only if you limited yourself to observing *vocalization* rather than *verbalization:* how linguistically useful noises can be produced, not how words acquire meanings. In anthropological jargon, Holz and Azrin were concerned only with the *-etic*, not the *-emic*—with the phonetics of sibilant production, not the phonemics of meaningful utterances.[8]

The same problem faces experimental psychologists in all cases where they hope to reach statistically significant results. For many years, behaviorists would recruit students as research subjects and treat them as interchangeable, regardless of their backgrounds. Each of them was referred to as "S": an anonymous, cultureless respondent. If they were hired to react to culturally neutral experimental stimuli—such as just-noticeable color differences—no problem arose. But as soon as the experiments relied on concept use or involved differences of meaning, there was no longer any guarantee that the backgrounds of the different research subjects would remain irrelevant; on the contrary, this uncertainty about the research subjects denied experimenters the opportunity to treat their responses as belonging to one-and-the-same class.[9]

These problems are special cases of a broader difficulty. At the outset we asked, "Why were the first social scientists so keen to be the 'Newtons' of social theory?" The activities of human beings are less like the motions of planets, or rigid spheres, than they are like the behavior of animals. So why should we think that the aim of the human sciences is to predict the future behavior of human beings, in the way that the aim of a physical science was (supposedly) to predict the future behavior of physical objects? The engagement of an experimental psychologist with research subjects in a laboratory is unlike an ornithologist's engagement with the birds he observes through binoculars: it is more often an interactive relation, by which research subjects and experimenter come to understand one another and arrive at shared discoveries. On occasion, indeed, the purpose of cooperation will even be to improve the subject's conduct and life plan. Thus, psychologists are in the business not so much of predicting their subjects' conduct as of helping them understand the options available to people in their situation. In the human realm the future is open, and will be affected by what the people involved do in the meantime: the subject matter of practical psychology is not forecastable futures, so much as futures that are within people's reach and so—to use Bertrand de Jouvenel's neologism—*futuribles*.

If this is true in individual psychology, it is no less true in such social sciences as Economics. When Alan Greenspan tells Congress that we risk renewed inflation, he does not hope that his prediction will be verified. On the contrary, his purpose in offering this forecast is to convince Americans that they must change their habits of consumption and saving, so as to avert this outcome. Greenspan would rather be Cassandra than Newton: he is hoping that people's changes of policy will lead to a better *futurible*, not predicting what will happen if things go on as they are. In American politics in particular, another distinction is also helpful. In theoretical analyses of economic or political problems, the solutions cannot be expected to be as definite as the answers at the back of a mathematics textbook. Real-life political and economic situations cannot be dealt with so simply. Often the best we can hope to do is to manage the situation we are in by acting in a way that helps to moderate the conflicts involved, while taking care to avoid adding still further complexities to the initial situation. In this area of experience, an honest practitioner will not pretend that he can achieve the kind of detachment that political and economic theorists suggest.

In anthropology, equally, the idea of "objectivity" needs to be taken in a sense that fits the purposes and methods of the discipline. Margaret Mead and Gregory Bateson's work, for example, was largely interactive. They did not treat the members of any community like the birds that an ornithologist tries to avoid disturbing; rather, they entered into the community's life closely enough to read it "from within," like a depth psychologist. Their methods of investigation no doubt entailed problems of their own, but at least they did not impoverish their material by keeping their subjects at arm's length. In the human sciences, that is, the line between bias and detachment is very hard to draw. Parents may claim to treat their children fairly, but those close to the family may know that in actual practice the favorite child gets more than his fair share. A judge may give every appearance of impartiality in presiding over a Court, yet he may—notoriously—give disproportionate punishments to defendants of color for what outsiders see as racial reasons. Similarly, we all learn to take witnesses' reports of automobile accidents with a large pinch of salt: some of them exaggerate their ability to say what they saw, while others are interested in escaping from a situation at only a minimal cost.

In a dozen ways, then, issues of *objectivity*—in the sense of a *bias*—are familiar for as long as we can recall. From the Judgment of Solomon on, literature and scripture have preserved stories showing how hard it is to treat situations "rationally" (without distortion) and also "reasonably" (without injustice). The sources of difficulty vary from situation to situation, but in general the word "bias" fits them all. We encourage parents to avoid favoring one child over another; we require judges to treat all defendants with the same procedural care; and we wish witnesses gave accurate accounts of events without their involvement warping their perceptions. In a word, we want all people to be *unbiased* or *objective* in their handling of such issues: this may be an impossible ambition, but at any rate it is an admirable one.

Behind the differing ideas of objectivity that play a part in the natural and human sciences, there lies a deeper point. For three hundred years, natural scientists—especially in physics—have been used to thinking of their objects of study as clearly defined and distinct. We are in no danger of confusing rocks with trees, or planets with gods, even though pre-Greek cosmologists around 800 B.C. encouraged people to think of the planets as divinities. By contrast, when we study human beings and their institutions, it is harder to divide the field of study for scientific investigation in a way that can claim complete objectivity. As Jürgen Habermas and the Frankfurt critics are right to insist, ways of classifying humans and institutions are based as much on the observer's moral or political attitudes as they are on intellectual considerations. In analyzing disputes about (say) industrial organization or electoral psychology, the causes of unemployment or the dynamics of political change, we must focus attention on the personal attitudes of the writers involved at least as much as on the intellectual content of their arguments.

Such comments carry serious weight, of course, only if they have a solid empirical foundation; but too often the Frankfurt critics argue only that people's opinions and interpretations are *liable to be* distorted by political interests, without doing the empirical work required to demonstrate that they *are in fact* distorted in this way. Yet the nature of "objectivity" in the human sciences can be clearly defined only if we keep our eyes open to the difference between the *liability* of scientific views to distortion, and the *actual* distortion of those views. In its extreme form, indeed, the posture of such critics seems to imply that they alone can view the contemporary situation "objectively." The views that they criticize (they argue) are distorted by class, gender, and other interests, which put blinders on those who adopt them. They themselves, however, claim to cut through the fog and get to the truth, without risk of being misled in the same way as those they are criticizing.

In the context of late twentieth-century philosophy, this argument belongs to what Paul Ricoeur calls the hermeneutics of suspicion: philosophical positions that attack the opposition by impugning their motives, not refuting their arguments. It is as if the Frankfurt critics had a space platform from which they can diagnose the thoughts of mortals on the Earth, without their own positions being open to question. Yet, once we allow motivation to be an issue, we are all in the same boat, and this stratospheric attitude is in danger of being a sham. Why do the critical philosophers think they are the only people having an impartial or unbiased position? How are they so sure that the hidden class, gender, or other interests that mislead those they attack, do not affect their own perspectives, too? If they are able to read their opponents' minds so clearly—seeing past surface rhetoric to the deeper interests behind it—why are they so confident that their own ideas are free from similar distortion and criticism? Seen from a truly impartial standpoint, the *hermeneutics of suspicion* must surely be balanced by an equally strong *hermeneutics of self-doubt*.[10]

Notice how this issue shifts the locus of objectivity in the human sciences. If we are seduced by the idea of an intellectual space platform from which other people's bias can be identified and corrected, we may assume that this is the unique locus for objective judgments about social, political, and other human matters. Recognized for the dream it is, this idea merely changes the subject. The pursuit of objectivity in the human sciences no longer depends on our ability to find a uniquely correct standpoint from which to arrive at proper judgments. No such unique viewpoint is to be found, and we are back where we started. In the social sciences as elsewhere, the problem of achieving objectivity is that of learning to counter our own biases. It requires us to make explicit, and to make allowances for, the interests and values that we ourselves bring to our research—whether this involves the intellectual activity of constructing social theories, or the practical activity of improving the institutions in which we ourselves participate. In such a situation, bias, impartiality, and objectivity are—at best—general norms that can acquire a specific force in practice, only when they are understood as embodied in particular kinds of situations and cases.

These arguments may leave mathematically-minded readers with a sense of loss. The dream of formal "algorithms" for guiding scientific procedures has a charm that will not quickly dissipate. For those who value mathematical exactitude above all other kinds of precision as the model for scientific inquiry, the alternative message of "different methods for different topics" will be a disappointment. Yet, over the centuries, we have been obliged to recognize a spectrum of different kinds of methods (in the plural) for sciences ranging from Newton's Planetary Theory—strictly factual and value-free, and in a style close to that of Euclid's Geometry—by way of empirical or functional sciences like geology, chemistry, physiology, and organic evolution, to those human sciences in which attempts to maintain value-neutrality finally proved vain.

If this spectrum resembles the similar spectrum of elements in the World of Nature that Aristotle introduced in Classical Antiquity—the *scala naturae*, or Ladder of Nature—this is no accident. Close to the human end of this spectrum lies the kind of inquiry widely referred to as action research, or sometimes as "participatory" action research. This is the kind of research in which the people working in an institution join in collective inquiries designed to show how well their institution operates. As in history or ethnography, this research is not directed at producing universal, abstract conceptual systems, but rather at local, timely knowledge of particular, concrete situations. As in civil engineering and clinical medicine, its goal is improving the state of the institution itself, not explaining its modus operandi in a purely theoretical spirit. Unlike ornithologists, who protect the objectivity of their results by hiding from the birds they study, action researchers draw the workers in an institution into the actual conduct of the research. So if, in this case, we are still to speak of "objectivity," it can no longer be equated with "detachment."

Above all, no one would pretend that the projects and procedures of action research are value-free. On the contrary, such research resembles (say) physiology in formulating research projects that will reveal the changes that it would be *good to achieve* as outcomes of the research. Far from the participation of the workers being an obstacle to the fruitful conduct of research, or a threat to the objectivity of its results, there may be no effective way of developing a fruitful action research project without the active involvement of the workers in the planning and execution of the research. Such research, that is to say, is guided by ideas about the differences between successful and defective institutions, and about the ways in which their working may be improved. Action research (one may say) is a "clinical" discipline, concerned not just with institutional *diagnosis*, but also with organizational *therapy*. Nor can the value commitments in such a project be criticized, in the Frankfurt manner, as distorting its formulation and execution. On the contrary, these criticisms have a real bite only where the value assumptions in an investigation are *hidden* or *unconscious*. In action research, by contrast, the first task is, typically, to make sure that they are well understood, and even stated as explicit policies.

A case history in management science can help to underline this point: it is told in Richard Gillespie's charmingly titled book, *Manufacturing Knowledge*.[11] This is a study of workers in the switch-testing section of the General Electric factory in Hawthorne, a Chicago suburb.

The significant feature of this project—from our point of view—was its failure to involve the participation of the workers concerned. The outcome of this study is often reported as showing that changes in the physical conditions of work—whether in the lighting level, or the color the walls were painted—always led to increases in output. But Gillespie shows that this account of the project is a professional legend, which does not represent its actual results. At a certain point in the project, Elton Mayo, an Australian management theorist, was hired to interpret its results. He brought to his interpretation conservative political attitudes that he did not state explicitly in writing his final report. As it turned out, he shared the interest of the factory managers in finding out how their workers could be used more productively.

In the Hawthorne study, the workers in question were a small group of immigrant women recently arrived from Eastern Europe, some of whom as yet spoke little English. Mayo's attitude toward these elderly women was patronizing: it never seems to have occurred to him that it might help if they felt personally engaged as partners in the research. He did not regard the women as totally passive, like an astronomer observing the planets' motions, but he gave the things they said about their work little more attention than ornithologists give to any incidental noises made by the birds they are watching. So the Hawthorne researchers perpetuated the superior attitude of "hard" scientists toward their objects of research, which had become habitual in organized Science since the mid-seventeenth century. Thus, the shortcomings of Mayo's work resulted, not from the general fact that all action research is flawed and unobjective as a result of the involvement of the workers, but from the fact that, in this particular study, his researchers' approach to these immigrant workers was *not participatory enough*.

Yet neither the success of scientific research nor the demands of methodological purity requires a social separation between working scientists and their research subjects. The situations in which action research takes the participatory road are so unlike those in which physicists undertake empirical research that the methods used in physics are, as near as makes no difference, totally irrelevant. As we cross the methodological spectrum from mathematical physics to action research, the values carefully screened out in planetary astronomy gradually reenter the picture. Just as a well-functioning heart is a *good* heart, a self-aware psychiatric invalid can have *good* ideas about her own treatment, and the interest of workers in their institution's workings can be an useful contribution to its *reform*.

The claims for Hard Science with which this section began—the search for general theories with timeless laws, the demand for a detached objectivity, and the insistence that investigations be "value-free"—are not (in Popper's phrase) demarcation criteria to divide truly scientific projects and disciplines from unscientific speculations: the Black from the White, the Saved from the Damned. They serve only to define the Newtonian pole in this spectrum, and at the opposite pole we find local, timely, and value-laden projects, each with its methods, organization, and type of objectivity. Darwin's claim that the theory of evolution was a genuine piece of Science was rejected by Karl Popper, Carl Hempel, and Noam Chomsky because its outcome was a historical narrative, which skeptics dismissed as "folklore," rather than a set of deductions from universal theoretical axioms. A similar criticism has been made of action research: "It may be OK in its own way, but don't call it 'Research,' let alone 'Science'!"[12]

Such issues of demarcation miss the point. Newtonian astronomy was supposed to reveal the Design imposed on Nature by its Divine Creator, who asked natural philosophers to think about Nature, not to change it. Action research, by contrast, is never an excuse for contemplating Nature dispassionately, but rather a way of devising *changes for the better* in the operations of institutions and organizations. Both its preoccupations and its methods are very far from the cosmological concerns of theoretical physics. But none the worse for that!

In putting *elitism* down as the final topic for discussion here, the goal is to replace the familiar dichotomy separating "hard" physical theory (*scientific*) from "soft" social practice (*unscientific*) by acknowledging a spectrum of fields with various procedures, all of which can be described—picking up the critics' chilly phrase—as being "OK in their own way." Intellectual elitism denies the titles of *rational, science,* or *research* to fields that depart too far from the Hard Science dream of theoretical physics; and Intellectual Democracy means taking the alternative route of letting each field develop methods appropriate to the basic goals of its enterprise. But it now appears that the terms *elitism* and *democracy* apply here in a social as well as an intellectual sense. This has to do, not with the vaunted superiority of hard sciences over other fields, but with the social relations between research scientists and their subjects. In the seventeenth century, natural philosophers confined their research to *physical objects:* these had no interests to express, nor did one need to consider their feelings. So the idea of objectivity embodied in "mathematical and experimental natural philosophy" placed rational scientists Upstairs, in a superior social position, and banished inert physical objects Downstairs, among the servants. This implication was, no doubt, unacknowledged by the philosophers themselves, but it did not deceive those about whom they theorized. In Cromwell's mid-seventeenth-century Commonwealth, political radicals were already vocal about this relationship, protesting that the language of Physics had the effect of debasing both Matter—"mass"—and the Lower Orders of society—"the masses."[13]

Once this social dimension of the idea of Hard Science is brought to the surface, we can see why *participatory* research is such a stumbling block to old-style methodology: it focuses attention on the need for management research to engage the participants in an institution in the organization of their own work. Yet craftspeople and factory workers are not inert physical objects without interests, perceptions, or feelings, nor are they whistling birds or growling animals, incapable of reflecting constructively on the activities their work involves. If we approach them from a position of superiority, as Elton Mayo did, we risk denying ourselves a valuable source of data, like a psychiatrist who neither talks nor listens to his patients; but if all participants are encouraged to enter the research on a footing of personal equality, they may come up with insights and proposals that the managers might not have thought of if they had not been involved.

To put the central point in an epigram: "A democratic (rather than an elitist) method in Science is a method for a democratic (rather than an elitist) Science." Those who elevate hard theoretical sciences above softer practical fields intellectually tend also to elevate scientists socially above the people or things that they study. Conversely, those who are ready to let any field develop procedures relevant to its own goals, on an equal intellectual basis, will be readier to let scientists admit their research subjects into the research activity itself, on an equal social basis.[14]

Does this epigram rely on a coincidence? Or is it a mere play on words? Neither of these is the case. The historical period in which Newtonian natural philosophy had unquestioned intellectual dominance was one in which intellectually advanced nations like Britain, France, and Sweden were class-structured in ways that harmonized the scientists' own professional interests with the political interests of the oligarchy. Until well into the nineteenth century, most working scientists were themselves aristocrats or gentleman, or else dependents of the aristocracy or the gentry, as ministers of religion, librarians, or secretaries. A few of them (it is true) were prepared to condone revolutionary activities, or even entertain revolutionary thoughts: these heretics included, among others, the editors of the *Encyclopédie* in France and Joseph Priestley in England. For most of the eighteenth-century scientific community, however, the important thing was—as the English say—to know on which side your bread was buttered, and most of the scientists were disinclined to bite the hand that fed them.

7

Practical Reason and the Clinical Arts

From Aristotle on, practical disciplines relied on "clinical" proce-
dures, which dealt in a timely way, not with universal, unchanging
structures, but with the particular problems of individual people or
situations. Our theories may help us understand why or under
what conditions such procedures work. But their practical success
need not depend on applying scientific theories, as the classical as-
sumptions require.

HALFWAY THROUGH OUR inquiries, we can see more clearly the
contours of the project we have embarked on. The aspects of life
that involve our Reason were seen as related to one another in different
ways at different stages in the history of society, or of philosophy and the
human sciences: in particular, during the thousand or more years from late
Antiquity to the Renaissance, in the four centuries from 1600 on, and during the twentieth century. We focused earlier on the challenge that the
new, exact disciplines of the seventeenth-century philosophers posed to
sixteenth-century humanism. In this transition mathematical ideas acquired a new prestige, at least for purposes of theorizing, so that physics
came to be seen as the star discipline. Yet, as time has gone on, the mathematicians in the Academy have begun to lose some of their primacy, and
their prestige has begun to rub off onto the more practical arts. So the second transition we shall be concerned with here is the tendency, in the late
twentieth century, for the practitioners to turn the tables, and look the
theoreticians squarely in the face.

How did such prestige attach to seventeenth-century physics in the first place? It sprang from the part that mathematics played in the development of a rational cosmology that was to displace earlier theological accounts of Nature. Seventeenth-century Natural Philosophy was a scholarly, not a practical enterprise. Cosmology had no day-to-day relevance to human welfare, so academics pursued it without being distracted by practical affairs. Though they did not underline the point in so many words, their attitude bears comparison with that in which Schumpeter spoke of the practical excursions of economic theorists as "dilettantic."

Even where theorists and practitioners presented their views in forms that were on their face similar, the preoccupations of the natural philosophers were quite unlike those of doctors, lawyers, or politicians in empirical substance. Philosophical theories reside in the Parmenidean World of Ideas, whereas "clinical" procedures belong in the Heraclitean World of Where and When. Modern philosophers explored the ramifications of the ideas around which their theories were constructed, but they did not add much fresh empirical content to our knowledge. Meanwhile, practitioners were continually adding to our overall empirical experience, in ways that might or might not pose a challenge to the current theories along the way.

Let us therefore carry our analysis of the dilemmas of Economics one step further. Here, the distinction we recognized earlier between the intellectual and institutional factors involved in the evolution of academic disciplines is directly to the point. The main source of tension between (say) the theoretical and clinical approaches to Economics lies not in the intellectual content of the discipline, but rather in the institutional arrangements that have determined how the discipline is understood. What has attracted attention for much of the twentieth century, and fuels Schumpeter's charge of dilettantism, is the prestige attached to pure theory in academic institutions: notably in Departments of Economics. But, on closer examination, this prestige itself turns out to have been a local and historical—in other words a changeable—fact about academic Economics at particular places and times. The emphasis on the centrality of pure theory has been a feature of academic life in the United States, and, more precisely, a feature of American Economics from the 1920s to the 1980s.

Scholars whose interests embrace both Economics and other disciplines can see the limited scope of this approach quickly and easily. Karl Polanyi, whose view of the subject was always embedded in a historical situation, had a subtler view. He refers to the need for the anthropologist, the sociologist, and the historian to study in their own ways the place occupied by the economy in the human societies in which people's livelihood is embedded. Twentieth-century economic analysis, in his view, had devised an analytical method that takes for granted the satisfaction of certain market conditions. Uncritical employment of this analytical method results in "an artificial identification of the economy with its market form." From David Hume and Herbert Spencer to Frank Knight, this identification places needless limits on our broader ideas about society and social life.[1]

The conventional wisdom in much of the American world of Economics—what we might better call the customary over-simplification—is a belief that academic economists have only one serious occupation, namely, the improvement of pure theory: only in this way do they contribute to the discipline in a manner worth rewarding. At the pinnacle of the institutional world, this attitude played a significant part in the choice of Nobel Laureates in Economics during the 1980s and 1990s. But, outside the narrowest sector of academic economists, a concern with mathematical theories has been less dominant, and the prestige of theory has been less exclusive. Instead, economic research has expanded in directions that involve a cross-fertilization of concepts and considerations of a strictly economic kind with historical and geographic, sociological and ethnographic inquiries that are not immediately reducible to economic ideas.

The difficulties that arose in our Bali vignette are just one sample of the larger range of problems created by trying to preserve the purity of scientific economics, and so placing limits on its human relevance. These problems frequently reappear in situations where the lives and practices of peoples outside the so-called "developed" or "mature" economies of (say) Western Europe and North America do not neatly fall under the would-be universal concepts and principles of the most highly esteemed theories.

Traditional agricultural techniques do not need to be associated with (say) religious institutions in order to be misunderstood. In much of Africa, as in Indonesia, the introduction of European methods of cultivation and systems of landholding is now seen to reduce, not increase, the productivity of local agriculture. For example, the long-term carrying capacity of rangelands in sub-Saharan Africa—the number of cattle that can in the long term be raised and put to work in those areas—was (it seems) underestimated by European onlookers, and even reduced, by imposing property boundaries of kinds customary in Europe itself. Older traditions, by which cattle from many communities and owners were free to range together across larger territories, finding food and water where the current year's weather allowed, have turned out to be more productive than the imported practice of fencing off farms and confining grazing herds to limited pastures. In the long run, the variations of weather from year to year have led to greater overall morbidity under these artificial European conditions than the traditional free-ranging practices might have done. In fact, the agricultural ecology of sub-Saharan Africa rarely if ever achieves economic equilibrium, and this places serious limits on the extent to which "equilibrium" theories can throw light on the success or failure of agriculture in these lands. (As I write, replacement of El Niño by La Niña—of unusually warm currents in the eastern Pacific Ocean by unusually cold ones—has redirected the jet stream, Texas has dried out, and the marginal areas of sub-Saharan Africa are having an uncommonly generous supply of rainfall. This will not, of course, last for long.)[2]

More generally, the cultural phenomena that are of greatest interest to sociologists, anthropologists, and geographers who look at the potential benefits of economic analysis compel scholars with interdisciplinary interests to look far beyond the narrowest concerns of economic theorists. From the 1950s on, the periodical *Economic Development and Cultural Change* has published many distinguished papers and reviews on interdisciplinary topics.[3] What historical or social factors, for instance, encourage and direct technological change? To what extent does the structure and culture of the traditional Chinese family serve as an engine, or an obstacle, to economic development? How are women's organizations contributing to the evolution of Indian society? (The continuing influence of Mahatma Gandhi is of interest here.) Inquiries of these kinds may not have carried a great deal of prestige in the leading circles of economists and American policy-makers in the 1980s and 1990s, but they have an important interest for the larger academic scene, and for the social and cultural practices of many countries.

All these points reappear most strikingly in the field of Development Economics. The successful union of intellectual and institutional innovations in the Grameen Bank, for instance, was helped by the fact that Muhammad Yunus was working on his home ground, and felt the essential facts of Bangladeshi village life in his pulse: he did not need a sociologist or a cultural anthropologist to draw his attention to them.[4] The same is true of (say) Partha Dasgupta, whose *Inquiry into Well-being and Destitution* has made important contributions to the subject. Dasgupta grew up in Bengal, and comes from a distinguished family of Calcutta Brahmins. So he knows the peoples he writes about by second nature, and did not need special training in cultural anthropology to develop his analysis.[5] On an even broader front, Amartya Sen—another development economist of Indian background—has given us a new grasp of the conditions under which famines occur: he has shown that the social and political obstacles to dealing creatively with natural disasters do as much as the natural disasters themselves to make famines unavoidable.[6]

For the rest of us, particularly if we live in the United States, economic understanding does not come so easily. To avoid the kind of disaster illustrated in the Bali vignette, we cannot afford to work in one discipline at a time, limiting ourselves to the abstractions of modeling Economics on a Newtonian "rational mechanics." Least of all can we afford to accept these limitations, if we are to develop "reasonable social sciences," concerned not with value-free facts but with actual human values and practices: if our grasp of these problems is to be at all exact, we need the additional perspective one can get only from the anthropologist, the sociologist, and the historian. Coming to understand how human lives go *well or badly*, *better or worse*, and how we can best help them fulfill their potential is the central task to be tackled if we are to achieve a practical grasp of social phenomena. But the human sciences can move in this alternative—or "clinical"—direction only if they build up their theories more on biological than on physical models, and so give up the myth of "value-free" science.[7]

Issues of human values may raise methodological problems, but the human sciences are no less *scientific* for abandoning value neutrality. The nineteenth-century physiologist Claude Bernard called his work "experimental medicine," not "the physics of the body." The subject of physiology was for him the difference between a well-functioning heart and a malfunctioning one; and if that was not a "value" difference, it is hard to say what is! From this point on, then, human scientists need no longer hesitate to study the differences between *well-functioning* and *malfunctioning* societies or cultures, organizations or personalities. That is just what the rest of the world can legitimately ask us to do.

This leaves me with only a last brief point to make about Economics. Even in pure theory, the grip of equilibrium analysis and the commitment to universality and stability are now loosening. In his analysis of increasing returns and path dependence in Economics, Brian Arthur quotes Schumpeter's *History* as follows:

> From the standpoint of any exact science, the existence of a uniquely determined equilibrium is of the utmost importance . . . Without any possibility of proving the existence of [a] uniquely determined equilibrium—or at all events, a small number of possible equilibria— . . . a field of phenomena is really a chaos that is not under analytical control.[8]

Writing as he did in the late 1940s, Schumpeter was not, of course, using the term *chaos* in the sense of late twentieth-century "chaos theory." Even before the development of that theory, he saw the idea of *equilibria* as indispensable to any economic theory that kept its subject matter under analytical control. By contrast, Brian Arthur challenges economists to look more carefully at the historical situations in which economic transactions take place, since these often make them exceptions to "universal" rules and principles. He has shown, for instance, that the success of technical innovations in several cases led to the commercial success of technically inferior devices, simply because they won a market position before there was any chance of a direct competition between rival products. Such an analysis has more in common, mathematically, with the "non-linear" mathematics of chaos theory than with the earlier, "linear" mathematics of the standard Newtonian analysis.

At this point, our road reaches a fork, and there are two alternative roads ahead. On the one hand, we can stay in the world of theory, and reformulate the human sciences in subtler terms, paralleling the new developments in physics made possible by twentieth-century critiques of Newtonianism. This is Brian Arthur's choice. He seeks to extend the reach of Economics, but in doing so he stays clearly on the side of theory. In writing about the commercial fortunes of rival brands of videotapes or typewriter keyboards, he does not seek to redress the failure of the less successful products in the market, but only to exemplify the theoretical phenomenon of "historical lock-in" with which his analysis is concerned.

On the other hand, we can now take the step from a *rational* to a *reasonable* view of the same subject matter. Muhammad Yunus surely conceived his redefinition of the concept of collateral in ways that refined the economic theory of Banking and Finance; but, for him, the top disciplinary priorities were always more practical than theoretical. His professional mission was to develop ways of tackling poverty and destitution in his home country, and this shows that his central concern was always with Practice rather than Theory. For us, likewise, it is time to turn the argument in a similar direction: namely, to the issues that arise across the board when we seek to put Reason to work in the realm of Practice.

In logical terms, the general ideas on which both theoretical and practical inquiries rely can be expressed as the major premises of Aristotelian syllogisms—"All A's are B's"; but the force of these premises is different in the two cases. In theoretical arguments, any statement of the form "All A's are B's" will be interpreted as meaning "*Any* A is a B": the use of the word "all" does not imply that we have counted every one and checked that it is a positive example in every case. On the contrary, as a theoretical generalization, it serves as a branch in the ramified tree of propositions that make up the whole theory: statements about particular cases are twigs, whose meaning is implicit in the general statement. On the other hand, in a practical argument, a general statement of the form "All A's are B's" will be taken to mean, rather, "*Every* A is (presumably) a B": this has generally—if not always—been the case on earlier occasions, and this experience entitles us to take this generalization as our starting point in facing new practical situations of an apparently similar kind. Thus, our earlier experience undergirds our practice on future occasions. Naturally, although our accumulated experiences may be secure for practical purposes, they cannot be deduced from any general principles in a strictly formal or geometrical manner. As Imre Lakatos put it, "In theoretical arguments, Truth flows downward from general statements to particular ones. Empirically, the contrary holds good: Truth flows upward from particular examples to broader generalizations."[9]

Still, the contrast between the general and the particular does not pit all theoretical conclusions against timely practices in the same way, nor has it always been interpreted by philosophers in the same way. For Parmenideans, theoretical principles are universal and permanent, in a way that practical experience cannot match. Practical fields like Engineering and Economics do not rest on cosmic abstractions, or claim the timelessness of the purest theories; yet the empirical generalizations employed in (say) bridge-building belong nonetheless in the World of Ideas, as the general facts that guide engineers when they embark on the tasks required for particular commissions on any individual occasion.

All of this was well understood 2,300 years ago, when Aristotle brought together his ideas about Ethics in his best-known work, the *Nicomachean Ethics*. To summarize a passage from early in this treatise:

> Matters of conduct have nothing fixed or invariable about them, any more than matters of health . . . Just as in the arts of Medicine and Helmsmanship, agents have to consider what is *pros ton kairon* [suited to the occasion].[10]

A sailor or a doctor may face rapid changes or unforeseen developments, and the need to act "as the occasion requires" puts the *timeliness* of his decisions squarely in the picture. The helmsman experienced in navigating the Aegean, for example, gains the skills that are needed when sailing in close waters. Standing at the helm of a boat, he will look for a way to steer between two close-by headlands against the wind, and he continually glances from side to side to judge variations in the wind or the depth of the water in order to recognize when the water is shoaling so rapidly that he must change tack. A physician too must be on the lookout for unexpected changes in a patient's condition, and for uncommon responses to medical treatment: these may be a sign that it is time to change the treatment, and find a new way of navigating the shoals of the patient's illness. One of the things that made Aristotle a perceptive commentator on the demands of practical reason, of course, is his background of having grown up in a medical family. The fact that he himself worked as a physician and was the son of a physician enhanced his understanding of *timeliness*, not just in Medicine, but in Ethics and practical fields of all kinds.

In the last thirty years, the contrast between clinical practice and biomedical theory has begun to be appreciated anew, but there was a time in the mid-twentieth century when most medicine was officially regarded as "applied biology." What made this interpretation fashionable was Abraham Flexner's 1913 report on medical education, which argued for putting biochemistry and physiology back at the heart of training. At the time, this change led to major improvements in the level of physicians' scientific knowledge. Rather than being a craft activity motivated by the sentiment, "It may be true in Theory, but things don't work like that in Practice," clinical procedures incorporated more and more advances grounded in the biological sciences. For quite a time, however, this change also encouraged a tendency for a new generation of doctors to overlook the non-technical aspects of clinical situations, whose significance was overshadowed by biological considerations. Only recently have the day-to-day arts of dealing with all of a patient's problems—technical and non-technical equally— won back their place at the heart of Medicine, along with clinical research itself. Although the range of diagnoses and treatments available to physicians today is continually being supplemented by new scientific work, the needs of timely clinical practice still take the central place, and the relevance to medicine of new physiological and biochemical knowledge is measured by its capacity to meet those needs.

This return to a clinical focus has been slower to carry general conviction as applied to psychiatry than it has in the more mechanistic parts of medicine. Even now, both inside and outside the Academy, many people doubt whether psychiatry has the same legitimacy as the harder biomedical sciences. Under a pretext of studying human phenomena, many writers today argue that human beings can be "reduced" to their genetic inheritance, their instincts, or their evolutionary history, while others isolate their cognitive and perceptual capacities, and try to replicate them in the form of computer operations. Howard Gardner quotes Erik Erikson as saying:

> The relativity implicit in clinical work may, to some, militate against its scientific validity. Yet, I suspect, this very relativity, truly acknowledged, will make the clinicians better companions of today's and tomorrow's scientists than did the attempts to reduce the study of the human mind to a science identical with traditional natural science.[11]

Why does he call mechanistic physiology "traditional"? For those who accept the need for methodological democracy, it will come as no surprise to find that one discipline's idea of what is "traditional" may be another discipline's poison.

To sum up: there is a moment in medical training when a young student faces the key task of clinical practice: *taking a patient's history*. To what extent is a patient's condition a result of earlier diseases, accidents, or other misadventures? To what extent must we explain it, rather, by the patient's family background, upbringing, and experience in life? And what pointers do we need to attend to, if we are to see just what the patient's problem is, and how it can best be remedied? These questions serve to define what I will here be calling "clinical" knowledge, and the contrast between a practitioner's reasonable judgments and a theoretician's rational computations will throw more light on the general differences between Rationality and Reasonableness.

Using a "clinical" approach does not mean giving up hope of establishing *general* truths. On the contrary, the term "universal" won a place in philosophical usage in just this kind of practical context, and the force of the term reflects its etymology. A *universal* was for the Greeks a *kat'holou*: this meant just the same as the English phrase "on the whole"—in the sense of "generally"—as it still does on the streets of Athens today. Aristotle did not claim that universal concepts were applicable invariably and without possible exception: in real-life situations, many universals hold generally rather than invariably. So, in medicine and other human disciplines, we must remember the difference between the general factual assumptions that support "reasonable" arguments in the practical arts, and the "rational" deductions that are the stock-in-trade of mathematically formulated theories.

The key feature of practical reasoning in the clinical arts, then, lies in their focus of attention. In theoretical physics and similar enterprises, scientists and philosophers are in the business of refining *general* features of the World; whereas in clinical fields, practitioners are concerned with what happens less on the whole (*kat'holou*) than on a *particular* occasion (*kat'hekaston*).[12] So the focus of clinical attention is on the particular *case*, which requires us to ask, "What is a *case*?"; and it is often easier to say what a case is *not*. These days people are so used to television courtroom dramas that their understanding of the term *case* is limited to the situations figured out by a fictional lawyer like Perry Mason. But that tells us only part of the story. What is particular in any given case is of course in part the *situation*, but it depends even more on the *person* or *people* whose lives a case affects;

and, even more, on the adventures (or *mis*adventures) that befall those characters. The use of the word "befall" in place of "happen" may look archaic, but it has the virtue of marking the fact that misadventures fall out of a blue sky, as happenings that we did not foresee and could not avoid.

Looking at typical cases, in this sense, we can start by thinking about time-slices in someone's life history. Life as we live it, in its daily concreteness, has a complexity that prevents experiences from being listed as neat, ready-made "cases": some misadventures must be considered from the angle of several professions at once. A countrywoman whose husband dies in a car accident will turn for advice to whoever is at hand. The accident may have affected her in many ways: legal, medical, financial, and even psychotherapeutic. She is unlikely to find all of these professions well represented in a small town, and the one to which she first turns may not be the one that is best equipped to help. Which clinical art will best answer her immediate needs? Whose help should she most urgently pursue? This may be the start of a long story.

Even if the woman consults a physician, it may take her only partway to an answer. The doctor's task is to examine her with several questions in mind. Was she too in the car when the accident occurred, and was she injured as well? Is that the cause of her weakness and lack of color, or does she have other problems? Does her poverty deprive her of an adequate diet, so that she has nutritional deficiencies? Or are her problems caused by viral infection, or blood poisoning, or an inherited kidney weakness? Medicine is so complex that a wise physician will keep his eyes open for half a dozen factors, and may even be ready to play a hunch that this patient's only medical trouble is the effects of shock. Before deciding what to do, the doctor must in any event think through a whole range of possibilities.

In his essay *Can a Doctor Be a Humanist?* Robertson Davies defines Wisdom as "that breadth of the spirit which makes the difference between the first-rate healer and the capable technician" and goes on to report his own experience as a young student at Oxford. Feeling unwell in a chilly Thames winter, he was sent by his tutor to consult his doctor, who "was not at all what I expected . . . He saw me in what must have been his consulting room, but it looked much more like a library, for it was lined with books and, because I can read the title of a book at forty yards, I knew at once that they were not books about medicine." The doctor asked him, "But why are you ill?" and was dissatisfied with his answers:

Why have these germs been able to get their hooks into you? Why are you ill in the way you tell me all your family become ill, when they have need of an illness? Is it a girl? What about your work? . . . You know, you shouldn't put so much emphasis on your work. Only second-rate people do that. And then, of course, their work eats them up. Whereas they, of course, ought to eat up their work. My work would eat me up, but I keep it in its place by climbing mountains. And, do you know, climbing mountains makes me a better doctor.

Robertson Davies adds:

Raymond Greene was indeed a very distinguished mountain climber, a greatly admired physician, and—this is not perhaps as irrelevant as it may seem—the brother of the novelist Graham Greene. And the London *Times* made it clear, to me at least, that he was a first-rate doctor because he never allowed doctoring to eat him up. He was a humanist first and a physician second.

The kind of doctor Robertson Davies praises as a humanist is not restricted by intellectual blinders: his activities are not so limited. Many of those who practice the clinical arts may set out to maintain the kind of spirit that Davies calls Wisdom, but the narrower their viewpoint and the more academic their preoccupations, the less likely they are to succeed.[13]

A report by another physician, my friend Eric Cassell, is also very revealing. He tells of being called to a distinguished medical school to go through the ritual known as Grand Rounds: unprepared appraisals of brand-new cases, designed to show colleagues and students how top-flight clinical practice is done. He was presented with a young black woman whose only symptom was that, two weeks earlier, she had begun to have blackouts in which she fell to the ground. The local experts could not make head nor tail of her condition; they ran all the biochemical, physiological, neurological, and cardiological tests they could think of, even to the extent of extracting spinal fluid by painful lumbar punctures. All of these tests had negative results. Nothing turned up to explain the blackouts.

Eric was faced on the one hand with a blank sheet, on the other with a living and breathing patient. So he turned to her and asked, "Tell me, my dear, just when did these blackouts begin?" She had never experienced anything of the kind (she replied) before the day, not long before, when her mother visited her apartment and—without any warning—dropped dead on the floor. "Oh, my dear," Eric replied, "how terrible that was for you"; and she immediately burst into paroxysms of grief. Hard as this is to believe, it was the first time she had been invited to speak for herself about just what had happened.

Rather than inadvertence, which would be professional incompetence, this failure to handle the case on a personal basis can be put down to the narrowing of attention we called "professional blinders." It is a failure that Aristotle would quickly recognize. In failing to ask when the symptoms began, the doctors forgot the role of *timeliness* in a medical history: they even implied that this part of the patient's history was irrelevant to a proper diagnosis. In that respect, they remind one of the economists that the Asian Development Bank hired to advise on the Bali irrigation project, who ignored the water temples because they thought that, as religious institutions, they could not be significant from an economic point of view. Temples were seemingly irrelevant to the technical questions they had been asked, so the economists regarded them as beside the point.

The idea that all the practical arts owe a debt to the skills Aristotle calls *phronesis* was not especially welcome to rational-minded thinkers in the modern period. Although, in its Latinized form *prudence*, this term keeps a place in words like *jurisprudence*, its broader implications are largely forgotten. The social scientists who set the academic pace in the first half of the twentieth century saw Aristotle as a whipping boy from whom they had nothing to learn. Even John Dewey, that moderate pragmatist, continued to regard Aristotle as someone whose ideas he could ignore—perhaps because he associated them with the dogmatic form of neo-Thomism taught by conservative-minded philosophers such as Mortimer Adler and others in his time. Viewed from the 1990s, Dewey's own ideas about "experimental logic" are not far distant from Aristotle's "topics": in particular, the concept of *phronesis* is still of value to us. So it is worth looking at the shifting emphasis in clinical medicine in the years after World War II—notably at the theological origin of the intellectual debates that have since become known as "bioethics"—especially because those same historical changes also throw light on the ways in which the practice of Medicine has responded to the successes of the new medical technology.

We live, it is said, in a culture of professionalism. Some people are happy about this: Alasdair MacIntyre sees the life of the professions as one of the contexts in which people can still experience at first hand the older, communal sources of moral obligation. Others deplore it: Ivan Illich regards professional solidarity as self-serving, and exhorts the laity to use all means at their disposal to frustrate or circumvent it. (He echoes George Bernard Shaw's earlier remark, "every profession is a conspiracy against the laity.") Between these extremes, the moral problems of professional life have become topics of active study for academics and the wider public, at universities, think tanks, and conference centers, and the daily press is full of stories about professional morality—or more often malfeasance, which makes better copy. Professional ethics is thus one of the topics of the present time.

This fact is not self-explanatory. From medieval guilds to modern associations of physicians and lawyers, professional groups have long had political and social power, and accepted responsibility for the exercise of that power. The rights and powers of medical practitioners are conferred by statutes that also impose legal restrictions on their use: in negotiating the agreements that confer their autonomy, they accepted accountability as well. Like most controversies that professional power gives rise to, this is ancient history; from Molière on, lawyers have been targets of ridicule: remember Mozart's *Così fan tutte*, Daumier's statuettes, and Dickens's *Bleak House*. (Shakespeare's Portia is perhaps the only truly lovable attorney in literature.) Yet professional life became open to serious academic analysis only recently; and we may inquire why lay people came to challenge the monopoly of professional physicians over medical ethics only after 1950.

The last fifty years have changed not just the activities of professionals, but the way in which outsiders perceive and criticize those activities. What is the source of these changes? In particular, what is at stake in the public's new attitudes toward the professions? It is hardly the case that we live today in a very different world from that of the mid-1950s: the nuclear threat has receded, and many people live somewhat more prosperous lives, but they do so in similar social contexts. Nor is professional life itself all that different from what it was fifty years ago. Some state legislatures have established new forms of clinical practice and professional self-discipline, but the general character of medical work has not changed much in these years, and—apart from "managed care"—the institutions in which physicians work preserve much the same legal framework.[14]

The more notable changes have come less from the side of the professions than from their lay clientele, from the new technical achievement of medical technologists, and from contemporary social critics: these are responsible for the weight of contemporary concern with Medical Ethics. Why, then, do the public's expectations about professional ethics differ so much now from what they were in earlier decades? Why do people demand so much more accountability and participation? One reason is that recent years have seen a dramatic increase in the range of things that medical practitioners can do for their clients: in the last two decades medicine has offered possibilities at "the edges of life"—in the neonatal intensive care unit or the geriatric ward—that were at most gleams in the eyes of research workers in the 1950s. The widening technical repertory of clinical medicine is not the only factor that has led to a critique of medicine, but it has certainly served as a trigger for change.

In the early twentieth century, it was presumed that professionals would be true to their callings; the few outsiders who questioned this belief faced a heavy burden of proof. Thus, before the 1950s, little criticism of medical practice originated outside the profession. The attitude of doctors toward patients in America was—as it remains in Japan—paternalistic or, to coin a gender-neutral term, *parentalistic*. Before 1950, the phrase "Doctor knows best" still did not raise a smile, and "unprofessional" conduct referred to practices that undercut the interests of the profession. (In England, a regular attorney can no more do the work of a "barrister" or leading trial attorney than a periodontist in America will trespass on the work of a dental surgeon.) In short, whenever moral issues arose within the professions, they were for a very long time kept under careful internal control. Morally and technically, William Osler of Johns Hopkins was a fine teacher of clinical medicine, but throughout his career he loyally helped colleagues keep the moral control of medical practice in the hands of their fellow-professionals.

In the twentieth century, one other academic group has written about the social role of professionals, namely, sociologists. Max Weber's essays on the "calling" at the heart of professional work are still classics, and American scholars like Robert K. Merton and Everett Hughes defined questions about the professions that are being pursued by young scholars today. Still, until the 1950s these moral issues were largely implicit, even for sociologists. The demand that social science be "objective" was still thought to impose an obligation to respect "value neutrality" by setting Ethics aside.

By a curious alchemy, this insistence on value neutrality affected lay attitudes to the professions, too. Before 1950, Americans took the question, "Is this man a *good* doctor?" to mean, exclusively, "Is he skilled and effective? Has he mastered, and does he use, the best available techniques?" By contrast, to question the *moral* aspects of a doctor's work was not generally acceptable. Even after the iniquities practiced in the Nazi concentration camps came to public view at the Nuremberg trials, they were dismissed as pathological: such issues were surely irrelevant to medical practice in any decent society. So those commentators who widened the debate on the moral aspects of medicine from the 1950s on, thus bringing them into the public forum, had to be individuals of unquestioned good faith, whose perspective was humane and comprehensive.

The people who were in this respect "the unacknowledged legislators of mankind"—as Coleridge described poets—were theologians. Joseph Fletcher in 1954, and after him Paul Ramsey, were the first people outside the medical profession to explain clearly that, since the Flexner report had increased the scientific content of medical education, clinical practice in America had become too technical, and had lost its earlier concern for the moral aspect of medical tasks. In moving from the atmosphere of the general practitioner's office to the bureaucratic setting of a hospital, likewise, the locus of clinical attention reinforced the "depersonalization" of medicine, at just the time when technological innovations were producing order-of-magnitude changes in medical treatment. From the point of view of a theologian, these changes in institutions and techniques raised questions about the choice of treatment—"Who may decide when life-support systems can be turned off?"—which were too far-reaching to be left to the unfettered discretion of physicians. Once the issues were stated in these terms, and presented in a practical context, doctors could no longer dismiss them as irrelevant, let alone attack them as politically motivated.[15]

At the moment when moral theologians began writing about the subject, the discipline of Bioethics was born, and the door was open to a tribe of "bioethicists." The debate had at first little of the color and passion it later developed. Taken as individuals, theologians may be passionate, but they look at their concerns *sub specie aeternitatis*, which encourages a certain patience. In the early days of American bioethics, the intellectual problems of the subject took on the shape they have kept ever since, but the publications and forums in which the debate took place were outside the normal arenas of social action. The late 1960s and early 1970s saw a sea change. In retrospect, those years were a crucial time in the political, cultural, and social history not just of the United States, but of all the Western World, comparable to (say) the 1610s or the 1840s. The resulting changes affected human activities across the board from the fine arts and the natural sciences to morals, politics, and education. Since the 1920s, European culture had been dominated by a respect for abstract elegance and intellectual excellence; in the 1960s this attitude was attacked for its lack of relevance to concrete human issues. So the focus shifted from Schoenberg to Mahler, from relativity to computer science, and from molecular biochemistry to genetic counseling.

Before the 1960s, American politics had been a *politics of consensus*. After 1965, issues of policy were still concerned with efficacious ways of achieving "national goals," but that phrase soon dropped out of political rhetoric as completely as "Doctor knows best" did from the debate about Medicine. In the next ten years, the politics of consensus gave way to the politics of sectional interests, as the special claims of racial minorities, women, or the elderly competed for political attention. In America, the confrontation was intensified by disagreements over the Vietnam War. Not that this war alone caused this transition: the social and cultural landslide of the late 1960s and early 1970s had been long in preparation. The crucial factor is what Jeffrey Stout called "the flight from authority." From the late 1960s on, claims to authority were resisted, and the parentalism of doctors was challenged, along with all other claims to know best. Bumper stickers on the cars of *bien-pensants* Bostonians read "Question Authority"; many people admired the books of Ivan Illich and Thomas Szasz; self-help medical books such as *Our Bodies, Ourselves* were received with enthusiasm; and Ken Kesey's cautionary parable, *One Flew over the Cuckoo's Nest*, won the support for the "de-institutionalization" of mental patients that later made its sad contribution to the epidemic of homelessness in America's cities.[16]

Around 1970, then, the assumption that professionals were true to their callings had weakened, and physicians faced the same shift in the burden of proof as all other authority figures. So no one found it odd when in 1974 Congress set up a National Commission to protect the human subjects of biomedical and behavioral research. ("From whom," one asks, "did they *need* protecting?"—"From the research scientists, of course!") Why were biomedical and behavioral scientists singled out for this critique? Many observers believe that Congress had wanted to control practicing physicians, not researchers alone; but there was no constitutional means by which they could lay down the law about professional activities in private doctors' consulting rooms. On the other hand, controlling the budget of the National Institutes of Health gave Congress the power of the purse over much biomedical research, both in major medical centers and at research universities. So, in 1967, NIH set up a system by which all proposals for federally funded research involving human subjects had to be approved by local "institutional review boards."

This was the visible and respectable tip of a larger iceberg. Meanwhile, more active political oratory started, much of it strident, some of which continues today in the campaign against the use of genetically modified crops. Some of this oratory was very responsible, but much was wilder and less well argued. When the National Commission held a public meeting in San Francisco to discuss moral objections to psychosurgery, it was disrupted. Even to discuss psychosurgery coolly or define the objections exactly was seen as immoral: the politically correct thing was to denounce psychosurgery and its practitioners root and branch, as an unmitigated evil. By the late 1970s, then, many American physicians and biomedical scientists were unhappy—at times paranoid—about lay criticism, and fell back to more defensive lines. Some of them denounced the whole NIH system of assurances, and the entire social, political, and moral critique of medicine, as unwarranted intrusions in the proper business of the medical profession. A Nobel Laureate at Harvard even argued at a public meeting in Washington that the NIH guidelines for recombinant DNA research violated scientists' First Amendment rights: this attempt to preserve a monopoly of control over scientific research was ingenious, but it went nowhere, and came at a stage when lay people no longer saw such professional self-control as sufficient.

By the early 1980s the atmosphere had cooled, and issues of medical ethics were addressed in a more theoretical spirit. The debate initiated by theologians in the 1950s was now restated in philosophical terms. With this change of intellectual focus, the locus of debate shifted from the corridors of Congress to colleges and universities, and to such new institutions as the Center for Biology, Ethics, and the Life Sciences at Hastings-on-Hudson, and the Kennedy Center at Georgetown University. Before long, the *Hastings Center Report* was a primary vehicle of publication in bioethics, to which philosophy instructors turned for material to use in the novel classes on "applied ethics" that they were beginning to teach in American colleges. The theological component was not lost: Daniel Callahan started the Hastings Center from a base not in academia, but as editor of a liberal Catholic periodical, and the religious interests of the Kennedy Center's sponsors were well known. Still, for professional philosophers, examples drawn from medicine had one special merit: they provided a fresh terrain on which to pursue, and fight out, theoretical disputes between (say) Kantians and Utilitarians. From the late 1970s on, then, bioethical issues tended to be framed in the abstract, general terms of moral philosophy. Moral issues in medical practice or research, and the delivery of health services, were reanalyzed so as to bring them under the theoretical wing of Philosophy, and integrate the general principles of bioethics into the academic structures of ethical theory.

At the same time, practical, social, and even political questions remained open to cool-headed analysis. The academic and professional talent on which the Kennedy and Hastings Centers drew made them a natural resource for those in the federal government who needed help or advice on problems in medicine and the health services. Thus, these centers developed a two-pronged attack on bioethical questions. On the one hand, they built philosophical foundations for the field; on the other, they were drawn back into public affairs to support the President's Commission on Medical Ethics, which succeeded the National Commission. The results of this two-pronged attack were not entirely happy. At centers and colleges from Galveston to San Francisco, from Minneapolis to Cambridge, Mass., such service activities paid institutional bills for the teaching of philosophy; but the intellectual gap between the concrete, particular questions of practice to which doctors and bureaucrats needed answers, and the abstract, universal issues of theory that philosophers were interested in disentangling, became clearer. However intriguing it was to reformulate the practical dilemmas of clinical medicine in philosophical terms, this made such dilemmas no easier to resolve in practice: John Rawls's *Theory of Jus-*

tice gives no specific guidance to clinical physicians. So, the philosophical phase of the late 1970s and 1980s was not the end of the story: in later years, the focus of bioethics in the United States has shifted yet again.

At medical schools and nursing colleges across the country, doctors, nurses, and paramedics taking courses in applied ethics found the abstractions of philosophical analysis too general and theoretical to be useful teaching tools. When required to master the definitions of "deontology" and "consequentialism," apprentice nurses dropped out in droves. Real-life cases they understood and enjoyed, but theoretical modes of analysis were less than ideal ways to resolve the quandaries of practice at the bedsides of individual patients. As a result, many clinical centers devised new ways of handling these moral problems, and of providing help to attending physicians who found the situations of particular patients raising special moral difficulties. One such experiment was an "ethics consultation service" that operates like the "consult services" in (say) cardiology, neurology, or psychiatry. An attendant physician who is perplexed about a patient's moral—not technical—problems calls in a colleague, or a team of colleagues, to go over the case records, talk to the patient and family, and give the physician additional advice about resolving his quandary.

But this procedure itself faces difficulties. Is clinical ethics a medical specialty in which post-doctoral certification can be required, as with other specialties? In operating an ethics consult service, can lay people be accepted as "clinical ethicists"; and, if so, do they need additional training? By "routinizing" this aspect of clinical treatment, physicians are winning back much of their earlier responsibility for the moral problems of clinical practice, in a way that Max Weber would have understood. Still, the physicians are no longer seeking to restore a total monopoly, or to keep the lay public at arm's length. In recognizing that medical practice unites technical skill with moral insight, they acknowledge (if grudgingly) that they cannot always make decisions about the moral issues of clinical practice single-handed, and are well advised not to try.

Sometimes, the best course is to hand the resolution of painful issues back to the patients and their families, supported by their spiritual advisers and other non-medical counsel. The moral aspect of medicine is thus reintegrated into clinical practice in a way that remains open to comment and criticism from outsiders, even from the lay public. As a result, physicians today more and more welcome the laity's taking part in the discussion of

the moral problems of clinical practice, and are ready to fashion procedures that let people with a legitimate stake in any given case become involved in clinical decisions, with their interests given proper weight and
respect. This brings into focus the relation of Ethical Theory to Moral
Practice, which comes onto center stage at this point: the central issue is
not the timeless question, "What general principles can be relied on to decide this case, in terms that are binding on everyone who considers it?" but
rather the timely question, "Whose interests can be accepted as morally
overriding in the situation that faces us here and now?"

8

Ethical Theory and Moral Practice

In place of abstract universal concepts, practical disciplines focus on particular episodes. Convincing narratives have a kind of weight that mathematical formulas do not. They allow us to revive moral argumentation in disciplines that, since the eighteenth century, had aimed at value neutrality; in the process, they bridge the gulf between Science and Literature.

WE COME NOW TO ONE of the most important issues in all these inquiries: the role of ethical theories—in moral theology, philosophical ethics, or any other variety—in our moral lives: the confused mixture of conflicts, puzzles and decisions, perceptions, judgments and reflections, desires, regrets and despairs, anxieties, disagreements or agreements to differ, and public commendations and condemnations, that constitutes our experience and practice in the moral realm. This is an issue over which abstract-minded philosophers and concrete-minded practitioners are deeply divided. A theorist like Alasdair MacIntyre does not believe that we can reach a well-founded moral position in any practical situation unless we are committed to some systematic theoretical position; meanwhile, practitioners do not see how such theories increase our confidence in untying the knots in which our lives enmesh us.[1] In this field, do theory and practice really engage on the same level? Or, like abstract psychological theories and our everyday understanding of mental life, are they merely ships that pass each other by in the night?

There is reason to believe that, in this case, there is a basic lack of contact. Those who reflect on the details in which the moral problems of clini-

cal practice are entangled turn for guidance to twentieth-century philosophical ethics in vain. Despite all the subtlety and depth they display in
abstract general terms, the conclusions of a book like John Rawls's *Theory
of Justice* provide no effective criteria for settling real-life disputes in actual
cases. Yet, if that is the case, what practical fruit can these theories bear?
Like the members of the National Commission for the Protection of Human Research Subjects in the 1970s, we must simply make what moral
sense we can of the stories of individual patients in the same way as literary
critics do when reading fictional stories by (say) Eudora Welty or V. S.
Pritchett.

The chief outcome of our discussion of Practical Reason is, therefore, a
recognition that the understanding of cases is inseparable from our views
about narratives: particularly, the kinds of narratives we call *case histories*.
Robertson Davies' distinction between "first-rate healers" and "capable
technicians" draws attention to two parallel styles of narrative in Medicine. Case histories are generally limited to issues that arise in the course of
clinical practice, as seen from inside the profession. But, when a clinician's
attention widens to embrace things about a patient that go beyond these
concerns, and faces human experience as a patient lives it, the resulting
narratives are more like those we look for in the writings of biographers
and even novelists. If we are to make progress at this stage, therefore, we
must consider explicitly the relationship between professional narratives,
whose place is in Law, Medicine, or elsewhere, and the literary narratives
that figure in stories for the general reader, which are not subject to the
same professional constraints.

The considerations introduced by adding personal narratives to case histories can go so far outside the normal run of clinical practice that they are
hard to generalize about. Let us begin by recalling the reasons why Eudora
Welty praised V. S. Pritchett as a teller of stories. "The characters he presents—all peculiar to themselves—have a claim on us that we cannot
deny": it is in fact their eccentricity that demands our attention. Alternatively, to cite another long-lived writer, William Maxwell, a former editor
of the *New Yorker:* "I wouldn't like to live in a world where nobody ever
told stories." Maxwell refers in particular to Lady Mary Coke, a "marvelous
eccentric" who divorced her boorish husband, slept in a dresser drawer,
and was convinced that the Empress Maria Theresa was trying to steal her
servants: "I was beside myself with pleasure over this woman."[2]

Nor is there any reason, in this context, to neglect that fine tale-teller Robertson Davies himself, since he cites such predecessors as Vladimir Nabokov in the twentieth century and Philip Sidney, a contemporary of Montaigne, in the last years of the sixteenth century. Some years ago (as Davies reports) Nabokov was asked what he regarded as the greatest quality in literary writing: he defined this by the Russian word *shamanstvo*—or "the enchanter quality." Nabokov echoes the definition that Sidney himself gives:

> He cometh to you with words, said in delightful proportions
> . . . and with a tale, forsooth, he comes unto you with a tale,
> which holdeth children from play and old men from the chimney-corner.[3]

Does this mean that narratives cannot serve as universal theories or general laws? That is on the whole a sound conclusion, though novelists sometimes give the impression that they think otherwise. In an appendix to *War and Peace*, Leo Tolstoy linked his story to a theory that history is moved by the same machine-like determinism as a locomotive. But, in itself, the story of *War and Peace* is not in the slightest "theoretical," and the intrusions of theory into the narrative tend to interrupt, rather than advance, the tale.

Elsewhere Tolstoy's preoccupation with railroad trains and locomotives is close to the heart of his stories, and other nineteenth-century novelists and playwrights shared this interest. In *Anna Karenina*, for instance, Tolstoy's heroine uses train journeys to escape from the moral conflicts in which her life becomes embroiled. These train journeys play a crucial part in the story, and from beginning to end we often find ourselves engulfed in clouds of steam from the engine. As for abstract theoretical ethics, however, Tolstoy has a low opinion of it. One of the more disagreeable characters in *Anna Karenina*, of whose insensitivity Tolstoy leaves us in no doubt, is a certain Professor Katavasov, a man who can hardly bring himself to take a moral stand of any kind without hedging it around with all kinds of theoretical considerations.

The theme of trains can be found in the work of other writers: Chekhov's play *The Three Sisters* is a story about three unmarried women with lives of provincial loneliness, far from the Moscow of their dreams, which is a long train ride away. The same is true of several of Thomas Hardy's stories: *Tess of the d'Urbervilles*, for instance, tells how a young farm girl from Dorset dreams of escaping to London by train, and so avoiding the fate that waits for her back home.[4] And as recently as 1998, in his remarkable novel about Virginia Woolf, *The Hours*, Michael Cunningham imagines Virginia using this device to escape her husband Leonard's relentless supervision:[5]

> On this side is stern, worried Leonard, the row of closed shops,
> the dark rise that leads back to Hogarth House, where Nelly
> waits impatiently, almost gleefully, for her chance at further
> grievances. On the other side is the train. On the other side is
> London, and all London implies about freedom, about
> kisses, about the possibilities of art and the sly dark glitter of
> madness . . .

What these storytellers have in common is a historical and cultural setting that is available to them in their own time. Science and Technology changed the raw material with which novelists and playwrights could work: some stories could be told only after the rise of the railroads created this new material for plots. Earlier in the century, Honoré de Balzac had taken it upon himself to develop a taxonomy of human characters, which (he hoped) supported his claim to be the Linnaeus of Social Life: each of his novels focused on a paradigmatic character, together with the professional skills he developed for his own purposes, skills that Balzac describes in digressions as long and detailed as those Herman Melville wrote for inclusion in *Moby-Dick*.

If we can usefully speak of anything as *generalities* in the field of narratives, it is the prevalence of widespread stories found in parallel—and in some cases vastly distant—cultures. Looking through the corpus of Sufi writings, for instance, we find tales that resemble closely ones familiar in the Rabbinical tradition: for example, the story about a judge who is about to hear his first case. The plaintiff husband gives evidence first. The judge at once leaps in to say, "You're right!" and the Clerk of Court reproaches him for running ahead. So the judge keeps quiet while the defendant wife gives evidence in turn; but, as she ends, he again bursts out, "You're right!" The Clerk reproves him once again: "First you said the plaintiff was right, then the defendant gave contradictory evidence and you said that she was right. Don't you see, you can't say both of these things at once?" "Do you know?"—says the judge sheepishly—"*You're right!*" This story has been told as often about an Imam as about a Rabbi.

Such parallel narratives are not alternative abstract theories; rather, they express shared experiences that are capable of striking home with us all. But the stories must be told out of good humor, and in all sincerity. As the Sufis also say:

> If a word comes from the heart, it will enter the heart; but if it
> comes only from the tongue, it will not get past the ear.[6]

In our own time, the work of one writer in particular is so directly to the point here that he is worth discussing at greater length. William Gass is both a novelist and a philosopher, and his critical writings on the relation between literature and philosophy are distinguished—so much so that it is unclear why the essays in his book *Fiction and the Figures of Life* are not more widely recognized as classics in their own genre. The explanation seems to be that they came out at a moment when the vogue for "deconstruction" was on the rise: Gass's interests were so contrary in spirit that his work had no chance of becoming fashionable.[7]

Speaking at first hand, Gass declares that the Novelist and the Philosopher are both obsessed with language.

> Both, in their ways, create worlds. Worlds? But the worlds of
> the Novelist, I hear you say, do not exist. Indeed. As for
> that—they exist more often than the philosophers'. Then,
> too—how seldom does it seem to matter? Who honestly cares?
> They are divine games.

The activities of novelists and philosophers may be divine games, but they are dangerous, and this danger is inseparable from their ambition:

> The esthetic aim of any fiction is the creation of a verbal world
> alive through every order of its Being.

As Gass tells it, the fact that the novel, as a genre, came into existence at a crisis point in the history of religion was no accident. In the mid-seventeenth century, formal theology lost its literary power, and Nabokov's enchanter quality passed to lay authors.

When God abdicates, the world becomes, for many novelists, a place not only vacant of Gods, but also empty of a generously regular and peacefully abiding nature on which the novelist might, in large, rely.

In the absence of God-made rules, the writer is left to make up for himself rules that "can be as many as the writer wishes, and of any kind he wishes. They establish the logic, the order of his world." Even in a world as vacant of Gods as Beckett's plays, Gass adds,

> I can replace my love for people with a love for principle, and even pursue a life beyond the grave as a program for the proper pursuit of this one. Bravo, Novelists and Philosophers; good show.

Yet Beckett's world is close to that of the deconstructionists: for him, as for Schiller and Weber, the disenchantment of things seems to rob us of any basis for reasonable moral judgments. In so empty a world, what place is there for discussing right and wrong?

This is not the conclusion that William Gass draws from the "abdication" of God. On the contrary, the trust we have in our own judgments, both about transparently clear moral situations and about those that are too confused to be clear, remains untouched. The idea of "disenchantment" is, for him, the outcome of a *theoretical* dispute, not a product of immediate experience; and, in another essay, he presents an imaginary situation about which, in his view, there is no reasonable doubt. He calls it *The Case of the Obliging Stranger*.[8]

> Imagine I approach a stranger on the street and say to him, "If you please, sir, I desire to perform an experiment with your aid." The stranger is obliging, and I lead him away. In a dark place conveniently by, I strike his head with the broad of an axe and cart him home. I place him, buttered and trussed, in an ample electric oven. The thermostat reads 450°F. Thereupon I go off to play poker with friends and forget all about the obliging stranger in the stove. When I return, I realize I have over-baked my specimen, and the experiment, alas, is ruined.

How can our moral attitude toward this failure admit of any doubt? Not only is such a case transparently clear, but it rests on general considerations that are equally clear:

> Any ethic that does not roundly condemn my action is
> vicious. . . . No more convincing refutation of any ethic could
> be given than by showing that it approved of my baking the
> obliging stranger.

To educated readers in a period of multiculturalism, here too, Gass's position will appear unfashionable. We are not supposed to admit, these days, that ethical matters are capable of such moral transparency. Yet, Gass retorts,

> These cases comprise the core of our moral experience. When
> we try to explain why they are instances of good or bad, of
> right or wrong, we sound comic. What we must explain is *not*
> why these cases have the moral nature they have, for that
> needs no explaining, but *why they are so clear*.

So as to disappoint all his critics, Gass goes on to explain that, just as many situations in his view are transparently clear, so too some are intrinsically *unclear*; "the unclear ones are more interesting, and there are more of them." Far from having convenient principles to which we can turn as a quick way out of these difficulties, there is little we can do to settle them except accumulate more facts that, like grains of sand, may help to tip the scale in one direction or another.

Once again, it is worth quoting a dialogue that Gass presents by way of illustration:

> "She left her husband with a broken hand and took the chil-
> dren."
> "She did! The ungrateful bitch!"
> "He broke his hand hammering her head."
> "Dear me, how distressing, but after all what's one time?"
> "He beat her every Thursday after tea and she finally couldn't
> stand it any longer."
> "Ah, of course. But the poor children."

"He beat them, too. On Fridays. And on Saturday he beat
the dog."

"My, my—such a terrible man. And was there no other way?"

"The court would grant her no injunction."

"Why not?"

"Judge Bridlegoose is a fool."

"Ah, of course, poor thing, she did right, no doubt about it.
Except—why didn't she also take the dog?"

Faced with this accumulation of fictional facts, whose relevance we cannot
doubt, the Philosopher has little useful to add. In this respect, unclear cases
no more turn on matters of general principle than clear ones. As we read
this dialogue, our sympathies tip from side to side, and we despair of summarizing its message in a simple generalization.[9]

"In the last resort," Gass adds, "it is our love for people which counts for
more than our love for principles." Set against any fully described problem,
abstract principles do not measure up. Why was it wrong to bake the obliging stranger? It is of little help to reply, "Because I could not consistently
will that the maxim of my action become a universal law"; or even, "God
forbade me, but I paid no heed." From a mixed bag of replies, the best that
Gass can proffer is, "Decent men remark it and are moved to tears."[10]

At this point, we are back in the world of Leo Tolstoy and Robertson
Davies. The oddity of all purely general replies is as extreme as the oddity
of the theories put forward by Tolstoy's caricature figure, Professor
Katavasov. The moral theorist, says Gass,

> may behave as if there were no clear cases because he is a ratio-
> nalist practicing deduction. . . . He is beguiled by the precision,
> rigor, and unarguable moves of logical demonstration. [As a ra-
> tionalist, he] is a man in love, not with particular men or
> women, not with things, but with principles, ideas, webs of
> reasoning; and if he rushes to the aid of his neighbor, it is not
> because he loves his neighbor, but because he loves God's law
> about it.[11]

Yet, at the end of the day, Gass is closest to Robertson Davies, for whom a
clear-headed moralist is "someone who observes the vicissitudes of life
[and] finds out as interestingly as he can that if (e.g.) you play with fire, you

will get burned."[12] With this step, the line between the novelist and the moralist becomes vanishingly faint, since both of them are concerned less with speculative theories about conduct than they are with the practical wisdom that shows itself in our lives.

Gass's essays are not set out in the classic analytical manner, but they succeed in raising crucial issues in Ethics: notably, the relationship—above all, the relative priority—of universal moral principles and particular ethical perceptions. Indeed, if Gass is right, the standing of "principles" in Ethics has been exaggerated for reasons that have more to do with the rationalist's beguilement by "precision, rigor, and the unarguable moves of logical demonstration" than it does with the task of resolving moral quandaries. On which side should we start? Before we get too far from Practical Reasoning, and from the moral aspects of enterprises like Medicine, Engineering, and Development Economics, let us focus on the relation of principles to cases in Bioethics, and see if similar relations hold if we broaden our attention to the professions generally.

Returning to the tension between theorists and practitioners, it is worth noticing that Alasdair MacIntyre insists on calling the discussion of moral problems in professions like Medicine "applied" ethics. For, by now, many moral philosophers accept this phrase, and it is widely used to name academic appointments and courses. The only difference is that, whereas MacIntyre argues for the appropriateness of this phrase, other philosophers simply take it for granted.

MacIntyre's case for using this name is one by-product of his more general theory of *traditions*. We grow up and live our lives, he claims, within the particular tradition into which we happen to have been born, and our basic ethical choice is whether to remain within our native tradition or convert to another. All our thoughts, feelings, and attitudes about moral issues depend on that basic choice, and the decision whether to stay or go can be rationally justified only by appeal to philosophical arguments about the merits of the two systems. Many people find this account very persuasive: many ethnic and religious communities do indeed have a systematic Code of Ethics for dealing with moral issues, and the individual members have little freedom to exercise personal judgment. The fundamental question is, "Are we happy to leave matters at that, or is there room for a deeper critique? Are such traditions governed by the intellectual authority of theoretical systems, or by the personal authority of religious or ethnic leaders? And is the systematic order of a Code of Ethics comparable to that of a system of geometry, or does it have a different kind of coherence, resting on a very different basis?"[13]

Clearly, the answers to those questions have changed more than once in the course of history: when, for instance, the emergence of a lay culture in the early sixteenth century undercut the exclusive *magisterium* of the Catholic Church. These answers also differ between people who lead lives confined to a single community, and those whose ways of life oblige them to balance off the demands of different institutions with different traditions. Most significantly for us at the present time, the answers differ also in ways that depend on whether the issues in question arise for the members of a homogenous group, or whether they have to be acceptable to people who come from different backgrounds, each with its own codes and practices.

Here, it is relevant to reconsider the experience of the National Commission for the Protection of Human Research Subjects. Instructed to make recommendations about the moral acceptability of enrolling young children in biomedical and behavioral research, the Commission discussed this issue for some six months, held public meetings to receive testimony from other people and organizations, and found it possible at the end of these proceedings to frame a set of proposals and conditions on which they achieved near-total agreement.

This agreement, however, extended only to the practical issues committed to them. Having voted to accept the recommendations, the Commissioners went home and spent a month writing statements about their respective reasons for accepting the recommendations. At this point Babel set in. Practically speaking, they were in agreement, and agreed what they agreed about. The thing they could not agree about was *why* they had agreed about it—what reasons they had for concurring in the recommendations. Their moral perceptions coincided, but the reasons they gave depended (at least partly) on their backgrounds. In short—and Aristotle would say the same—their shared certitude about their perceptions was greater than the certainty, or uncertainty, that each of them felt about the general systems to which they were professedly committed.[14]

This outcome is one that MacIntyre's account cannot accommodate. As he tells the story, the rational way to decide a practical question of morals is to interrogate yourself about the demands of your native or adopted tradition, and stand by them. Practical solutions to moral quandaries will then be "applications" of the wider system of beliefs embodied in the tradition's Code. If the National Commission had followed this course, the result would have been not consensus but deadlock: Protestants, Catholics, Jews, and skeptics would have felt obliged to take stands on different systems of doctrine, and any consensus would be a pure coincidence, without any sound foundation.

The trouble with MacIntyre's position is the same as that which we encountered in the case of "applied sciences" in general. In Physics as much as Ethics, individual cases in all their particularity cannot be simply "deduced from" universal and general principles of a theoretical kind: at best, theories can be required to "make sense of" the ways in which we succeed in dealing with particular cases. Theory (so to speak) is not a foundation on which we can safely construct Practice; rather, it is a way of bringing our external commitments into line with our experience as practitioners. This insight has influenced bioethical theory and the moral practice of clinical medicine only in the last thirty years or so.

MacIntyre's reply is that the apparent consensus to the recommendations of the Commission was artificial: whatever their differences in class, race, gender, or religious affiliations, all the members of the Commission were middle-class Americans, and ended by voting like middle-class Americans. To see the truth of his claims, he concludes, we would need a Commission whose members included also Tibetan Buddhists, Orthodox Jews from Mea Sharim in Jerusalem, and other traditional communities. This response is too powerful to ignore, but it underlines again the ambiguity of MacIntyre's term *tradition*. One of the successes of the United States has been to create traditions of its own that are humane and middle-of-the-road enough to attract Americans from very different backgrounds. This does not mean that the consensus that the Commission achieved was arbitrary, let alone irrational. Rather, it shows us one kind of situation in which we can fairly speak of a consensus about moral questions as resting on a sound basis in shared experience.

We cannot, of course, deny that in some countries most people might object to the Commission's conclusions, which were not as transparently clear as (say) William Gass's *Case of the Obliging Stranger*. In a more exotic locale than Bethesda, Maryland—for instance, a Lhasa monastery—it might well be more difficult to organize an effective commission. But that does not mean that MacIntyre is right to conclude that there is no chance of people with different backgrounds reaching a reasoned agreement on moral issues. The Commission's debates went on for months without any of the bargaining or arm-twisting common enough in legislatures. If we accept MacIntyre's interpretation as the only rational conclusion, our mistake is the error of all rationalist philosophy: assuming that ethical theory and moral practice alike must be grounded in principles whose relevance is timeless and universal. On the contrary, all we can reasonably require is the existence of a forum—such as the Commission—in which initial differences of opinion can be narrowed down as far as possible, as a result of discussions whose procedures its members accept as sound, in respects shared by those outside the forum who have to take notice of the outcome.

It may sound obvious to say so, but the proceedings that govern the debates that lead to consensus in the natural sciences, too, are not that different in form. What marks some of these debates—whether scientific or moral—as being more reasonable than others is evident only if we look in detail, not at matters of form, but at the substance of the issues involved. All knowledge may be in the service of human interests, but it is not always clear whose interests count in a given debate. Issues that were once the prerogative of a physician to resolve are now deputed to a patient's family or spiritual adviser. Problems that an academic economist previously felt qualified to solve single-handed now need to be kept open until the members of the affected community have spoken for themselves. Decisions that the U.S. Army Corps of Engineers used to make about flooding a fertile agricultural valley to create a reservoir now have to be subjected to the formalities of an environmental impact inquiry. In each case, we are moving back into a period when medicine is again a human art, engineering a device for meeting human needs, and economics is seen as a matter of political economy and not just mathematical calculation, so that the academic cloister and the political assembly have complementary tasks to perform.

Any chronicle of bioethics must, therefore, underline the attitudes to practical reason that have come to the fore since the 1970s in all of the human arts. When the ideals of theory embodied in natural philosophy won acceptance in the seventeenth century, intellectual fields that had been vigorous in medieval academic debate were expelled from philosophy. One of these was Rhetoric, another was case ethics—the analysis of "cases of conscience" which Pascal violently satirized in his *Provincial Letters*.[15] The idea of "moral philosophy" in its contemporary sense—as a branch of *theory* independent of the practical problems of pastoral counseling or the confessional—was an academic innovation invented by Henry More and the seventeenth-century Cambridge Platonists. Yet when case ethics—or *casuistry*, as it was renamed after 1700—lost its place in the Academy, that was not the death of it. On a humbler level, it survived within the churches, while rising like a phoenix in Literature. The novelist Daniel Defoe earned a living by writing agony columns on moral quandaries for a wider public, publishing them in the periodicals of his time as a kind of Ann Landers. But the limits of a newspaper column were too great. Defoe needed elbow-room to develop narratives about people's lives and troubles that came closer, in detail, to their real-life experience. So the casuist turned into a novelist, and set an example that did much to shape the development of the genre in the years that followed.

For Henry More, by contrast, case ethics lacked theoretical significance; and the same was true for his nineteenth-century admirer, Henry Sidgwick, who revived Ethical Theory in a form that lasted into the mid-twentieth century. In deciding whether to take Holy Orders, so as to remain a Fellow of Trinity College, Cambridge, Sidgwick played the casuist himself, and wrote a competent *casus* about his own situation; but, as he remarks in an autobiographical note, he had little patience with the taxonomic moral classifications relied on in (for example) William Whewell's standard textbook of practical ethics. Casuistical arguments, Sidgwick complained, lacked the "certainty" that a philosopher would demand of mathematical arguments. Instead of accepting this as one of the inevitable differences between Ethics and Mathematics, he tried to shift attention back to theory: surely, it was not as impossible to construct a "moral geometry" as Aristotle claimed!

So, at the close of the twentieth century, the discussion of moral problems in the professions is taking us behind abstract theory to the case method, and this concern with practice is not confined to medicine and other well-disciplined professions. The difference between approaches to ethics grounded in universal principles and those shaped by the traditions of case morality, respectively, was understood in Antiquity by Aristotle and Hermagoras, Cicero and Quintillian, and was handed on to the medieval Pastoral Theologians. Today, the work of Sissela Bok and Paul Ekman on lying, and that of Michael Walzer on the morality of war, are parallel strands in the contemporary renewal of casuistry, and these authors would not flinch from accepting this description.

In a theoretical science, Aristotle had argued, we account for particular phenomena about which we are *uncertain* by referring them to general principles of which we are *more certain;* but in practical affairs our experience is usually the other way about. We are more certain about the rights and wrongs of particular cases than about the general principles we appeal to in explaining them. I *know that* my headache was relieved by taking an aspirin with greater confidence than I can *explain why* taking an aspirin relieves those headaches. The National Commission for the Protection of Human Research Subjects found itself repeating the same pattern. Once again, it seemed, Ethics was on the side of Practice, not of Theory; and the kind of knowledge that it embodies is concrete, practical wisdom, not an abstract, theoretical grasp.

Finally, let me close off a blind alley: the difference between practical philosophy and its theoretical namesake is not a contrast between two academic disciplines, each with its own abstractions. In countries from Scandinavia to Australia, universities have used the terms "theoretical philosophy" and "practical philosophy" to label departments that focus, respectively, on Ethics and Political Theory, or on Logic and Metaphysics. In an academic setting, however, both these sets of topics are discussed in the same abstract terms. (The phrase "political theory" makes the point.) In our present argument, by contrast, theoretical philosophy is a field for imaginative but abstract speculation, while practical philosophy is a field, either for policy decisions, or in most cases for *actions*. To this day, many academic philosophers are puzzled by Aristotle's claim that the conclusion of a "practical syllogism" is an *action;* perhaps we are beginning to see why that puzzlement is misplaced.

We need not, like some contemporary writers, look for a *Theory* of Practice: that is not the point. At a glance, such a program may seem to agree with Wittgenstein's ways of thinking; but that (I argue) is the reverse of what he claimed. "Theories" (more exactly, "appeals to theory") are *practices* that have specific parts to play in particular disciplines. Appealing to a theory does not reveal the discipline's metaphysical foundations. Rather, it is a *trope* or *topic* that operates alongside other kinds of scientific reasoning: classification, demonstration, analogy, and the rest. The collapse of Foundationalism destroyed dreams of a comprehensive Theory (with an uppercase "T") as a rational framework overarching or supporting our everyday concepts, but the varied roles of theories (with a lowercase "t") in practical disciplines means that they still deserve, and reward, philosophical reflection.[16]

This may be the reason why so many constructive projects in philosophy today—so many of the "legitimate heirs" of traditional philosophy—start by reflecting on the "forms of life" in one or another of our practical fields: law, medicine, and other areas. So, as the twentieth century ends, the more abstract and universal of the seventeenth century's excursions into theoretical, speculative philosophy may be beyond repair, but practical philosophy survives the wider academic wreck.

9

The Trouble with Disciplines

The value of disciplinary procedures is beyond doubt; but, by now, the ways in which professional activities are organized keep alive intellectual activities that have already outlived their value. As a result, the revival of more humane and reasonable ideas proceeds more slowly than it need do.

WE HAVE NOTED the difference between those for whom the culture of professionalism strengthens our ethical traditions, and those who view professional communities more skeptically, as self-serving and untrustworthy: Alasdair MacIntyre is our example of the first, Ivan Illich our representative skeptic. Not surprisingly, this contrast can be stated too sharply; some qualifications demand our attention. So let us take up again the discussion of disciplines that we started earlier. The organization of activities into "disciplines" began (we saw) for two distinct kinds of reasons. Both of these were already operative in the final years of the religious wars from 1550 to 1650, but they became dominant only in the twentieth century. While noting the development of disciplinary practices early in the modern period, my emphasis here is on the factors that encouraged academics to carry "disciplinarity" to damaging extremes, most notably during the Cold War.

The factors that concern us are, of course, not only those associated with an intellectual division of labor, but also those that arise from the working of our institutions. Most contemporary universities are sharply fragmented into departmental units, each of which is devoted to a single discipline. This tendency is most obvious in Economics, and remains especially powerful there. Some years ago, I served on a committee charged with recommending tenure or promotion to faculty members in a range of subjects covering all the Sciences and the Humanities. The committee was made up of eighteen scrupulous and experienced colleagues from a broad range of subjects, who studied at length the dossiers submitted by the departments in support of their preferred members. The Department of Economics petitioned the Dean to promote four of its members from Associate to Full Professor; our task was to read carefully the inchoate documents included in their dossiers. Academic economists rarely publish entire books, so we were given a batch of papers to read in various branches of the subject, and at our meetings we were unanimous that the case for two of the promotions was stronger than for the other two.

Was this the end of the matter? No. Once our recommendation had been made, the Department sent a delegation to comment on our judgments. This was a bizarre occasion. The delegation entered the room, and the Chairman soon reached the boiling point. Rather than expand on the arguments in the dossiers, he unleashed a comprehensive denunciation of the committee. His theme was clear: the opinions of non-economists on the merits of economists were valueless; the entire procedure for promotion and tenure should be treated as null and void, and the Department of Economics should be left free to twist the Dean's arm as they pleased.

Even in the late twentieth-century Academy, matters rarely reach so drastic a point. Yet the institutional conflict in this case is closely associated with intellectual issues from the other main stream of disciplinary concerns. If economists are unhappy about the views of their colleagues, this is in part because they regard themselves as guardians of values that represent the mission of their discipline. Here as elsewhere, the interpretation they gave to Economic Theory was one that ignored all considerations of history and culture, and confined itself to abstract, mathematical reformations of economic theory. They were anxious to put the same spin on Economics that Henry Sidgwick had put on Ethics, when he complained of the untheoretical character of case ethics. Both tendencies (as we saw) had historical roots in the seventeenth-century program for a strictly rational cosmology, and, to this day, echoes of the abstract, non-empirical branch of mathematics known as "rational mechanics" survive in the social sciences in arguments about "rational choice."

The mission of protecting the narrowly defined core values of a discipline severely limits the options available to even the best young members of departments that run their affairs as that Department of Economics was doing. Those junior scholars who are attracted to currently unfashionable parts of any discipline soon learn the price of wandering from the straight and narrow path, and only the obstinate and the odd ducks among them persist in doing so, rather than let their own intellectual inquiries be distorted and frustrated. So, in the professional activities of tightly structured disciplines, conformity is more highly valued than originality; or, rather, originality is tolerated only for as long as it reinforces the core values of a department. (The same scenario is reenacted in Departments of Psychology and many others.) This is what I mean in saying that disciplinary emphasis on the technicalities of the human sciences imposes on newcomers to the subject a set of professional blinders that direct their attention to certain narrowly defined considerations, and often prevent them from looking at their work in a broad human perspective.

In underlining the damaging extremes to which "disciplinarity" has too often been carried in twentieth-century academic life, I should not (of course) be understood as ignoring the advantages that it has brought to our ways of thought ever since the seventeenth century: disciplines would never have become established as they have, if they were not productive. So, while making some helpful points about the trouble generated when disciplinarity is pursued in an exclusionary spirit, critiques presented in the name of "interdisciplinarity" must, in turn, acknowledge the debt that interdisciplinary ideas owe to the very disciplines on which they are parasitic. Only within a world of disciplines can one be interdisciplinary: it is the vices of each style of thought (as Steve Shapin puts it, from a sociologist's point of view) that make possible the virtues of the other.

This relationship between the disciplinary and interdisciplinary aspects of our thought is not by any means unique. The vices of churches are best denounced by true believers, even by clergy themselves; the shortcomings of governmental action can be understood by those who are responsible for it at least as well as by those who criticize it from outside governmental institutions; without the protection provided by an effective State, those who look forward to its "withering away" have little chance of advancing their views in public. (Watching countries like Sierra Leone and the former Soviet Union collapsing—though in different ways—into ineffectiveness, we rediscover the reasons why philosophers from Thomas Hobbes on were so zealous in attributing absolute powers to the Sovereign.) Still, for all their practical virtues, the social by-products of "disciplinary" organization continue to afflict people at universities and centers of research, whenever they seek to reform such institutions.

Nor were these tendencies ever confined to the Academy alone: they were influential in the rival churches and among their political supporters four hundred years ago; and they acted as fuel for a century and a half of conflict. Martin Luther's hope of "reforming" the Catholic Church led only gradually to a breach between the two branches of Western Christendom, and the Thirty Years' War found the Habsburg rulers of Austria-Hungary in an ambiguous position. The Emperor himself was committed to the Catholic cause, yet in his own capital of Vienna no less than 70 percent of the population had (it seems) gone over to the Protestant camp. If Austria was to carry the banner for Rome, strong measures were called for. The Emperor quickly made it clear that Lutherans had three options: they could convert, they could hide their opinions, or they could emigrate. The Habsburgs threw their prestige and effort into the Catholic side of the balance: they regarded anyone who continued as a Protestant as an Enemy of the Dynasty. So began a persecution that outstripped what the Bourbons from Louis XIII on would visit on the Huguenots in France. Outside Austria, eleven families of the Bohemian nobility refused to convert, but in Austria itself the Court and aristocracy remained solidly Catholic. Meanwhile, the main body of Lutherans—mostly craftsmen and professionals—chose emigration: after the 1620s, Austria lost so many skilled workers that its economy, notably in iron and steel, was so damaged that it did not fully recover for some two hundred years.

There remained the great bulk of the Viennese population: the lower middle class, the minor civil servants, and those laborers who pretended to neither wealth nor education. Even if it had occurred to them to emigrate, they could not afford to do so; yet they had no desire to renounce their Protestant loyalties. As a result, most of them chose the humbler path of an outward conformity to Catholicism quite divorced from doctrinal commitments. It was as though these classes said to the authorities, "Very well, we will *act* as Catholic as you please, but please do not ask us to *believe* anything!" Faced by authoritative doctrines, they opted out; those who thought about such matters at all became skeptics—at best, like Hans Thirring, "skeptics committed to peace and humanity." Those who lacked any skill in argumentation learned to avoid offending the authorities by saying whatever their interlocutors wanted to hear: "As you say, Sir!" Thus, the agreeableness of the Viennese first developed as a cover for skepticism. What Paul Feyerabend wrote about Nazi sloganeering in his autobiography was true for them, too: "I did not accept it, I did not oppose it; the words came and went, apparently without effect."[1]

For such people, professions of belief were both pretentious and inseparable from the social pretentiousness of life at Court. The whole body of the lower classes in Vienna formed a secret society, whose expectations and private jokes were hidden from the Court hierarchy. In Mozart's *Marriage of Figaro*, the servant Susanna does her best to answer Count Almaviva as he wants, but keeps slipping up, repeating "Yes" even when he has switched to wanting "No," and vice versa. In this, Mozart is a typical member of the lower orders, and much of the charm of his operas is that he did not—nor did he need to—pillory his aristocratic characters. Presented with Almaviva or Don Giovanni, Mozart's fellows laughed up their sleeves, clasping him to their breasts and honoring him by loving parodies of his own productions. (In the film version of Peter Shaffer's *Amadeus*, Milos Forman shows a troupe of hostlers and serving maids, footmen and amateur musicians, staging a pantomimed opera. No one in the audience is laughing more wholeheartedly than Mozart: as he knows, they are laughing *with* him, not *at* him.)

This skepticism, as the Viennese will admit, can verge toward hypocrisy. On the Schwedenplatz, by the canal edging the northern boundary of the Inner City, there is a rugged stone monument marking the site of the Gestapo headquarters during the National Socialist period. This monument betrays no sign of the enthusiasm with which Hitler's forces were greeted when they entered Vienna in 1938: after 1945, the Austrians claimed to have been the first victims of Hitler, and their conformity to Nazi expectations matched their earlier conformity to Catholicism after 1620. Not that the Court complained about this lower-class skepticism: when the Cardinal Archbishop of Vienna took his bishops out of the First Vatican Council rather than endorse the new Doctrine of Papal Infallibility, the Emperor Franz Joseph wrote a letter to his wife, criticizing Pope Pius IX's policies and applauding the Archbishop for refusing to approve them.

Both intellectual and institutional tensions survive within the Church. A colleague trained in the Jesuit Order tells me that he was long convinced that a good Christian could never be faced by true conflicts of moral obligation: God must have ordered the World in such a way that such conflicts simply would not occur. (He has now revised his opinion.) If anything, these tensions have grown under John Paul II. Twenty years ago it seemed that there might be some relaxation of Church doctrine with regard to birth control, but the doctrinaire leadership of the Bavarian Cardinal Ratzinger holds lay opinion at bay in much of the industrialized world. Moral dogmas installed in the seventeenth century—against the tenor of earlier teaching—continue to be insisted upon, even if they amount in practice to little more than counsels of perfection. (Do we not all live through these compromises? Going back to England after a year in Australia in the 1950s, I was shocked to see that there was a column of small ads on the front page of the London *Times* headed "For the Epicure": not having become enough of an epicure myself to appreciate it, I at first viewed this concern for the palate as a sign of Britain's moral degeneration!)

In the academic world, the gravest impact of disciplinary tension has fallen on the social and behavioral sciences. For convenience, we may look at International Relations, which emerged as a distinct academic discipline after the First World War. The Department of International Politics at the University of Wales, Aberystwyth, was the first specialized department in this field, and the University of Southern California followed in 1924. These departments were not called into existence out of the blue: they were set up in response to a historical occasion, which is worth defining. In the eighty years since then, clear divisions have emerged between scholars who base the mission of International Relations on different core values. Two main streams of opinion are often referred to as "realism" and "idealism"; and it is widely assumed that, of the two, realism has dominated the field for much of the past century. Yet it is more accurate to say that, for much of the last half-century, the realist tradition has dominated the study of International Relations in *American* universities. Earlier, a vigorous counter-tradition of liberal internationalism was evident, notably in Europe, and this tradition was, in retrospect, more idealist than realist.

From the last years of the nineteenth century up to 1914, European scholars and activists were well aware that the Westphalian idea of the State had its limits, despite having played a large part in the political reorganization of Europe from 1648 on, and so challenged all unqualified claims to "national sovereignty" on behalf of the existing Powers. The first Nobel Peace Prize was awarded in 1901 to Jean Henry Dunant, founder of the International Committee of the Red Cross, and between 1901 and 1939 many of the Peace Laureates had this liberal internationalist background. Certainly this was true of Norman Angell, the 1933 laureate: he was a leader in moves to set up an overarching League of Nations. His early books *The Great Illusion* (1910) and *Foundations of International Polity* (1914) were widely read, not least in Germany: they underlined the value of non-governmental agents, and the growing importance of the global economy, with a clarity hard to improve today. There was also an extensive European movement to set up global non-State institutions, to overcome the limits of the Westphalian dispensation. Much of this activity was centered in Belgium, which was the first state to make legal provision for international—in contrast to intergovernmental—institutions. Meanwhile, the work of Marconi on radio communication allowed the coordination of time zones in distant countries: an agreed signal, sent from the Eiffel Tower in Paris on July 1, 1913, enabled clocks to be synchronized across the world.[2]

The World War from 1914 to 1918 was a historical trauma after a long period of general stability, and its military horrors, much worse than those of World War II, set off the debate that gave the discipline of International Relations its intellectual underpinning. The first Chair in the field, at Aberystwyth, was in fact named for Woodrow Wilson, the President who had helped to promote the League of Nations, only to see the United States Congress refuse to let America join. That is the situation out of which the dispute between the realists and the idealists arose.

At the outset, it was not an intellectual debate among academic theorists: it was a struggle between *internationalists*, who were happy to see the power of the Westphalian State limited, and *statists*, who sought to strengthen it. As early as 1912, there was a sharp exchange between Norman Angell and Admiral Mahan, who reviewed *The Great Illusion* for the

North American Review. (Mahan was the leading American advocate for a large fleet of battleships—the counterpart of intercontinental ballistic missiles in the Cold War.) So the debate between realism and idealism began as a dispute about practical policies, not abstract theories; and, as the British historian E. H. Carr was to argue, political thought was inseparable from political action. If Norman Angell was the prototypical "idealist" in this debate, E. H. Carr was cast as the representative "realist," though the substance of the debate (we shall see) was very different from that which developed after 1948.[3]

From our distance, the complexity of E. H. Carr's mind is easy to recognize. Born in 1892, he joined the Foreign Service in his twenties and, in the course of his duties of monitoring the affairs of the new Soviet State, he developed a fascination with Russian culture. While his colleagues were at the Ballet, he immersed himself in the novels of Dostoevsky, even publishing a new biography of the author. Later, his duty was to track the activities of the League of Nations for the Foreign Office, but he finally left the service and worked as an editorial writer for the London *Times*.

Politicians on the Right in Britain called Carr "the Red Professor of Printing House Square." Living in the Great Depression and seeing the impotence of the governments in Europe and North America in the face of mass unemployment, Carr became skeptical about liberal democracy and attracted by the idea of a planned economy. As a result, historians today admire his open-minded, fourteen-volume *History of the Soviet Union* (1950–1978) more than they do his work on International Relations. His most recent biographer writes of him as attracted by "romantic dreams of revolution"—though in the 1930s you did not need to be a romantic to feel that there must be a better way to run a State than that of European governments in the 1920s. Until Germany invaded Russia in 1941, Carr's refusal to be consistently anti-Soviet did not recommend him to representatives of "respectable" opinion, who tended to apologize for the Nazis. Right-wing conservatives like Lady Astor happily entertained the German ambassador and champagne salesman Ribbentrop at Cliveden on the Thames for house parties and dinners like those portrayed in the film *Remains of the Day*.

Carr's mixture of opinions was an uncomfortable one. He found the uncritical internationalism of believers in the League of Nations naive, but saw the anti-communism of pro-Nazi sympathizers as sterile; and he refused to give up either the idealism of his political goals, or the realism of his political analysis. This makes him hard to pin down. In ten pages of text, he can write both of the following passages: "Politics are made up of two elements—utopia and reality—belonging to two different planes that *can never meet*"; and "the State is built up out of these two conflicting aspects of human nature. Utopia and reality, the ideal and the institution, morality and power, are from the outset *inextricably blended*." The best summary of Carr's position (as Hayward Alker hints) would be the Kantian epigram, "Idealism without Realism is naive, Realism without Idealism is sterile"; but this summary still omits his preoccupation with the development of the Soviet Union—so much so that many readers are puzzled that Carr, the theorist of International Relations, and Carr, the historian of Soviet Russia, could have been one and the same person.[4]

Any historian understands the problems that arise if a major thinker's ideas cross cultural boundaries. Wundt's psychology gave birth to quite different offspring when it was transplanted to America and Russia: E. B. Titchener at Cornell saw simplified ideas of sense perception in his work, while A. R. Luria in Moscow found in Wundt the intellectual foundations for a new psychology of cultural development.[5] E. H. Carr's views had the same ambiguous reception in Cold War America, for two reasons: first, the methodology of the behavioral sciences in America from the 1960s on was very different from that of historiography in Britain between the Wars; and second, the political situations in post-war Europe and America were also developing in quite different directions.

As for the contrast between political situations: the questioning of the Westphalian State visible in pre-1914 Europe began again after 1945, in both theory and practice, in the way we associate with Jean Monnet and Robert Schumann. This has led most recently to the establishment of the European Union, and the introduction of the "Euro" as a common currency. So, except where American examples dominate, the discussion of International Relations in European universities has been historically broad-based, and avoids hard-line statist assumptions. (The author who comes to mind is Raymond Aron: his urbanity is represented in the United States today by his student, Stanley Hoffmann of Harvard.) As for American anti-communism: from the late 1940s on, it was possible to condemn all liberal internationalists as unpatriotic, and to discredit the newly established United Nations, notably after the Alger Hiss affair. But the book that dominated longer-term discussion was Hans Morgenthau's *Politics Among Nations*. This work analyzed problems in essentially statist terms, and its tendency was carried further by later writers such as Kenneth Waltz, who took it for granted that the only significant agents in international affairs are governments of sovereign states.

By the 1970s, the academic study of International Relations in America was also caught up in a larger intellectual project, which arose out of arguments about "method" in the behavioral sciences. These aimed at developing theories of international behavior that were value-neutral and (wherever possible) compatible with the mathematical algorithms of neoclassical Economics. For his part, Carr's political ideals meant that Realism in the field of International Relations could never be value-neutral. Its ideals might not be naive, but a Realism that called for value neutrality was inevitably sterile, so Carr the historian was not attracted to abstract, let alone axiomatic theories. Abstraction always had its price: that of setting aside all factors that are irrelevant to a given theory, and tolerating blinders that cut off from view the "other things" that must be assumed "equal" for the purposes of a theory. In short, the man who began as a foreign service officer, was a critic of Russian literature, yet above all was a *historian*, could never be a pure Westphalian Statist, indifferent to the limits of the traditional system or the need for transnational institutions. Realism and Utopianism may be treated as opposite poles of a theoretical spectrum; but for someone like E. H. Carr, exchanging arguments about which one of the two programs is theoretically superior to the other was a game barely worth the candle.

Though the debate between Realists and Idealists started around World War I, the mathematical dreams of rational choice theory took a central position in social science only as the Cold War intensified. This began from a debate about the problem of "The Prisoners' Dilemma." The question this problem raised is, "How can two prisoners whose chances of winning a release depend on each other's choices maximize their individual chances of release, without knowing each other's choices?" In the field of International Relations, the interest in this problem was enhanced by the American perception that any problem of real importance in international affairs involved a similar *two-person game*. (In political science and economics, rational choice theory had broader agendas.) In America, the opposition between the United States and the Soviet Union made this the key problem for discussion.

Both nations might have been better off if they had cooperated and avoided the race, yet the dominant political strategy was for each of them to arm to the teeth. This superpower rivalry was so crucial that the "rational choice" approach was very attractive, and departments of International Relations in the United States began to concentrate on formal methods of analysis, setting historical and cultural factors aside as being empirical, and so intellectually weak. At a stage when global misjudgments risked devastating consequences for the world, the rational choice theorists still valued mathematical elegance over empirical fact.

Even in Economics, where the assumptions underlying rational choice theory are less grossly simplified, its arguments are still too abstract to be helpful. The classic paper published by George Stigler and Gary Becker in 1977 denied that there were theoretically significant differences of taste between human agents. Ironically, their title for this paper was the Latin tag *de gustibus non est disputandum*—"tastes are not to be argued about." In Latin, this phrase concedes that everyone is entitled to decide these things in personal ways, but Stigler and Becker reverse its meaning, claiming that seeming differences of taste are a theoretical illusion. Yet surely (we respond) the point of talking about "tastes" lies precisely in the fact that one individual will have a taste for sweets (say), while another prefers savories. For economists to assure us that both these tastes are, from their point of view, theoretically indistinguishable—both of them are a definite taste for *something*—is intellectually vacuous.[6]

None of this would get much mileage from empirically-minded natural scientists. For them, explanations to the effect that something is theoretically intelligible, just because it is *something*, confront Karl Popper's objection that any decent explanation must explain *what is in fact the case* by showing what distinguishes it from *what is in fact not the case*. This is why rational mechanics had eventually come to seem out of date in Europe. Aside from the demands of a system of dynamics meant to apply to the real world—as Newton's dynamics originally was—the only merit of rational mechanics was its mathematical elegance, regardless of factual correctness; and the abstract nature of rational choice theory puts it at risk in the same way and for the same reasons as rational mechanics. Elegance is not enough.

Some other examples will put flesh on these mathematical bones. In the biological sciences, would-be explanations often fail because the theories they invoke are too general to account for the phenomena under discussion. By 1950, biologists may have had a good grasp of the empirical facts about heredity—many of which are now explained in terms of molecular biology—yet for a long time it was premature to speculate about any theory of heredity-in-general, which could trace those phenomena back to mechanisms explicable in quantum mechanical terms. At some future time, we may perhaps be able to do just that; but the best that we can do for now is to show how quantum mechanical processes might generate something in the way of self-replicating offspring, and biologists at the Santa Fe Institute are currently working on such arguments.

Peter Medawar, for instance, graduated from Oxford in the 1930s and was ready to embark on a research career. Given his intellectual brilliance, he was a natural target for older biologists working in puzzling fields; he was besieged by people who wanted him to study embryological development and morphogenesis, and in later life was asked to explain why he declined those invitations in favor of the more pedestrian-seeming subject of immunology. His reason was that in 1939 there was no way for biological theorists to get a grip on embryology: there was a chasm, and no conceptual machinery was available to bridge it. The program we know as molecular biology was barely thought of before Crick and Watson published their paper on DNA in 1962. Then and then alone did it become transparently clear why the problems of embryology had resisted theoretical analysis for so long. As Medawar commented, it is no good trying to improve your skill in tennis by playing against people you have no chance of beating: you can learn only by choosing opponents who are not-too-much-better than you are yourself. A strategically savvy scientist will therefore choose problems that are not completely out of his reach.[7]

The disciplinary problems that we find in the social and biological sciences do not spare Psychology either. When Paul Samuelson introduced rational choice theory to Economics, as early as the 1930s, he hoped to do for the subject what Skinner's Behaviorism had done for experimental psychology. Yet, after 1945 particularly, there was less and less agreement about the core values of Psychology, or about what methods any psychological science should employ. Up to the 1980s, indeed, there was so much internecine conflict among professional psychologists that it became doubtful whether one could even talk of a *singular* Science of Psychology at all. Sigmund Koch, who began his career working on the "little magazines" of the pre-1939 New York literary scene, insisted that we should refer to the whole field of study in the plural, as *the psychological sciences*. At most, he argued, the core concerns of these fields of study overlapped, and this meant that they lacked the key features of any strictly compact discipline.

As so often, this insight went back to Antiquity. In the *Categories*, Aristotle had discussed the different things we can say about human beings, and the kinds of meanings these statements had. In the book as we have it, he discusses nineteen kinds of statements we make about our fellow humans, and the predicates that go with them. Does this mean that he thought that there were nineteen (and *only* nineteen) such categories? To draw this conclusion would be the worst scholasticism. (He might as well have said fifty-seven.) Aristotle's aim was, of course, not to create a definitive list of categories, but to deny the *singularity* that philosophers had too easily demanded.

If this is true in Psychology, the same can be said of Biology. In a fine lecture entitled "Time in Biology," J. B. S. Haldane challenged the assumption that the whole of biological theory can be integrated into a single logical system, let alone an axiomatic system. There are and will remain—he said—at least four distinct, coexisting bodies of biological theory that operate on different scales of Space and Time, each of which develops a set of concepts that fit those scales. His distinctions are still worth pursuing.[8]

At the minutest level, the atoms and molecules in an organism take part in physical and chemical processes that obey the same laws as such processes do in the larger world: as Claude Bernard had insisted, the distinctive features of living things arise not from their disobeying the laws of physics and chemistry, but from the distinctive "niches" or micro-environments in which such processes take place. On a more familiar, everyday scale, the individual organs of a body contribute to an organism's life, in ways we describe in terms that go beyond the material language of physics or chemistry: so, at the boundary between the micro-structural and the everyday, we may speak about the very largest macromolecules (for example, sub-parts of genes) as having functions analogous to those of physiology.

Going beyond the range of immediate experience, physiology is supplemented by developmental biology, which includes embryology and morphogenesis: the term "kidney function" refers to an individual at a particular time, with a particular age. The way in which competent cells in an embryo differentiate into parts of a kidney rather than a muscle, and the way this develops over the individual life-span, is the topic in turn for a third group of biological theories and ideas. The same is true again if we widen our view still further to include changes that affect entire populations of organisms, whose rates of reproduction and survival modify the distribution of features among their members. The usual example to illustrate evolutionary change occurring at an observable rate is that of melanism in moths in industrial areas. As the trees near factories became soot-covered, moths with darker wings and bodies were said to be less liable to be eaten by birds than those with lighter wings, so that in time they formed a larger part of the population. The actual story now turns out to be more complex, but the elementary processes of organic evolution provide a field of biological study, with its own subject matter—populations—and its own time scale—from years to millennia.

Four scales of time and space, four sets of concepts and categories: that was the recipe Haldane developed for biological theory. Nor is there any hard and fast boundary between the biological and psychological sciences. As our understanding of the neurology of experience and behavior increases, we can "place" personal, social, and cultural aspects of human behavior alongside their physiological aspects. Cultural change thus takes place on a scale and at a rate intermediate (for Haldane) between development and evolution. Of course, cultural changes also have evolutionary consequences, so that culture is becoming yet a fifth category of concern to theoretical biologists.[9]

A final question has to be faced: "Are disciplines bound to run into these sorts of troubles, inevitably, or at a certain stage in their historical development?" The answer is, "Not necessarily, but there is a standing risk of their doing so, for sociological reasons." The organization of late twentieth century universities has encouraged a narrowness of preoccupations that has ended by rewarding participants who remain closest to the middle of their chosen intellectual road. Yet this way of organizing intellectual work is not inevitable: even in the most focused of subjects, a few individuals or groups can attract attention to broad and humane issues. Fifty years ago, for instance, writers on political economy like Gunnar Myrdal or Friedrich von Hayek had international reputations in the economic profession, despite their interest in such political and philosophical issues as "the logic of liberty" and the ill-effects of racial discrimination on the prosperity of American society, while Hazel Henderson continues to keep environmental issues before the public today at a time when economists are, for the most part, inclined to retreat onto narrower ground. As a result, Amartya Sen is not alone in analyzing the nature of human needs, the political conditions of economic success, and other questions that take him far beyond the mathematical bounds of orthodox economic theory.

What goes for Economics holds true also in Engineering. There is a tendency for academic engineers to train their students only in the techniques of nuclear reactor design, or Web page management, without teaching them to think in the ways that any practicing engineer is forced to think, about the potential effect of a major project on the real human beings whose lives would be changed by its actual realization. Fortunately, some working engineers are more reflective and humane than the majority of their academic colleagues: there is, for instance, one successful contractor based in the New York area who realizes the moral depth of the issues arising in his profession, and is ready to compare the conflicts that face him in his practice with those depicted in *Hamlet* or the Greek tragedies.[10]

There are even some fields of professional work in which it is impossible to pick out any techniques as the distinctive trademarks of the enterprise. The best of cultural anthropology, in the tradition of Gregory Bateson and Margaret Mead, has an intellectual freedom today at least as great as that of Myrdal and von Hayek. (I mentioned earlier Mary Catherine Bateson's book, *Composing a Life*.) The field of participatory action research, whose methods I discussed at length, has a similar freedom of investigation. And management research has the same potential breadth of vision—not, to be sure, in the style of Elton Mayo, that conservative Australian, but in the continually rethought ideas of Peter Drucker or, most recently, Ian Mitroff's studies of the role of spirituality in the life of senior managers in industry and commerce. None of these activities relies on a single core set of academic values and techniques; instead, they bring a broad range of professional skills to bear on problems arising in a particular situation, thus exemplifying the distinctive merits of "clinical" research.[11]

A particularly good illustration of this point is provided by the professional activity known as occupational therapy. Consider again our countrywoman (Chapter 7), whose misfortunes made her situation a poignant and intractable case: those best placed to help in her resulting personal crisis would in fact be occupational therapists. For, unlike doctors or lawyers or others with specialized training, occupational therapists do not concentrate their attention on a narrowly defined set of factors. Whereas specialists like doctors and lawyers are trained to adopt a selective viewpoint, looking for the specifically "legal" or "medical" implications of any situation and ignoring those that do not "count" medically or legally, the professional task of occupational therapists is to pay attention to an individual's actual needs, of whatever kind. They quickly come to understand that, in talking with a client or patient or human subject (however you label them), they cannot afford to exclude *anything* from consideration. There is in their field no way to draw a line between things that do, and do not, "count." As a slogan, they might well choose the Latin tag, *nihil humanum a me alienum puto*: "nothing human is, from my point of view, irrelevant."

Given the rise of professions and disciplines from the eighteenth century on, one central intellectual concern of the social sciences has been (as we saw) *prediction*. But the goal of "social prediction" takes for granted a future whose seemingly ineluctable character it should be our ambition to figure out in advance. Yet that is what occupational therapists are *not* trained to do; rather, their task is to help people *make something* of their futures. To recall Bertrand de Jouvenel's term, their concern is only with *possible* futures that we can reasonably hope to *bring about*— as he calls them, "futuribles."

What this means, of course, is not just that the academic social sciences are too narrowly concerned with abstract issues, which have little direct bearing on the complex situations that are the daily fare of occupational therapists. It also means that the whole project of orthodox social science rests at best on an oversimplification of human life and experience, at worst on a methodological error. Social scientists who are philosophically committed to their enterprises may insist that we have no capacity to "make" our own lives: the things we do are determined by hidden causal factors. But that is a metaphysical slogan, not the outcome of experimental demonstration. What needs to be shown is to what extent subcellular biochemistry in actual practice forces us to act as we do, or prevents us from acting as we choose; and everyday experience teaches us not to worry unduly about such compulsions. Drinking too much alcohol may prevent us from walking in the direction we choose; but, equally, we learn that avoiding excess immediately restores our ability to tell left from right, and act accordingly.

What, then, can we say about the status of occupational therapy as a profession or discipline? As occupational therapists avoid the exclusionary viewpoints of more orthodox disciplines, we may be tempted to call it a profession *without a discipline*, but advocates of the profession are not pleased by that description. They are more interested in developing an "occupational science" that would provide an intellectual foundation for their clinical activities, and they are unwilling to admit that this "science" could be any less respectable a "discipline" than the biomedical sciences that inform the activities of clinical medicine. As a political tactic, this insistence may be powerful, but as methodologists we may ask, in return, that the advocates for occupational studies treasure the openness to all the vicissitudes of life that makes their enterprise such a special activity. Nothing is more enriching than to get professional help from someone who has an open ear, and an open mind, toward whatever is of concern or interest to their fellow-humans. As Jeremy Bentham put it in an epigram that is less cynical than it at first sounds, "The best way to influence people is to appear to love them, and the best way to appear to love them is to love them indeed."

To speak generally: if by the end of the twentieth century professional activities have developed a highly disciplinary character, which has distorted their fulfillment, we must try to grasp the source of those troubles. It is not the intellectual focus of the discipline that has this effect; rather, it is the style of social organization in which disciplinary work is done. In a word, this is at bottom not an intellectual but a sociological phenomenon. The narrow departmental system of organization in American research universities so fragments fields that cultural anthropologists and social historians cannot collaborate effectively with (say) many highly reputed economists. So it is often the social structure of learned institutions that—for better and for worse—finally determines the intellectual focus of disciplines. Ours is not an academic world into which a Friedrich von Hayek or a Gunnar Myrdal would fit very comfortably, or would feel that he could make his distinctive contributions to the betterment of human understanding and welfare.

10

Redressing the Balance

So far, we have focused on things that upset the balance between our ideas of rationality and reasonableness in the last four hundred years, most of all in the twentieth century. If we now turn to more constructive arguments, what hope does our own situation—intellectual and institutional, political and cultural—hold out for healing the Wounds of Reason?

I N SOME RESPECTS, the Age of Modernity is ending as it began, but in ways that undo many of the seventeenth century's changes. With two world wars and the inter-war years, the time from 1914 to 1945 was, in effect, a second Thirty Years' War, and its effects on the diplomatic map of Europe were as striking as those from 1618 to 1648. The parallels extend to some surprising details. Historians have noted that the general crisis of the early seventeenth century in Europe was aggravated by a short-term climatic change referred to as the Little Ice Age. In Virginia Woolf's imaginative novella *Orlando*, the main character attends winter festivals and royal celebrations on the Thames in London at which the river is frozen so hard that whole oxen were roasted on the ice. Did the severity of the weather encourage the harshness of seventeenth-century life and thought? Certainly, much of Northern Europe lost its marginal agricultural land to cultivation at that time, and laborers who had previously made a living on the land found no other work than as mercenaries in the rival armies of the Catholic and Protestant powers. Since 1950, conversely, global warming has, if anything, made the climate of the region easier, and has done little to hinder cultural relaxation. So nowadays many people, scholars and poli-

ticians equally, regard the end of the twentieth century as marked by a decline of the Westphalian System of sovereign states established after the
first Thirty Years' War.

That system played a major part in supporting and maintaining the new
ideas and procedures of the time. From the Peace of Westphalia emerged
the forms of the world in which we live today—forms so familiar that we
forget that they were then brand-new. The Peace introduced three novel
elements: a new system of States, a policy for Church/State relations, and a
concept of rational thought. Political power was vested absolutely in each
individual Sovereign. In each State, power was exercised from the top, and
outside states did not meddle in its affairs. Religious conflict was overcome
by a compromise that took over a thesis—*cuius regio eius religio*—previously formulated for the Treaty of Augsburg in 1555: under this formula,
every Sovereign had to choose the Church for his or her realm. So, for the
first time, the Westphalian System created "established" churches—Anglican in England, Calvinist in Holland, Catholic in Austria, and so on.
Finally, the new idea of Reason took as its starting point Descartes's claims
that knowledge must have the certainty of a geometrical system, and that
opinions unsupported by such a rigorous theory were just that—nothing
but unsupported opinions.

On its face, these three aspects of the Westphalian System—Absolute
Sovereignty, Established Religion, and Logical Demonstration—may appear distinct and separate. As a matter of practical politics, however, they
had two significant things in common. First, all of them operated
top-down, and gave power to oligarchies—political, ecclesiastical, or academic—that supported one another. Second, they formed a single package. Voltaire commented, "One leaves Paris, where Space is Full and everything happens through Vortices, and reaches London, where Space is
Empty and everything happens through Attraction."[1] The three elements
of the Westphalian settlement in fact formed an ideological package, so
that questioning any one of its components was regarded as attacking
them all.

In this respect, heresy could get one into serious trouble. In eighteenth-century England, Newton's physics had more than empirical authority: it mapped God's Plan for the Creation and supposedly demonstrated the stability of the Solar System, so its success was political as well
as astronomical, bolstering the odd mixture that passed for respectable

opinion in England: a close alliance of the Anglican Church, the Hanoverian Monarchy, and Newton's astronomy. The minister-scientist Joseph Priestley, who challenged this mixture, got himself into hot water by talking at the same time as a Nonconformist in religion, a Republican in politics, and a Materialist in philosophy. He was not just a man of unusual beliefs (they said), but a troublemaker; not just a Dissenter, but a Dissident.[2]

This alliance of Anglican Religion with Newtonian Mechanics and Constitutional Monarchy came in time to form a unitary Ideology, whose attractions only reinforced the sense of God-given superiority that seemed to justify the English in their imperial mission and provided a model for all other countries—a stance that would be taken over in the late twentieth century by the United States. In the manifesto that, in 1857, Richard Chenevix-Trench used to launch the campaign that finally led to production of the *Oxford English Dictionary*, the aim of this enterprise was not just to set a new standard in lexicography—which it did—but to show how strong were the claims of English to become a Language for the whole World—which today it shows signs of doing for quite other kinds of reasons.[3] (Of course, in the aftermath of the Westphalian settlement, similar claims were made for French, which for a century and more was the general language of diplomacy and society across Europe, from Paris to Moscow and beyond; and to this day French government policies look back nostalgically to that time.)

One basic defect of a public ideology, however, is that people cannot present unorthodox or unfamiliar views without being accused of enmity to the Powers-that-Be. Priestley was a Unitarian minister in Birmingham, but, once he had spoken in support of the French Revolution, the Birmingham Mob did not permit him to explain his opinions—let alone listen to him, to see if they might learn from his views. They preferred to burn down his place of worship and his home, and to drive him out of town. Nor was this intolerance merely English. After 1650, all European States demanded exclusive loyalties: no citizen was a subject of more than one Sovereign. Established religions expected their adherents to avoid the churches of other faiths; in this respect, the English could be as unforgiving to Papists as the French and Austrians were to Protestants. As for Rational Knowledge: from Leibniz on, most philosophers demanded formal deductions, rejected Rhetoric as irrational, and the rest. Thus, the Westphalian Settlement imposed exclusive attitudes on religious, political, and intellectual life alike.

Things had not always been that way. Medieval rulers in Europe never exerted the exclusive sovereignty that Nation-States later claimed; after Thomas Becket's murder in Canterbury Cathedral, the Church shamed Henry II of England into changing his policies. Nor was Sovereignty tightly linked to Nationhood: the Habsburgs' subjects spoke not just German, but Polish and Portuguese, Magyar and Dutch. Nor need religion everywhere be always exclusive. Most people in the West are so used to practicing one-and-only-one religion that the open-mindedness of other peoples comes as a surprise. Japanese friends of ours, visiting Chicago for Christmas, sang the carols at the Fourth Presbyterian Church on Michigan Avenue from memory; many people in Japan (they explained) include in their lives ceremonies from three different religions. It is quite common to be baptized in a Shinto ceremony, to marry in a Christian service, and to be buried as a Buddhist, so that the three religions peaceably coexist. Nor do philosophers always demand formal proofs: if things go well, they need not reject humanist ideas outright. Diderot's concern with physics was pragmatic, not ideological, and the *Encyclopédie* had practical interests, too. By contrast, when things went badly—in the Thirty Years' War, the French Revolution, or the First World War—they were tempted to ask for greater rigor. At times, therefore, the history of philosophy in the Modern era has been something of an intellectual seesaw.

The Westphalian Settlement was, then, a poisoned chalice: intellectual dogmatism, political chauvinism, and sectarian religion formed a blend whose influence lasted into the twentieth century. To put it more exactly: the Westphalian System *ended* as a poisoned chalice; initially, its terms met the needs of the time. Nation-States, Established Religions, and Formal Rationality were at first effective ways of ordering life and thought so as to minimize, and temper, the conflicts among different countries or religions. For three centuries, from 1650 on, the states of Europe lived in what has been called the International Anarchy: each of them went its own way without fear of outside criticism. This was practicable only because the established Church was also an emasculated Church, with State and Church tied together at the ankles in a three-legged race; so the State escaped the indignity of being exposed to moral reproof from its own citizens. Even in philosophy, the charms of Rationalism were reinforced by the needs of the day. Leibniz hoped that his formal arguments might succeed where Diplomacy and War had failed, ensuring agreement between rival religions whose followers had devastated his native Germany. Still, after a time, these devices outgrew their initial efficacy; and now, at the end of the terrible twentieth century, they need to be replaced, as new institutions come on stage. Above all, the facts of global interdependence are no longer compatible with claims to entirely unfettered Sovereignty—especially as nowadays such claims are most stridently made by rulers who are also villains.

For a seventeenth-century image of the State, Hobbes chose a sea monster he called Leviathan. This was a natural image for a theorist from the British Isles. (Today a nuclear superpower recalls the 900-pound gorilla who sleeps where he pleases.) As matters stand, the general interest lies less in increasing the force of the Nation-State than in moderating it: nongovernmental organizations (NGOs) that reduce the power of States have a growing influence, serving as those voluntary associations that Hobbes criticized as pathological, calling them "worms in the intestines of Leviathan" that must be "purged."[4] Meanwhile, we see States joining together in larger units that limit their Sovereignty, such as the European Union.

The NGOs remind us of a time when Sovereigns were subject to outside reproof. Institutions like Amnesty International are not emasculated: as voices for the conscience of humanity, they keep their distance from Nation-State Governments, which are the agents of violence, and from corporations, which are given to pollution. NGOs cannot compel governments or industries to act in ways that would please them, but in suitable cases they can shame them into changing their policies—a reminder that the Politics of Shame can be as fruitful, on occasion, as the Politics of Force. Here again, the Westphalian System has outlived its efficacy, and the earlier tensions between Church and State are reemerging, but on a new level. From now on, governments and corporations need to retune their ears and listen to unofficial institutions that speak, not for the special interests of a particular nation or party, but for the "decent opinion" of humankind.[5]

Even scholars who recognize the contributions of NGOs, however, sometimes underestimate their autonomy, and the influence this gives them. They see NGOs less as transnational elements in global Civil Society, which is their long-term role, than as based in a given State, or in the administrative structures of the United Nations organization. True, NGOs are incorporated as charities, businesses, or other entities, and this requires them to accept oversight by State agencies. But in this they are no different from any other charitable or commercial enterprise; that in no way makes them State agencies. Still, there are clear contrasts between those NGOs based in Europe or North America, which operate on private contributions, and the quasi-autonomous organizations in Mainland China (say) that claim to be nongovernmental, but operate entirely on funds from the State and follow a State-approved policy. Highly visible NGOs like Amnesty International or Greenpeace are fully effective, too, only if accredited by the U.N. authorities. Yet, in accepting this necessity, they hold the U.N. at arm's length. They remember that the United Nations Charter starts, "We, the People of the United Nations": Member States of the U.N. owe their standing as "members" to their role as political representatives of their Peoples. Thus, we can judge NGOs realistically only by seeing how they enter into public affairs on the international and transnational levels in actual fact.

Consider, for instance, the relations between Care International and the authorities in Afghanistan. Over the last few years, relations between Afghanistan and most outside powers have been highly tenuous. It has scarcely been possible for governmental or even inter-governmental agencies to tolerate the constraints the Taliban authorities place on Afghan women, notably on the education of girls; some humanitarian and charitable agencies, as a result, have felt obliged to withdraw from the country. Care International found a way to continue serving its mission by exercising diplomatic powers that were not open to any government agent. Negotiating with the Afghan authorities, Care emphasized the need of war widows to earn an income by going out to work, and also the need to set up day care facilities for children of both sexes, in order to permit the mothers to work. This point having been made, they asked for a document authorizing them to move around Kabul on this mission. This was not, by itself, a perfect defense against interference by the self-appointed Guardians of Virtue, but it allowed them to claim official permission, and avoid the punishments to which their activities might otherwise expose them.

Once these centers were in operation, they became places where, under the general heading of day care, elementary education could be provided to young girls and boys alike. If the Taliban's local agents were uncooperative, it might happen that the repairs to Kabul's water supply in which Care International was also involved were, coincidentally, delayed. In this way, the transnational NGO negotiated with a foreign agency in terms that would be unacceptable on a formal, government-to-government level.

Day by day and year by year, the outlines of the Westphalian Settlement—political and religious—have thus been progressively eroded. The final element was, of course, the intellectual one. In both Natural and Human Sciences, a leitmotif has been the importance of *prediction;* and this requires radical reinterpretation. In neither Physics nor History do we have unqualified confidence in our ideas on this subject. Since Poincaré, the business of making predictions has become a pragmatic affair, which no longer has a strong basis in ideology: this is true of predicting what natural phenomena we should regularly (as a rule) *expect,* but it is also true of the regular (or rule-governed) conduct that we may *expect of* our fellow human beings.

In the world of natural events, the benchmark is still the Great Lisbon Earthquake of 1755. As physicists still recognize, the Lisbon earthquake "shattered the contemporary European belief in a benign, predictable Universe based on the spectacular success of linear mathematics, such as Newton's theory of gravitation." It was no good taking it for granted that Newton's dynamics allowed one to calculate the orbits of the planets, and that the same theory would eventually account for all physical phenomena. In practice, as we have seen, the theory was of limited value, and it remained necessary to rely on empirical observation. Careful study of the happenings around a volcano often make it possible to give advance warning of an eruption: the 1980 eruption of Mount Saint Helens is a good example. In the case of earthquakes, however, we can neither rely on theoretical calculations alone, nor accumulate enough advance signs of a quake to justify (for example) evacuating the population. The revolution in physics in recent years means that unpredictable changes are likely to occur in the course of the processes involved.

As a recent authoritative statement put it, "The hypothesis to be disproved is not that earthquakes *are* predictable, but that they are *not:* the practical question now is, How far should we now go in trying to judge the predictability of such processes?" An exchange by specialists in the field does little to improve our hopes. The historical record of earthquakes provides reasonable estimates of the general hazards in a particular location, but none of the specialists involved thought that it was, even now, a realistic goal to predict any individual earthquake accurately enough to justify (say) an evacuation.[6] Here, as elsewhere, we are concerned more with *risks* than with *forecasts*. And, since such risks can never be wholly eliminated, we can account exactly for these natural events only in retrospect, if at all.

In this respect the convergence between the Natural Sciences and the Humanities would have come as a surprise to eighteenth-century academics. Listen to Timothy Garton Ash on the collapse of the Soviet Union:[7]

> Did not the events of 1989 show, once again, the folly of any
> attempt to predict the future? Which of the countless models
> and theories of political science, or from the academic field of
> international relations, suggested that the world of Soviet
> Communism would end in that way, let alone at that time? As
> one American scholar ruefully observed, "None of us predicted
> these events, and all of us could explain why they were inevi-
> table."

Having visited Vienna twice in the summer and fall of 1989, I know what he means. All my friends were aware of the fragility of Eastern Europe. No one was surprised that, when Otto von Habsburg—the inheritor of the family name—arranged a "Europicnic" in an enclave of Hungary embedded in Eastern Austria, the movement of people through an abandoned customs post near the picnic site was the first pebble of a human avalanche; yet, to the end, they estimated that Czechoslovakia would take ten years to "go West."

All told, then, the distinction between the determinate (if unpredictable) Natural Order and the far less regular course of Human Affairs, which lay close to the heart of the modern World View, is no longer taken for granted as strictly as it was, either by Voltaire or even by Poincaré. In the twentieth century, physicists have to accept deviations from a strict classical determinism that Leibniz would have abhorred; yet, in everyday experience, these are only samples from a long and familiar list. To take an extreme example: does it make sense to claim that one might have predicted the composition of Beethoven's Ninth Symphony as early as 1820? A detailed prediction of this achievement would have meant writing out the score of the whole symphony four years before it was actually completed!

These *inconceivable* predictions may be extreme, but there are other familiar ones that have no counterpart in the physical sciences. Two people in a close interaction, eye to eye, may reach a point at which the most precisely informed onlookers cannot say which will blink first. Again, the abstractions involved in physics, by which the planets Mercury, Venus, and Mars (say) are renamed, for the purposes of calculation, "freely moving bodies attracted by a heavy center of force," are a source of much of the intellectual power of physics, but the complex and concrete interactions typical of human affairs largely resist that kind of abstraction. There, we are dealing with individuals rather than classes, and the differences among those individuals frustrate generalization.

The idolization of Newtonian prediction is only one factor that led to the imbalance in our ideas about Reason. More basic was the attitude that John Dewey called "the quest for certainty": the belief that the very heart of philosophical logic resided in the principle of non-contradiction, which was invoked to guarantee the necessity of philosophical argument. In the twentieth century, too, analytically-minded philosophers continued to prefer fields of experience in which our beliefs could be given a quasi-geometrical foundation to those in which that seemed impossible. Once more, disciplines like Physics came out ahead, and were seen as intrinsically rational, while the rationality of fields such as Ethics, in which no agreed analytical proofs seemed to be available, was called in question.

Aristotle himself had no illusions about the principle of non-contradiction. It does not show us anything about the *substance* of our reasoning; rather, it is a warning against claims that are internally inconsistent in *form*. Somebody who asserts both that "p" and that "not-p" at the same time, without realizing what he is doing, trips over the meaning of his own words. Not that all statements of the form "p and not-p" automatically fall into this trap: if we ask a friend whether it is raining, and get the reply, "Well, it is and it isn't," we understand what he is saying perfectly well. Indeed, there are some situations in which we may deliberately say things that appear contradictory: subjected to a hostile interrogation, I may do this simply to gain time, while the questioner wonders if I am an uncooperative witness. The validity of the reasoning embodied in an utterance can, thus, be understood only with an eye to the situation in which it is made. (It is *pros ton kairon* once again: the occasion, more than the form, determines the meaning.)

If the idea of rationality is problematic, that of "irrationality" is even more difficult. If formal logic were truly the science of rationality, we would expect irrationality to show itself in errors of formal reasoning. To the extent that we unwittingly speak inconsistently, our lack of attention may deserve that description; but, in a broad sense, the term *irrational* applies to situations that do not involve formal reasoning or even language use at all. When Edmund Burke says, for instance, "Inconsiderate courage has given way to irrational fear," he is talking about states of mind, not beliefs or propositions; and this applies to inattention as much as to courage and fear. In phobias, tics, fugues, and other uncontrolled reactions, it is the same: a woman who freezes at the mere glimpse of a snake reacts "irrationally," and this reaction prevents her from giving a "reason" why she acted in that way. (If she could speak coherently about her response, that would be another matter. The question is then whether her account is "reasonable" or "unreasonable": we are back in the land of empirical opinions, not formal theories.)

The seventeenth-century philosopher who best exemplifies both the significance of the relations between Reason and Rhetoric, and their inner tensions, is Thomas Hobbes. In an analysis of the changes in Hobbes's position during his long career, Quentin Skinner has mapped the twists and turns in his attitudes as the century went along. Born in 1588, Hobbes grew up in the culture of Renaissance humanism, and became strongly attracted to the natural philosophy of Descartes and Mersenne only in the 1630s. Meeting Mersenne on a visit to Paris (Skinner comments) "appear[s] to have aroused in [him] an obsessional interest in the laws of physics, and above all in the phenomenon of motion." As Hobbes himself says, "there is only one thing in the whole world which is real . . . [A]nyone who wishes to understand physics must first of all make a study of the laws of motion." Only in 1650, after King Charles I's execution, did he complete the *Leviathan* and return to his earlier, more charitable view of Rhetoric. In Chapter IX of *Leviathan*, for instance, Hobbes retracts his earlier attack on rhetoricians: rather than seeing "Rhetorique" as concerned with tracing "Consequences from the Passions of Men," he reclassifies it together with Logic, as tracing "Consequences from *Speech*." Between them (he says), "ethics, logic, civil philosophy and rhetoric . . . arise out of the contemplation of Man and his Faculties."[8]

We would do well to follow Hobbes's example. Rhetoric is not a *rival* to Logic; rather, it puts the logical analysis of arguments into the larger framework of argumentation. If you present a train of reasoning forcibly and vividly, you do not seek to convince your hearers by arousing their passions; instead, you try to give them a fuller and easier grasp of your substantive claims. Rhetorical tricks are on occasion used to evade or conceal a substantive point, but that once again is a matter of what *may* happen, not what *must* happen: overall, the act of arguing still has the dual role of seizing the hearers' attention and using this to convince them of a well-founded claim.

It is time to state the general position at which the argument of this book is directed. Jürgen Habermas's lasting contribution to ideas has been to insist on the connection between knowledge and reasoning on the one hand, and human interests on the other. Our interests may be, but are not necessarily, personal or class interests, and so render our language liable to distortion; at the same time, we know that some interests are shared by all human beings. Yet these interests are not necessarily shared in all cultures and periods alike: many of them overlap, or change slowly enough to be understood across cultural or historical boundaries. (Everything may be in flux, but this flux need not be so severe and rapid that we cannot even *name* things as they *change*.)

To come to examples: achieving intelligibility by avoiding incoherence is a formal interest; but it is not our only interest. Respecting the principle of non-contradiction rarely does any harm, but by itself it conveys nothing substantive either. Revealing the grain of the natural world, which the seventeenth century called the Laws laid down by the Creator, is a substantive interest, but not our only interest. In the 1950s and 1960s, John Ziman likened the motivation of young students entering graduate work in the physical sciences to that of postulants entering the medieval monastic orders. In earlier times their interest might have been to achieve personal Sanctity; now it is to win a reputation for revealing scientific Truth, and this requires them to avoid (for example) the distractions of politics or other unscientific activities, so as to escape the counter-reputation of being "unsound." Allowing for the fact that the grain of the world runs differently in different fields of study is another legitimate interest: failing to allow for these differences may (as we saw) generate the kinds of disputes that dogged psychology for thirty or forty years.

So we may go on. Reason embraces more shared interests than are listed here. Ethics, law, politics, aesthetics, and even rhetoric have their distinct contributions to make. Are these other kinds of reasoning any the less serious, for being "value-laden"? By now, that should appear a foolish question. Interests and values are inextricable: the avoidance of formal incoherence, and understanding how the natural world affects our everyday lives, are interests as value-laden as any other human enterprises. Indeed, this way of presenting the relations between formal and substantive—morally neutral and value-laden—aspects of the Reason evokes resonances with the overall plan of Aristotle's own philosophical work. Two thousand years and more were not without effects, but these changes merely overlay certain basic similarities.

When Aristotle put avoiding contradictions and respecting the essences of different species together under the heading of *Analytics*, he was a man of his time: the idea that Formal Logic was an abstract intellectual game with symbols became current only after the work of David Hilbert and other mathematicians in the years around 1900. It took until the late nineteenth century, too, for Darwin's arguments against fixed organic species to win widespread acceptance: until then, the belief that things of many kinds have permanent "natures"—what is nowadays called "essentialism"—could not be wholly ruled out. Formal logic today is no longer linked with botany and zoology as it was in Aristotle's *Analytics*. Whereas a new *Prior Analytics* might include not just subject-predicate logic, but Russell and Whitehead's propositional logic as well, scientific ideas about the grain of the natural world are now as evolutionary in the field of cosmology as in zoology and botany, and so fully empirical. So we now have grounds for distinguishing sharply between the formal implications of the Law of Non-Contradiction and the substantive principles of taxonomic classification embodied in contemporary biological systematics.

Nor are philosophers today as tempted as they were from the 1920s to the 1950s to find formal reasons for ruling out some familiar scientific inquiries as logically illegitimate: the attempts by Hempel, Popper, and Chomsky to discredit Darwin's ideas about evolution now appear dated. As in politics, tolerance and democracy are winning out over elitism in methodology, and over imperialism in the philosophy of science. To that extent, the imbalance in European ideas about Rationality and Reasonableness shows healthy signs of correcting itself.

For the rest, Aristotle's *Organon* and its associated works are still a useful guide to a balanced view of Reason. We give reasons for the things we do, the ways we vote, and the movies we admire; we find fault with the reasons of the same kinds that others offer in turn; and we have a subtle grasp of the ways in which our reasons depend on the subjects we are discussing, will or will not carry weight with others, and are most effective when addressed to a hearer's feelings or interests. (Quakers call this *speaking to his condition*.) Little of this has to do with formal or substantive analytics; most of it has fallen out of the catalogue of academic philosophy courses; yet we can all be said to "know a lot" about these things, as is clear if we take the trouble to study everyday conversations.[9]

Let us take a final look at the traditional War between Logic and Rhetoric. English speakers still see terms like *rhetorical, pharisaical, casuistical,* and *sophistical* as criticisms meant to distract attention from the merits of unconventional ideas. We need to correct that impression, and rescue is at hand. Moral casuists and students of rhetoric are raising their heads again, not always under these traditional names; and many departments of English or Communication discuss rhetoric without apology. Meanwhile, analytical philosophers are less preoccupied with desituated propositions and more with local and timely utterances—"speech acts" that call for analysis in terms more rhetorical than formal. So (we may argue) analytical philosophy has itself moved on from Aristotle's *Analytics* to the *Categories,* the *Topics,* and the *Art of Rhetoric.* Moral problems in medical practice, too, are being handled less by strictly theoretical analysis than on a "case by case" approach. Scholars like Sissela Bok and Michael Walzer are reviving styles of argumentation more congenial to medieval moral theology than to philosophical ethics in the tradition of Henry

More and Sidgwick. The Pharisees and Sophists are less widely defended, and have farther to go; but at least we can ask why all of these enterprises were denied academic attention for so long.

Two points are worth making. Students of rhetoric were always ready to analyze the solidity or weakness of substantive arguments, and the only people who rejected their analyses as superficial were philosophers with a stake in formal logic or a universalistic theory of knowledge. Honest casuists today discuss the ethics of war, or the limits to the use of life support for terminally ill patients; by contrast, people who want ethical theory to be moral too often dismiss casuistry as corroding general moral principles. Yet how does studying the merits or defects of particular arguments undercut a general, formal account of Reason? And how does scrutinizing the things that carry weight in particular cases corrode medical ethics? What the attacks of logicians and epistemologists lack is a serious concern with the details of particular situations, and few moral theorists are in any hurry to resolve the bedside problems of individual patients.

Yet, if moral philosophy and formal logic handle general, abstract questions, while rhetoric and casuistry focus on particular, practical problems, there is room to accept a fair division of labor. The critical attacks on rhetoric and casuistry, sophistry and pharisaism, share a common burden. By focusing on timebound practical issues, pedestrian thinkers (the critics claim) distract us from larger and more general ideals. By contrast, philosophers and prophets lift our eyes from the mundane world, and measure transient problems by a more comprehensive and enduring standard. From the standpoint of the Ideal, opinions (*doxai*) based entirely on transient experiences seem to them no better than lies. Certainly, we need not deny poets and dreamers their day, but such complaints are overstated. Reflecting on universal and eternal principles is fine, so long as they keep some links with the spheres of life on which they seek to throw light; but ignoring the urgent demands of daily life is less praiseworthy than deplorable—the behavior of an intellectual ostrich.

Even the philosophers of Antiquity employed two distinct standards of judgment. Early in the *Nicomachean Ethics* Aristotle criticized Plato for demanding in Ethics a kind of exactitude and necessity that is appropriate in Geometry, but not to human situations or the moral issues they entail. Where Platonists insisted on general principles in every field of human thought, Aristotle asked us to aim at whatever kinds of generality the nature of our particular problems justified. In this, he was more tolerant of Sophists and Casuists than those who called for the Universal and the Eternal in facing every kind of problem, on all kinds of occasions.[10]

The division of labor that is required by a more balanced view of Rationality and Reasonableness is, accordingly, clear enough. To sum it up in our own terms:

> Let students of rhetoric analyze particular substantive arguments and leave general theories of rationality and knowledge to the philosophers. There is then no occasion for conflict, let alone insults.
>
> Let physicians develop ways of resolving the moral problems that arise for their patients in clinical practice case by case, and leave comprehensive ethical theories to moral philosophers. Here too there is room for a truce.
>
> Let sophists give timely, circumstantial advice, fitted to given occasions—here, not there; now, not then—and leave the search for timeless, universal principles to metaphysicians.
>
> Let Pharisees interpret the literal content of the Moral Law, as it relates to everyday situations, and leave it to the Prophets to throw fresh light on the role of the Spirit in a religious life.

In each case, we can achieve a détente if scholars will only stick to their lasts.

Yet even this proposal is too irenic to help. In each dispute, one of the two sides is ready to compromise, while the other is intransigent. Rhetoricians do not seek to abolish formal logic, nor do casuists reject moral philosophy. Sophists do not attack a concern for the eternal; and the most literal-minded Rabbinical readers of Torah can read the Law in a proper spirit. In general, then, workaday practical people no more need to discredit the theories of philosophy than casuists, sophists, and the rest. They are ready to be judged by their particular products, if the others will do likewise. It is the abstract theorists—formal logicians, metaphysicians, or moral philosophers—who are threatened by appeals to practice or experience, and resort to insults as a defense. Yet what do metaphysicians, logicians, or moral philosophers have to fear? Their scorn for practicality is shown in their debasement of the very term *sophist*. They paint skilled craftsmen as intellectual deceivers, contrasting everyday mastery of practical experience with the dream of permanent truth. Just because the experience that leads to practical wisdom, however long and deep it has been, is always incomplete, we are not to trust it: theoretical understanding, they insist, is superior because it grasps Certain Truths once and for all, in a self-validating insight.

Plato's followers offered a Dream of timeless Truth and Certainty unattainable by timely human experience. Yet the content of this Dream is more lasting than its charm, which works better for some people than others: in some regions, such as Latin America, the critique of practical wisdom has never been as sharp as in Europe or North America. Powerful defenders from Montaigne to Dewey, Wittgenstein, and Rorty have argued that we must not take this Dream at its face value. So let us ask, in conclusion, "What leads individual humans, or even whole peoples, to seek Eternity, Universality, and Certainty, despite such vigorous replies from the Skeptics?" The twin questions, about individuals and collectives, are inseparable. In Dewey's book *The Quest for Certainty*, he found the origin for the Platonic Dream in anxiety; yet it is not clear, in retrospect, if he thought of anxiety as an individual affliction, or as shared by a whole population. If he had firmly supported the collective reading, he might sooner have faced a question he ignored: "Why was this Quest so seductive in Descartes's time, rather than (say) a century earlier or later?" In facing this problem, he might have linked the collective anxieties of a particular time to the individual anxieties of writers like Blaise Pascal and John Donne, who passed their lives within the period in question.

Another source of the Dream was aristocratic disdain for the professional Sophists as money grubbers. The idea that the philosophers' hostility to the crafts had a class basis was first popularized by Benjamin Farrington, yet despite some intuitive plausibility this approach adds little to Dewey's "anxiety" story. In the long run, we need a richer account of why some people are unhappy with workaday experience, or knowledge that is subject to revision, and so open themselves to the appeals of Eternity, Universality, and Certainty. Aristocratic attitudes can, in any case, be read several ways. Farrington linked Platonism to class envy, but we might expect this to work in reverse, with the lower-class Sophists criticizing the posturing of upper-class Platonists, not the other way around. In cultures where honor plays a major part in people's status and self-esteem, upper-class youths will avoid activities in which failure is in the cards, threatening their status in ways beyond their control. So class envy is hardly relevant. Where honor was at issue, cobblers did not resent the gentry, for they knew what they did best: it was the gilded young who had something to lose in their own eyes, compared with the practical skills of Athenian cobblers.[11]

Blaise Pascal fell between these extremes. The Jansenist theology he espoused was popular in the aristocratic circles he frequented, but, in his self-esteem, he displayed a split personality. At Court, he had a brilliant reputation as a mathematician (a flair that later gave his name a place in computer science); away from Court, he feared that this reputation was bought at the price of his own Soul, and he strove to be worthy of Grace by renouncing his intellectual talents. This dream of Redemption generally went hand in hand with a scorn for worldly productivity: Salvation by Grace, not Works, appealed to those who neither wished nor had to earn a living as stablehands, charcoal burners, or printers. At the level on which commitments shape self-esteem, and vice versa, Pragmatism was for Dewey an egalitarian position that revived the theological belief that Grace without Works, or Theory without Practice, are fruitless in the same ways, for the same reasons.

As we move into this last phase of our inquiries, one thing especially needs to be emphasized. I spoke initially of reason "losing its balance" in the seventeenth century, and put this down to the obsession with formal Theory at the expense of everyday Practice that elevated Euclidean deduction above all other kinds of reasoning. But it was no part of my agenda to tip the scale entirely, or to elevate Practice, in turn, at the expense of Theory. What I intended to do was, indeed, to restore a proper balance between them: to recognize the legitimate claims of "theories" without exaggerating the formal attractions of Euclidean reasoning, and to defend the lessons of actual "practice" without denigrating the powers of theoretical argument.

Richard Rorty draws a useful distinction between talking of the role in philosophy of (an uppercase) "Theory" meant to embrace all knowledge in a comprehensive system, and the pragmatic utility of separate (lowercase) "theories" that are put to use in different activities for different purposes. For instance, in talking over how to present a civil case for damages, two trial attorneys may consider whether it is better to treat it as a straightforward tort issue, or whether to rely on (say) "agency theory"; and similar choices face us in other activities. Such alternative theories typically make no exclusive or overarching claims on our loyalties or understandings: they have no ideological status and make no pretension to universality. Nowadays, many social scientists use the terms "model" and "theory" as interchangeable, and switch between different models to account for one or another kind of social, political, or cultural phenomenon, without this having any grandiose implications on the level of high Theory. At this point, the Balance of Reason is fully restored, and we can set the old disputes about their relative superiority or subordination aside.

Such questions about the relation of theory to practice have been in dispute from 1650 on, and have been the central topic here. A disdain for practical skills, opinions based on experience, or the chances of a given occasion, was used to justify subordinating workaday practice to abstract theory, and this subordination shaped the agenda of European philosophy for three hundred years. Today we find ourselves in a very different situation. Instead of a humble subordinate Practice being answerable to a superordinate self-validating Theory, the two realms now have an equal relationship. Theory is not intrinsically superior to practice. Appeals to theory are themselves a kind of practice—one more *topos*, Aristotle might say. With the decline of Cartesian foundationalism, claims to self-validation do not carry their earlier weight: we need not choose between knowledge based on experience and knowledge based on claims to self-evidence. Instead, the question is, "What forms of life support, and rely on, one or another variety of substantive knowledge?"

In this respect, Dewey was right to suggest that Pragmatism is not just one theory on a par with all others. Rather, it represents a change of view, which puts *theorizing* on a par with all other practical activities. From now on, honestly productive craftsmen need not apologize for vulgarity, nor do we need to put logic above rhetoric, ethics above casuistry, metaphysics above sophistry, or the Prophets above the Pharisees. For the time being, that game is over; and when Plato declared that Gorgias and the Sophists prostituted their skills by setting up "knowledge shops" (*phrontisteria*), it was he who was guilty of a vulgar libel. Academic jealousies turn out to be as old as the Academy itself.

If we accept a pragmatic view of theorizing, however, it is not hard to escape from the imbalance in our ideas about Reason that we have inherited from Modernity, and restore to our other ways of thinking and acting the legitimacy that an egalitarian approach requires. On this approach, no single mode of theoretical reasoning has hegemony over all others, let alone holds the central position in intellectual and practical life that the Newtonian cosmology assumed at the hands of Laplace and Cournot. Instead, theories operate simply as "models" of the phenomena that they represent. These models are of many kinds. For intellectual purists, axiom-systems such as those Duhem insisted on are a real option. Or we can use graphs, maps, and other two-dimensional representations; physical models—real or imagined—like those Maxwell and Lodge wrote about; or computer graphics that display changes too complex to calculate with pen and paper. If a representation pulls the phenomena together in a way that makes intelligible sense, giving a systematic grasp of the field concerned, that is enough: the vivid image of airflow over a wing is both very memorable and entirely intelligible. No kind of explanatory representation can suit all kinds of phenomena, but one or another model has practical results that meet the needs of some particular natural or human science, and the empirical limits of the model are thus explicitly recognized. This accomplished, all kinds of thought or action that engage our Rationality or Reasonableness have their proper scope and limits, and the traditional Balance of Reason is reestablished.

The idea that Natural Philosophy guarantees the certainty of ideas about the Order of Nature rested on the belief that our empirical knowledge needed such a system—in either its Cartesian or its Newtonian form—as its *foundation:* a footing to ensure its stability. In the 1980s, the discovery that no intellectual system can do this provoked a reaction against foundationalism in general, and Cartesianism in particular, which marks the transition from Modernity to Post-Modernity. Yet, in retrospect, we might have seen this coming sooner. As early as 1902, Poincaré had shown (for example, in *Science and Hypothesis*) how little we gain from putting our knowledge on a quasi-geometrical foundation. It was not just that the discovery of non-Euclidean geometries undercut the "certainty" that Descartes credited to Euclidean geometry; any empirical understanding that can be framed in terms of one set of geometrical axioms (Poincaré saw) can with minor adjustments be put in terms of another. What security, then, did the Cartesian theory add to our everyday knowledge? Is it not just as effective to rely on the accumulated experience of our practical lives? Pragmatism is an honest foundation for knowledge, and avoids the specious claim that only abstract, self-validating Theory gives us genuine Certainty.

There is in any case reason to think that the appeal of foundationalism sprang from the elitism of the literate. For it assured people that we *truly* know only those things that we can express in *words*—and even that we know only what we can explain using a full-scale intellectual theory. Diderot would have demurred: his respect for craftspeople led him to reject such intellectual snobbery. Inarticulate knowledge must not be despised: we grasp theoretical ideas only if we have sufficient experience to give them meaning. To change the image, pre-verbal knowledge is the root from which intellectual claims get their sense; the words in which we make those claims are, rather, their top growth. The following two chapters will investigate explicitly this relationship between verbal and non-verbal knowledge.

II

The Varieties of Experience

Rationalist philosophers are impressed by subjects in which "knowledge" consists in a grasp of a formal theory. Pragmatists argue rather that, even in the physical sciences, knowledge may be tacit, or unspoken. Instead of all knowledge being based on a single kind of experience, we must acknowledge a spectrum from the verbally articulate to the unspoken.

O NE FINAL STEP completes the restoration of a balance in our ideas about the Rational and the Reasonable, and helps to counteract the deep-seated intellectualism of Modernity. If a philosophical foundation is to give our ways of dealing with the world any kind of certitude, pragmatism is as good a starting point as any of the philosophers' systems from Descartes on. I say this with a certain wry sincerity. In writing *Human Understanding*—one colleague complained—I did not mention my debt to the pragmatists; more seriously, he might have complained that I arrived at a position close to pragmatism, and even moved from Britain to the United States, before I had done more than glance at the works of the leading American pragmatists.

If pragmatism is admissible as a basis for understanding language, experience, and theoretical knowledge, of course, we need to take William James seriously: not just his classic lectures on *Pragmatism* or his pioneer work on *The Principles of Psychology*, but also his best-selling book, *The Varieties of Religious Experience*. (Those who fear being trapped in the world of formal doctrines and Church authority may read James's title as meaning "spiritual" or "deeply personal" experience.) James did not discuss out-of-body experiences, the higher consciousness, or other subjects fashionable today. As he told it, any or all experiences can be put to religious use, and he placed no weight on the need to mark off some experiences as exclusively religious; so we leave his book with a deepened concern for the spiritual aspects of all experience.

Why did he pay such attention to religious experience? This was, not least, out of loyalty to his father, Henry James Sr., who was a renowned Protestant preacher in Boston. Coming from a distinguished Beacon Hill family, William James spent most of his career in Boston, aside from the early, abortive attempt to become an artist that took him to Paris and ended in an emotional breakdown. This interest in the fine arts had a healthy effect on his philosophical work. He was never tempted to confine himself to the narrow circle of topics that are sufficient for most academic philosophers. All the same, in his views on language, experience, and theoretical knowledge, he inherited two related problems from Kant. First: given the personal nature of sensations, how can we avoid lapsing into solipsism? How, that is, can we justify transcending the boundaries of our own existence, and see the world as open to other human beings like ourselves? Second: if those sensory experiences are to serve as starting points for knowledge, how can we give a truly interpersonal account of the kinds of knowledge we share with our fellows?

Once again, the key word is "variety": James had an eclectic view of experience, and did not restrict himself to the standard five senses, of sight, hearing, touch, smell, and taste. In his *Principles of Psychology* as well as in *Pragmatism*, he was ready to rely on his own early memories. Wittgenstein liked to cite a report James gives of seeing something fall far below him into the water, and recalling his associated sense of loss. His family later filled out this event. He had a beloved cap that he once wore when leaning over the guard-rail of a ferry boat in a stiff breeze; when the cap fell from his head into the Boston Harbor, he was deeply upset. Nor did James's discussion of sensations rule out kinesthesis—inner bodily sensations—as a possible basis for knowledge. For a rationalist, such experiences cannot support substantive claims about actual situations in a shared world. From a pragmatist's point of view, however, there is no objection to regarding (for example) the visceral sensations a test pilot experiences when engaged in rapidly turning high-speed flight as "confirming" that he is pulling out of a dive, and giving him sensory "verification" of this fact.

The second question—how we can reconcile personal sensations of a directly experienced kind with any more objective (or, as Kant would say, intersubjective) claim to knowledge on the level of understanding, rather than mere feeling—was no easier for James than it was for Kant himself. Both philosophers did their best to talk in unprejudiced terms about things that are (so to speak) out of cognitive or intellectual reach. Where a Diogenes did no more than gesture, Kant felt he must at least dignify the object of this gesture with a neutral title: the *Ding-an-sich* (or "thing in itself") unqualified by human observation, let alone human naming. In doing so, however, he failed to place that which was "out of reach" *sensorily* also out of reach *conceptually*.

James did no better. Without repeating Kant's move, he recognized the problem, but continued to argue as though it did not exist. He left it quite unexplained whether the "stream of consciousness," which was for him the source of all knowledge, is our own exclusive possession, or is shared with others. This problem remained unsolvable until Wittgenstein dealt with it in his later years. In the *Tractatus*, he had insisted that "Whereof we cannot speak, thereof we must remain silent": we must, that is, avoid dignifying what is beyond conceptual grasp with so much as a name. In the *Philosophical Investigations*, all that can be certain is that all meaningful language can be shared by all language users. So Wittgenstein leads us by the hand, and hints at how we can follow a series of steps that take us ever closer to the nameless things we cannot refer to directly, without actually reaching them. He caricatures the older view of "inner" sense experience with his image of a beetle hidden in a private box, to which each individual alone has access.[1]

The contrast between a balanced approach to the functions of Reason and one in which that balance is upset can be illustrated by contrasting the pragmatism of James and Dewey with the intellectualism of the Platonists and Cartesians. In a balanced account, all the different kinds of knowledge that we have recognized in these inquiries are treated with equal respect; in an unbalanced account, there is a systematic preference for the kinds of knowledge that are articulated in language, and most of all in the language of formal theory. (By these standards, a contemporary like Alasdair MacIntyre is as much of an intellectualist as any Cartesian or Platonist.)

The intellectualist puts the different kinds of knowledge in an honor roll, with an understanding of pure mathematics, or *episteme*, at the head of the roll. The misguided priorities of social science, in trying to ape Newtonian astronomy, are a direct outcome of this choice. Close behind *episteme* comes *techne*: the kinds of instrumental knowledge that are typically presented as sets of printed rules having a theoretical *raison d'être*. (Recall the attempt to analyze the thousand or more things that could go wrong with a copying machine *in theory*, as contrasted with the oral culture, transmitted by word of mouth, that actual copier repairers develop for discussing their problems.)[2] Lower down the honor roll are the various kinds of practical knowledge that we master for reasons of survival and other human needs, such as the practical skills of *phronesis* embodied in the arts of clinical medicine or sailing. The farther we go down the roll, the smaller is the part played by formal reasoning or language, and the larger part takes the form of those non-formal practical activities that Michael Polanyi has called the "tacit dimension" of science.[3]

As a physical chemist with experience on both the practical and theoretical sides of scientific work, Polanyi was one of the first writers to say, unambiguously, that much of what natural scientists know or take for granted "goes without saying" because there is no occasion to mention it explicitly in published papers. Such papers (he saw) report only a small fraction of the information we need if we are to follow their arguments in full detail. The things that go without saying are familiar to both authors and readers. If questions are raised about them, the authors may at first hesitate to reply, and then begin, "Oh, I see what you mean . . .": though articulate about such matters, they are not fully at ease with them. This tacit dimension of knowledge (as we shall see) is not relevant only to scientific work: in early life, we all learn to deal with situations in ways that involve habituation rather than explanation. Whether this involves behaving politely in company or mastering the multiplication tables, these kinds of learning are effective, without our being able to explain why we have reason to trust them; and, if this is true of the things that other people teach us, it is true even more of the skills we acquire in dealing with the world by ourselves, so that we do not even need to be taught them.

In this way, Polanyi cleared the ground for our own central point about Logic and Reason. Scientific knowledge is richer and more complex than most non-scientists would assume, given what schools and the media tell them. Too often, scientific reports for the lay public do no more than assure us that some bare unsituated formula like "$E = mc^2$" is the Key to understanding the Universe. Such a report is worse than useless: it hides from us the task that Einstein used the equation to perform, and the particular situation in which he introduced it. Instead, we are faced with a naked contrast, between formulas or words set apart from their normal background, while we lack a lifelike picture of the practical work involved when scientists look to a new intellectual procedure to tackle a problem.

So interpreted, Polanyi's picture of scientific knowledge is a parable for knowledge in general. I have distinguished here the conceptual grasp of a theory; the techniques we master as ways of dealing with practical problems; and the private perceptiveness needed to put such techniques to use in a variety of situations. Aristotle liked to insist that all these different kinds of knowledge—*episteme, techne,* and *phronesis*—were orchestrated by the broader wisdom he called *sophia.* Yet they all take for granted a certain articulateness, and thus ignore the special skills of those who master their crafts to good effect, without saying much about them. (From J. M. W. Turner to Alexander Calder, the history of art is full of examples of people whose creativity lay in their hands, not their tongues.) Knowledge of crafts has always been, and still is, grounded in manual experience rather than a theoretical foundation: the experience from which it grows is a product of acting, not of using language. So, as a final exercise, let us turn to one last species on the list of Varieties of Knowledge: what the Greeks called *metis*—that is, knack, wit, or cunning.

There is a kind of perfection that belongs not to the idealized realm of exact science but to the realm of skilled and experienced practice. A story in the Taoist text *Chuang-tzu* (also spelled *Zhuangzi*) tells us about the cook Ding, who by reflective practice refined his skills as a butcher to a point that was beyond improvement. (Zhuangzi lived around 320 B.C., and was skeptical about traditional Confucian precepts, which he regarded as too rigid.)[4]

This anecdote appears in the last chapter of the reported teachings of Zhuangzi. The cook Ding is carving an ox for his Lord:

> As his hand slapped, shoulder lunged, foot stamped, knee
> crooked, with a hiss! With a thud! The brandished blade as it

sliced never missed the rhythm, now in time with the Mulberry Forest dance, now with an orchestra playing the Ching-Shou.

His Lord congratulates him warmly, exclaiming, "That skill should achieve such heights!", but Ding insists that mere skill is not the point:

> What your servant cares about is the Way: I have left skill behind me. When I first began to carve oxen, I saw nothing but oxen wherever I looked. Three years more and I never saw an ox as a whole . . . I rely on Heaven's structures, cleave along the main seams, let myself be guided by the main cavities, go by what is intrinsically so . . .
>
> A good cook changes his chopper once a year, because he is a hacker. A common cook changes it once a month, because he is a smasher. I have had this chopper for nineteen years and have taken apart several thousand oxen, but the edge is as though it were fresh from the grindstone. At this joint there is a natural division, but the chopper's edge has no thickness: if you insert what has no thickness into a place where there is a division, then, what more could you ask: there is, of course, ample room to move the edge about. That is why, after nineteen years, the edge of my chopper is still as though it were fresh from the grindstone.[5]

Zhuangzi distinguishes "small" from "great" knowledge. A run-of-the-mill cook "would, no doubt, measure the width of the cleaver against the width of the space into which it must be inserted." Cook Ding, for his part, "visualizes the edge of his cleaver as being without thickness, and inserts it into what he visualizes as a space, in looking at the parts of the ox as two discrete objects he intends to separate." Ding's great knowledge "is not perception that measures and categorizes. It tries to use what cannot be measured in an entirely practical way."

Reading this passage, I recall a class in which Wittgenstein talked about the skills of field geology. When we watch experienced geologists on a hillside using geological hammers to cleave rocks and see what they consist of, it seems so effortless and intuitive: they turn rocks over in one hand, then choose where to tap them, and they fall neatly into halves with their internal structures clearly presented. This is not a skill that relies on formal inferences from a scientific theory, nor does it even use a specific disciplinary technique. Would it be highfaluting to call it the Way? There may be no other convenient name for it.

The difference between *metis* and *phronesis* is subtle but important. The passage in which Aristotle introduces *phronesis* refers specifically to medicine and helmsmanship, but nothing he says there suggests that this kind of practical knowledge is wordless. A doctor or a helmsman can typically name the signs or symptoms that require a change of course, though sometimes experience will sharpen these skills beyond what anyone can articulate. In his book *Sources of Power*, Gary Klein reports a fire chief's account of a near-disaster in which a hunch led him to order his men off the fire scene just a moment before the floor on which they were standing collapsed into a basement that he did not even know existed. In retrospect, he saw what inarticulate knowledge must have sharpened this hunch, though at the time he could not name the factors that went into sharpening it: all skilled craftsmen have a knack for such wordless knowledge that goes beyond anything that they can point to.[6]

Isaiah Berlin referred to this special knack in his lecture on Political Judgment, as broadcast in 1957:

> We resort to metaphors. We speak of some people as possessing antennae, as it were, that communicate to them the specific contours and texture of a particular political or social situation. We speak of the possession of a good political eye, or nose, or ear, of a political sense which love or ambition or hate may bring into play, of a sense that crisis and danger sharpen (or alternatively blunt), to which experience is crucial, a particular gift, possibly not altogether unlike that of artists or creative writers.

Of course, he goes on to say,

> We mean nothing occult or metaphysical; we do not mean a magic eye able to penetrate into something that ordinary

minds cannot apprehend; we mean something perfectly ordinary, empirical, and quasi-aesthetic in the way it works.[7]

It is the same with doctors and sailors: some cases do not "smell right," so that a doctor will act conservatively, his "hunch" being that what looks like (say) influenza may in this case turn out to be meningitis. Some patches of water likewise "look tricky" and are best avoided by a prudent helmsman. Indeed, while craftsmen may be able to learn from their experience, and can even hand on to their apprentices a sensitivity to possible risks, it is doubtful if this kind of unspoken knack can be clearly explained or directly taught.

This brings us to the word "knack," which is one of the standard translations of the Greek *metis*, along with "wit" and "cunning," and it is worth noting that none of these terms need be derogatory. Yet the contrast between *metis* and *phronesis* quickly leads us further. Neither Plato nor Aristotle uses *metis* except in reference to that tricky character, Odysseus, who is described as *polumetis*, or multi-skilled. Being publicly visible, the Sophists could not be ignored and had to be libeled, but the wide distrust of intellectuals for manual crafts, and the *anthropos polumetis* who possesses them, made craftsmen easier to ignore. This scorn for cunning among the academics of Antiquity has been hard to outgrow. Some of it survives to the present in the classic work on the idea of *metis*, Detienne and Vernant's *Cunning Intelligence in Greek Culture and Society*.[8] They quote a famous story from Book XIII of Homer's *Iliad* in which Nestor prepares his son Antilochus for a chariot race:

> It is through *metis* rather than through strength that the
> wood-cutter shows his work. It is through *metis* that the helms-
> man guides the speeding vessel over the wine dark sea against
> the wind. It is through *metis* that the charioteer triumphs over
> his rival.

Neither the skills of the wood-cutter nor those of the helmsman are shady, only those of an unscrupulous charioteer. Antilochus is crafty, and capable of unfair maneuvers; knowing this, Nestor says to him, as Father to Son, "The man who knows the tricks wins the day, even with mediocre horses." That seems all right to Nestor, and to Detienne and Vernant. For the rest of the discussion they forget about the honesty of the wood-cutter and the self-confidence of the helmsman, and claim that the essential features of *metis* are

> pliability and polymorphism, duplicity and equivocality,
> inversion and reversal . . . qualities which are also attributed to
> the curve, to what is pliable and twisted, to what is oblique
> and ambiguous as opposed to what is straight, rigid and un-
> equivocal.

In the development of the English language, a similar slant has been put on the word *knack*, and the associated words *craft*, *guile*, and *dodge*.[9] From 1225 to 1842, the primary sense of *knack* was that of "a mean or under-handed trick"; only recently has the word been used to refer to "adroit or ingenious methods of doing something, clever expedients." Given the slow spread of literacy, the earlier citations in the *Oxford English Dictionary* are, of course, largely upper-class usages, and this unbalances our view of the matter. So, for the rest of this argument, we may set aside the dictio-naries, and focus instead on neutral moral or social experiences of kinds we are familiar with in our everyday, pre-theoretical life.

Michael Polanyi's picture of the tacit aspects of scientific knowledge thus helps to dissolve away the intellectualist accounts of the Philosophy of Science that were in fashion in the earlier part of the twentieth century. In a way that harmonizes with Wittgenstein's later positions, he shows how scientific terms and statements acquire their meaning from associa-tion with particular constellations of human situations and actions. Of course, there need be nothing in this relationship that will come as a sur-prise to anybody but an academic philosopher: even in baseball, things people utter in the course of a game—"Strike!", "fly ball," and so on—are intelligible only to people who know what part those terms play in the course of that sport.

We can take it, then, that all scientific knowledge is a balance of the theoretical with the practical, the verbal with the non-verbal. Textbooks and papers are made up of words, but there are other aspects of scientific work in which the non-verbal component plays the chief part in showing how Nature works. The facts that computer graphics nowadays have the power to convey are near-impossible to represent in words and formulas alone: for example, the way that air flows over and under an aircraft wing—in particular, the color differences that highlight vortices in the airflow, and the pockets of vacuum that create "lift." These representations may be scientific rather than artistic, but they undercut any excessively verbal or intellectual view of science.

The question we must face is, "Can we, as philosophers, develop a *fully verbal* account of knowledge?" It is harder and harder to answer that question in purely positive terms: everything that has come to light in these inquiries points the opposite way, to a pragmatist analysis of a kind that goes beyond anything that James adopted. For now, the cutting edge is the claim that much of our knowledge is *pre*-theoretical or *non*-theoretical. Some people argue that different cultures think of the world differently because the languages they use to report what they find are not fully intertranslatable: therefore, everything we say is theoretically slanted, and there can be no non-theoretical knowledge. Yet this argument has some implausible consequences. Suppose that two people of different backgrounds meet in a desert, and find a man lying on the ground with a bad wound in his leg. Even if they share no common language, they can both see that the bleeding is so severe that the injured man risks dying. Far from requiring sophisticated medical knowledge to give sense to this conclusion, the most unsophisticated kinds of peoples will interpret such situations without difficulty. So, with the best will in the world, it is hard to make sense of an argument that the process by which our two men have arrived at their shared view was handicapped by the "incommensurability" of their ideas.

Recall Remarque's famous novel about life in the trenches during the First World War, *All Quiet on the Western Front,* in which a Christmas truce allows the combatants to talk to one another in No-Man's-Land, after which they are less willing to go back and start shooting at each other again. Most of them, on both sides, would rather be allowed to go on dealing with one another in the way that the armies' medical personnel were permitted to do: members of the U.S. Army Medical Corps, for example, are allowed to treat the wounded of both sides in battle, though a private soldier doing the same would risk being punished for fraternizing with the enemy.

This is not to deny that much medical language is theory-laden—only to insist that much of it is not, and that a good deal of medical knowledge is non-verbal. Nor is it to deny that, in many cases, the line separating the intuitively obvious from the sophisticated grows fainter every year; it is only to deny that very much follows from that fact. It is one thing to see—or even to say—that the wound in the injured man's leg is bleeding profusely, quite another thing to suggest that he has (say) a hematoma. Even further, it is one thing to say of someone: "He died in a car crash," and quite another to say: "His brain scan went flat, but the life support machine maintained his heartbeat until it was switched off by Court Order." The increasing technicality of medical practice presents us with more and more ambiguous examples, in which people of different backgrounds may find it hard to agree on a common description; but nothing in them discredits all our non-theory-laden insights.

Let us recall once again William Gass's essay, *The Obliging Stranger*. Although there are some cases about which nothing clear can be said (he argues), this does not mean that there are no clear cases at all. The fact that someone's leg is bleeding profusely, or that she died in a car crash, is something we can often just *see:* a medical examiner or a coroner may need a fuller technical statement of the case, but this will merely explain and amplify—not nullify—the original perception. At this point, then, a clarification is needed. The powers of recognition we show in transparently clear cases are easily misunderstood. In the 1920s and 1930s, for instance, Fascists and Nazis in Italy and Germany pointed to the fact that we often "see" things we have no need to "explain" in order to justify their anti-rational or downright irrational ideologies. Healthy young Aryans, the Nazis argued, could recognize the evil in a Jewish face at a glance, with the same confidence that Aristotle found in our ability to recognize a figure as a triangle, or an action as cruel.[10]

One victim of this Fascist and Nazi misrepresentation was Friedrich Nietzsche. His attacks on Christian Ethics were read as endorsing the Nazis' own ruthlessness, and his praise for an Ethics of the Will was hailed as making him a good Aryan. This distortion is especially evident in Leni Riefenstahl's 1934 propaganda movie, *Triumph of the Will:* the Hitler-jugend is presented as uncompromising in his commitment to freeing Germany from the influence of decadent Jewish Thought and Art. This adoption of Nietzsche as a Nazi culture hero was a special piece of historical irony. Nietzsche had been conscious, rather, of an affinity between his ideas and those of Ralph Waldo Emerson: he had, in fact, meant his Super-man to be the counterpart of Emerson's Oversoul. Søren Kierkegaard as well rejected the theoretical grandiosity of Hegel's philosophical system and rebelled against the Puritan intolerance of institutional "Christen-dom" in favor of a gentler kind of Christianity. Nietzsche shared his con-clusions, both about Hegel's shortcomings and about Christian Ethics as it was taught in the Lutheran Church, to which Hegel had declared lifelong loyalty. Any such moral "code" was for Nietzsche "an Ethics for servants," who were ready to be ordered about according to a set book of rules.[11]

Nietzsche, however, meant to contrast Church Ethics not with ruthless violence, but with a refusal of any unthinking submission to guidance by others: what Kant called the "heteronomy of the Will." Emerson, of course, had no access to Kierkegaard's work, which was widely available to European and American scholars only after being translated from Danish into German around 1905; yet he understood the significance for Kant of the value of any independent individual having a Good Will. That is the core element in Kant's own moral theory, and remained so for Nietzsche, though transformed into something less universal and more active. It was Nietzsche's *Genealogy of Morals* that first emphasized the need to consider moral concepts as the products of historical evolution, and so to some de-gree as cultural variables; but all three writers—Kierkegaard, Emerson, and Nietzsche—clearly accept the primacy of *epieikeia* (fairness) over *nomos* (law) and *phronesis* (practical prudence) over *episteme* (intellectual grasp) as differentiating moral good sense from any rationalistic commitment to a formal theory of Ethics.[12]

In conclusion, some points of terminology—even of lin-guistic difference—call for our attention. What holds good for Peirce, Polanyi, and Feyerabend in the philosophy of science does not necessarily hold true for epistemology in general. These men all started with an inter-est in questions about the physical sciences, and we must not jump too quickly to general doctrines from points they made along the way. The things people say about the inconsistency between ideas of knowledge or ethics as between any two cultures may seem attractive if we muddle them with the points Paul Feyerabend made about *incommensurable* observa-tions. Any such equation is a mistake. Feyerabend's points were, precisely, about scientific experimentation, and thus cannot be extended without disastrous results to experience in general. In deciding when there is reason to modify theoretical concepts in physics, for example, we interpret our experimental observations in terms that already link them to the given theory. Different theories impose different demands, and the "fit" between any given theory and the experiments used to establish it are specific and ad hoc. Clearly this is not true of all kinds of "experience": it was intended to be, and is, relevant only to one particular variety of experimental observations in physical science, and it only rarely has any direct application to our familiar experience of other human beings.

Curiously enough, this distinction is more easily made in English than it can be in French. Notice the key contrast between the nouns *experiment* and *experience*. English has two distinct words for these things, but French has only one: *expérience*. Where we speak in English of performing a scientific experiment, the corresponding phrase in French is *une expérience scientifique*. French scientists use the adjective *expérimental*, the verb *expérimenter*, and even the general noun *expérimentation*: the meanings of these words in French are just what the corresponding English words imply. But the only word in French for a particular experiment, performed in a particular place and at a particular time, remains *expérience*; the term *expériment* has not yet taken root either in French science or in scientific journalism.

Go back far enough, and we can find the same difference in English. In the late fourteenth century, John Wyclif published one of the first English translations of the Bible, and hesitated over which word to use. In translating Genesis, chapter 42, verse 15, his first edition (1382) read: "Now I shall take experiment of you"; but, in the second edition six years later, he replaced the word "experiment" by "experience." The *Oxford English Dictionary* gives the same definition—the action of trying anything or putting it to the proof—for both words; but, for the word *experience*, the dictionary marks this meaning as "obsolete." The second definition of *experience*—"an operation performed in order to ascertain or illustrate some truth; an experiment"—is also labeled as obsolete. (The last clear example is from 1649: "They will tell you a story of I know not what experiences they have made, when alas they never know that an Experiment must hold in all its parts." Comparable uses of the word continue to 1763.) On the other hand, a different sense of *experiment*—actual observation of facts or events considered as a source of knowledge—is listed as in current usage, with examples dated throughout, from Langland (1377) to the present.[13]

As for the standard meanings of the word *experience*, these the O.E.D. presents as follows:

> "the fact of being consciously the subject of a state or condi-
> tion or of being consciously affected by an event,"
>
> "the events that have taken place within the knowledge of
> an individual or a community, mankind at large, either during
> a particular period or generally,"
>
> "knowledge resulting from actual observation or from what
> one has undergone,"
>
> and "the state of having been occupied in any department of
> study or practice, in affairs generally, or in the intercourse of
> life; the extent to which, or the length of time during which,
> one has been so occupied; the aptitudes, skill, judgement, etc.
> thereby acquired."

We recognize in these definitions such maxims as "Experience is the best school, but the fees are very high"; or an airline pilot's reference to his career as having included "fifteen years' experience in multi-engine commercial jets." Writing a book on *Glaciers of the Alps*, the Victorian scientist Tyndall modestly remarked, "I have had but little experience of Alpine phenomena."

The sense in which Wyclif used the word "experiment" in his 1382 text is, therefore, not obsolete, but current; and the related sense of "a method, system of things, or course of action, adopted in uncertainty whether it will answer the purpose" has been current since 1594. But the central meaning—an action or operation undertaken in order to discover something unknown, to test a hypothesis, or establish some known truth—dates at least from 1362, and displaces the noun *experience* after the publication of Isaac Newton's *Principia* in 1687 and John Locke's *Essay Concerning Human Understanding* in 1690. Locke is already writing of "a man accustomed to rational and regular Experiments," and the use of "experience" in this sense is increasingly rare from 1700 on.

None of this lexicographical detail implies that there is anything wrong with the French language; it is worth looking at here only because, for once, English displays an unusual subtlety. The operations we refer to in

English as "experiments"—undertaken in order to discover something unknown, to test a hypothesis, or to establish some known truth—are (as Feyerabend was right to see) experiences of a very specific kind, and untypical of experiences in general. His arguments about the incommensurability of observations made in the course of scientific experiments do not imply any claim about the cultural relativity of all sensory experience. If we have inarticulate, pretheoretical, or untheoretical experience, so be it. This only adds to the Variety of Experience, from *episteme* at the intellectual pole to *metis* at the pragmatic, non-verbal extreme.

12

The World of Where and When

Everyday experience reinforces the recognition that the seven-teenth century stood the human situation on its head. Like Virginia Woolf's novels, the essays of Montaigne convey the texture of the world we live in better than any theory. Thus, pragmatism and skepticism are the beginning of a wisdom that is better than the dreams of the rationalists.

I CAME TO SEE HOW RICH and varied are the terrains in which pretheoretical knowledge is grounded only when my wife and I spent seven weeks living in a converted barn near an upland village above the Dordogne, in the old French region of Quercy. In my generation, we learned to appreciate Central France from Freda White's book, *Three Rivers of France*. On earlier visits I had seen the painted caves at Lascaux before they were closed to tourists, and had been enchanted by the wildflowers of spring and early summer. But, since those days, I had got to know Montaigne's *Essais*, and was eager to visit the Tower in which he wrote them, not too far from where we planned to stay.[1]

As we reached Quercy, the sense of familiarity intensified. Its valleys are broader and more generous than those of the English countryside I grew up in, and further east we would have run into the volcanic country that played a part in the history of geology. Many of the May flowers that we saw were familiar from gardens in England: a little ahead of the English seasons, there were love-in-a-mist, peonies and lilacs, wild gladioli and the first day-lilies, yellow potentilla and pot herbs. In cracks in the stone walls, vetch, wild geraniums, and bedstraw were growing. At the barn itself, the yellow stones contained crevices from which lizards would dart out. Indoors, the cast-iron fireplace stove reminded us of New England: its name plate bore the name Franklin, and it had been made in a factory we already knew in Vermont. The agriculture was less familiar. In place of England's wheat and oats, there were walnuts and asparagus, tobacco and maize— "corn" to Americans. The fields and orchards were populated by geese and ducks, and the local cuisine included plenty of *foie gras*, washed down with a coarse red wine from Cahors.

By the end of our stay, the seasons had advanced. The sheep that had earlier wandered every morning up the field across the lane, and back as the afternoon wore on, were carted off to higher summer pastures, under the system that Fernand Braudel calls *transhumance*. Meanwhile, the colors of the wildflowers took on the purple or yellow of late summer, and the ditches were full of the local variant of Joe Pye Weed. The hillsides were purple with Fireweed or yellow with St. John's Wort and Evening Primrose, and the highway verges wore the gold of Mount Etna Broom, whose ability to flourish on the barren screes of a volcano was celebrated by Leopardi in his poem, *Il Fiore nel Deserto*.

In the garden hollyhocks replaced peonies, butterflies swarmed over buddleias, and at last the goldfinches arrived to harvest the first seeds. Finally, the harvest got under way. By the last weeks of June, hay was cut and stacked, and the corn shot up at an accelerating pace. We knew the Vermont motto, "Knee high by the fourth of July," but in Quercy the fourth of July saw the corn shoulder high and the tobacco ripened; we went in search of the last bottles of the previous year's walnut oil. Being at the same latitude as Vermont, around 44° north, Quercy enjoys the benefits of the Gulf Stream, and its farmers are ahead of the game.

Is this kind of "nature writing" offensive to people of a truly philosophical bent? If so, they need to think again about the foundations of our knowledge. Many basic skills of traditional life—such as the use of different plant species to produce indigo as a dyestuff for the blue of handwoven carpets, just as it is still used for jeans today—developed in parallel in different parts of the world without any particular scientific foundation.[2] These thoughts struck me as we drove down to Bergerac, and on to Montaigne's home village. Not that these kinds of knowledge are confined to Nature: each morning I listened to BBC World Service News, with a signature tune long familiar from evenings in California.[3] Cycles of experience imprint our minds: radio schedules, botanical and agricultural seasons, or the commanding regularities of the astronomical year. Though less physiological than the circadian rhythms of waking and sleeping, these cycles build themselves into our awareness of the World.

Is this kind of knowledge relevant only to ways of life more primitive than ours? On the contrary, it is increasingly to the point for people who aim at self-sustaining modes of existence such as are possible, for instance, in Northern California, with its local quick-flowing rivers to generate electricity, an agriculture suited to the temperate climate, and pastureland suitable for wool-bearing sheep. None of this, certainly, would strike Montaigne as anything but a matter of course. Until the 1590s, he remained as skeptical about the possibility of a comprehensive theory of nature as he was about the philosophical teachings of Antiquity. His *Essais* go out of their way to avoid all formal theories, and try only to show what it is to live a truly human life. He barely names the stars and planets, which were a staple of earlier philosophy and cosmology; the *dramatis personae* of his essays come from the repertory of literature or history. Alexander the Great or Julius Caesar, Virgil or Seneca, mean more to him than Orion or Betelgeuse, Mercury or Jupiter.

What kind of a man was Montaigne, as he gazed across this landscape? Historical dramas from Hollywood have accustomed us to hefty, energetic heroes, so it is hard to accept a Lord of the Manor who is barely five feet high, and lives in a house proportioned to people of his stature. But the evidence is there: the building, the narrow doors, the low ceilings and winding stairways tell their own story. If I think of our everyday experience as belonging to the World of Where and When, a world in which everything we say refers to a particular time and place, without claiming any abstract, universal validity, Montaigne lived in the World of There and Then. Better nutrition and genetic evolution now mean that we share the land with people several inches taller and far sturdier than our predecessors, but in other ways Montaigne's *Essais* show us how little has changed in the ways we lead our lives. Indolence, vanity, moderation, constancy, and not least cowardice—the mother of cruelty—are no different now from what they always were. Professional academics may dismiss Montaigne as a philosopher, because he ignores the technical issues they profess to find important. For the rest of us, he remains the preeminent philosopher of everyday experience, the writer who succeeded in focusing on things that really matter.

In reinstating Montaigne as a philosopher, these chapters seek to restore the balance between the theoretical and the practical in European thought that has been upset since the seventeenth century. Hegel's *Phenomenology* concedes that "sensory experience" as the British empiricists thought of it—already a theoretically tainted notion—has a certain priority, but he insists none the less on the intellectual centrality of the theoretical. So today, when we are overwhelmed by an addiction to theory, the task of recovering our awareness of inarticulate practical experience takes a cool head and a steady vision. Here, we may look at two twentieth-century writers who are in other ways very different: Ludwig Wittgenstein and Virginia Woolf.

The skeptical role of Michel de Montaigne in sixteenth-century Europe was played in the century just ended by Ludwig Wittgenstein, with one curious variation. Those of us who attended his classes in his last years at Cambridge felt privileged, and regarded that experience as being more unique than it really was. To sit in his sparsely furnished room at Trinity College, Cambridge, was to watch a deeply reflective man judging his own ideas by standards more stringent than any that we knew existed, and no serious-minded student could shirk the task of deciphering the demands that Wittgenstein imposed on himself. It was no less impressive to see him "at leisure"—the phrase sounds almost frivolous—on, for instance, his weekly visits to the house in Chesterton Road where G. E. Moore, who had preceded him as Professor of Philosophy, lived with his formidable wife, Dorothy. Then, the richness of Wittgenstein's cultural background and the intensity of his musical interests illuminated conversations that cried out to be recorded almost as much as his classes.

The most striking thing about the Wittgenstein we knew then was the depth of his personal commitment to ideas. His deepest intellectual contemporaries at Cambridge in the years before 1914 struck him—John Maynard Keynes tells us—as shallow and brittle. This was still the case in the 1940s: he was too aware of what is at stake in the World of Ideas ever to toy with concepts, as Bertrand Russell was liable to do. Having grown up in Habsburg Vienna, where the blood of intellectuals was often spilled—not least that of his colleague Moritz Schlick—Wittgenstein found the

Bloomsbury Circle's playfulness morally unacceptable. With the abolition of the Monarchy and the fragmentation of the Habsburg Empire after 1918, he felt more and more out of place in the world. Everything seemed to him to have lost touch with the culture of Mozart and Schumann that he had learned to love in childhood, in the Alleegasse.[4]

Faced with Wittgenstein's blend of moral seriousness and intellectual concentration, those of us in his last audiences could not tell to what extent his classes were the unique product of an unusual personality, or to what extent they were the mark of his radical or even unparalleled originality as a philosopher. We were not to be blamed for this failure. We did not come from Linz or Innsbruck, Aspen or Grinzing: we came from Hampstead or Kansas, from India, Australia, or Palestine. Without understanding the cultural and intellectual debt that "young Ludwig" owed to Central Europe generally—notably to the German-language *Kulturkleis*, and above all to Vienna itself—we could not separate the personal novelty of Wittgenstein's thought from the un-English features of his cultural inheritance.

By now, however, half a century after his death, with much of his *Nachlass* more or less adequately published, and all the material in the first authoritative biographies, we can better distinguish the personal aspects of his work from their cultural roots, and begin to assess his place in the history of thought. As a result, we see him in a broader historical context. Why, in his lifetime, did his teachings appear to have no clear parallel in earlier philosophy, and confronted his hearers and readers with the special challenge that comes with radical novelty? What are we to make of Wittgenstein's claim to show that all previous philosophy was inherently fallacious, or even dead, so that his methods of philosophizing were "the legitimate heir of the activity that was formerly known as 'philosophy'"? Like the theological claim that God is dead, the apocalyptic claim that Philosophy too is Dead provokes historical irony. Wittgenstein died in 1952; by the 1970s, more teachers of philosophy existed than at any earlier time in history. So, to paraphrase Mark Twain, claims about the Death of Philosophy were at the very least exaggerated; yet it had been quite some time since Wittgenstein's forerunners had made the same claim, and we can learn something about the future of philosophy, as well as its past, if we build those forerunners into the ancestry of his ideas.

Let me define two landmarks from which (as I see it) any historical analysis can triangulate. The school of philosophy to which Wittgenstein's later approach can best be compared is that of the Pyrrhonists or "classical skeptics." Others have remarked on this parallel. Brian McGuinness mentions it in the first volume of his biography of Wittgenstein, and the same point has struck other writers too: Phillip Hallie in *The Scar of Montaigne*, Arne Naess in his essays on Pyrrhonism, and Avner Cohen in his discussion of earlier authors (ancient and modern) who had announced Philosophy's Death.

I must clarify this use of the term *skepticism*. Many twentieth-century writers use this name for the views associated with Descartes's use of the Method of Systematic Doubt or the destructive arguments in David Hume's *Treatise of Human Nature*. Classical Greek philosophers, however, would not call the arguments of this Modern Skepticism—in Hume or Descartes—"skeptical" at all. They would see them as a variety of "negative dogmatism": a readiness to deny all those things that other philosophers assert. For the Greeks, true skeptics resisted with equal force the urge to assert philosophical generalizations, and the urge to deny them. The core of Pyrrhonism, as taught by Sextus Empiricus, was to recognize when claims to knowledge and certainty were too comprehensive and grandiose to fall within the scope of our experience, and avoid *either* asserting *or* denying them.

When Wittgenstein called the urge to debate philosophical questions, or to insist on philosophical doctrines, a "temptation"—one that may be natural, but needs to be held at arm's length—his citations predominantly came from the last 350 years—roughly speaking, from the Modern era that begins with Descartes. There are exceptions: his *Philosophical Investigations* open with a quotation from Augustine, and he later comments on passages from Plato's *Theaeteus*. Still, for the most part, we can gloss his argument effectively with examples that do not date from before 1630.

In this, Wittgenstein's critique of philosophy is like those of other twentieth-century writers. Dewey's Gifford Lectures, entitled *The Quest for Certainty*, written in 1929 in the aftermath of Heisenberg's first papers on quantum mechanics, attack seventeenth-century philosophy for taking too passive a view of perception, and rigidly separating the Observer from the Observed. He calls on twentieth-century philosophers to reject the seventeenth-century model of the Mind as an Inner Theatre, and to re-state their concerns in pragmatic terms. Richard Rorty's book *Philosophy and the Mirror of Nature* also disowns the program for philosophical theory dominant since Descartes, as relying uncritically on a conception of the Inner Mind framing a representation of the Outer World that we have, by now, good reason to reject.

Yet (we may ask) why do so few of these writers cast their nets back before 1600, or inquire to what extent earlier philosophers had been tempted to overrun the limits of language—*an die Grenze der Sprache anzurennen*, in Wittgenstein's phrase?[5] Before the 1630s, the European scene had been marked by a speculative vigor and a tolerance of varied opinions that van-ished during the Thirty Years' War, and by 1650 the demand for doctrinal certainty was firmly entrenched. From then on, as we have seen, the domi-nant trends in philosophy focused on issues of theory, while the matters of practical philosophy that were discussed from Aristotle on, in Antiquity and the Middle Ages, lost their philosophical standing. Before 1620, Montaigne's essays, particularly his *Apologie de Raimond Sebond*, had re-mained best-sellers; they presented the skepticism of Sextus Empiricus, who expounded the two key insights of the Classical Skeptics: that we can know nothing about the world of experience with complete certainty, and that any attempt to prove the superiority of one abstract, universal doc-trine over its rivals is a product of human presumptuousness.

Descartes, of course, tried to defeat Montaigne's skeptical gambit by of-fering the *cogito* as his "indubitable truth" to serve as the foundation of all intellectual knowledge. Critics of Foundationalism today agree that this attempt to give knowledge a logically secure basis failed, like all later at-tempts; and, despite all that has happened on the intellectual scene since 1640, Montaigne's gambit still stands out, as reinforcing Wittgenstein's feeling for the hidden seductions of Foundationalism. Not that Witt-genstein and Montaigne were alike in all ways. Personally, at least, they were very different men. Montaigne enjoyed the life of a recluse in his Tower near the Dordogne, but had earlier been an effective magistrate and diplomat; he was at ease in the world of public affairs, and we cannot imag-ine him, like Wittgenstein, agonizing about "logic and my sins."[6] Wittgenstein's moral perfectionism was more like the painful self-criticism of the tormented mathematician, Blaise Pascal, than like the urbane toler-ance of such humanists as Erasmus: he saw clearly that the seven-

teenth-century quest for certainty and intellectual foundations was fallacious, but for personal reasons he was drawn to the moral rigorism of
Pascal, Kierkegaard, and the Jansenists.

Even after we have buried the corpse of Foundationalism,
then, the less grandiose enterprises that belonged in the practical tradition
of rhetoric and case ethics, history and jurisprudence, have present-day
successors that keep us busy enough. These enterprises are all in one way or
another practical, pragmatic, or pragmatist. This is not to equate them
with what Karl Otto Apel and Jürgen Habermas have called "universal
pragmatics": despite a proper concern with *praxis*, their Frankfurt program
is as prone to excessive generalization as its theoretical predecessors. What
marks off "practical philosophy," rather, is its avoidance of premature generalizations. In practice, we never know in advance how far the results of
reflective analysis can be carried, but must decide this in the critical light
of practical experience. That makes our practical enterprises so *very* modest and experiential that Wittgenstein himself might not have chosen to
call them "philosophy." But a reasonable and modest Classical Skeptic will
not fuss about this; as I recall Wittgenstein half a dozen times saying about
such boundary-drawing issues, "Have it your own way!" What matters is to
see how much pre-Cartesian practical philosophy resurfaced in the last
thirty years, and took a place near the heart of the philosophical debate.
That accomplished, we can leave purely theoretical philosophy, whose
death sentence Wittgenstein and others have pronounced, to wither on
the vine.

To see how Practice provides an occasion for philosophical clarification,
consider the following problem. Many American physicians still think of
their task as therapeutic: their business is to treat injuries and cure ill-
nesses. They deeply believe that, if a patient dies, they have failed, so once
death becomes inevitable they are tempted to withdraw, thinking there is
nothing more they can do. Their patients, not surprisingly, *feel* abandoned, as they *have been* abandoned. As onlookers we can challenge the
model of treatment on which the physicians rely: are there not other models? If a dying patient suffers in ways that a doctor might have prevented or
mitigated, then and only then (we may reply) has the physician failed. Palliation—easing avoidable suffering—is as much a part of medical treatment as providing antibiotics, or other curative therapies. Yet, from work-

ing in hospitals on the moral problems of clinical medicine, I know how hard apprentice physicians trained in Scientific Medicine find it to stop subjecting dying patients to pointlessly heroic therapy, and move to gentler, palliative modes of treatment. They still tend to see the first patient they "lose" as a total failure; it takes more mature physicians to see that the manner of a patient's dying is no less a mark of success or failure than the fact of his or her death.

What makes this issue philosophical? The difference between curative therapy and palliation is not a scientific discovery, but a contrast between two parts of medical practice—a contrast as radical as that between two ways of seeing an ambiguous figure. The young physician, Wittgenstein would say, confuses the "grammar" of the term *treatment:* he mistakes a part for the whole, and sees curative therapy as comprising the whole range of medical procedures. The purpose of correcting this confusion is then less intellectual than moral: errors of perception in clinical medicine are professional failures, and can impose a price in terms of the patient's suffering. In this respect, practical philosophy has the full seriousness—not to say earnestness—with which Wittgenstein encouraged his students to avoid following philosophy as a profession, but to take up a more humanly useful line of work, such as Medicine.

Similar issues arise in psychology and psychiatry. Confusions about mental life, and about the language we use when speaking in "mental" terms, are not the monopoly of professional philosophers. People who manage psychiatric hospitals, work in hospices for the dying, or deal with the laws governing the use of organs in transplants, must think also about human experience and personality if they are to treat patients with justice and love for as long as they are alive, and apply humane standards to decide when their lives have come to an end. So the muddles that Wittgenstein found in theoretical psychology reappear in the practice of law and psychiatry in potentially more damaging forms. Debates about the idea of brain death, or the withdrawal of life support machines which prolong the bodily functioning of brain-damaged patients, are thus more a matter of practical philosophy than of scientific medicine. We cannot resolve such issues without knowledge of the relevant scientific and medical facts, but those facts alone do not force us to agree on an answer. For that, we must reflect on the alternative ways in which these facts can be viewed, and the clinical implications of taking each view. (As Alvin Weinberg puts it, these questions are not just "scientific" but "*trans*-scientific.")[7] Once again, we have to choose between coexisting aspects of our professional activities, in which the price of mistakes can be both substantive and needlessly painful.

Nor are medical examples the whole of the matter. In regard to the Environment, deeply rooted ideas about how the lives of different creatures are linked, or how they affect and are affected by human lives and actions, shape debates on industrial or agricultural policy. Thus, the philosophy of nature is not merely theoretical: its implications are practical, and there is room for a philosophical analysis of the concepts used in debates about ecology, too. Theology apart, does it make sense to talk about the Worlds of Nature and Humanity as forming "the scheme of things"—as an ecosystem, or a system of ecosystems? How are we then to balance the importance of creatures of different kinds? Do all forms of life have equal value in the grand scheme of things—equal value (we might say) in the eyes of God? If so, must we protect Smallpox Viruses as energetically as we do Pandas? Clearly, this is not just a technical question. So, in this respect, those of us who like to reflect philosophically on the World as we find it after the death of the Cartesian tradition are not affected by the supposed Death of Philosophy, and do not lack occupation.

Given Wittgenstein's concern with humanly useful work, one might have expected him to read Aristotle more charitably. But, like Dewey, he saw Aristotle as out of date—particularly because the new symbolic logic swept aside Aristotle's syllogistic approach as surely as seventeenth-century natural philosophy had dismissed his physics. The corpus of practical philosophy in Aristotle and others, which was unaffected by the twentieth-century critique of epistemology, seems to have been closed to Wittgenstein himself. It need not have been so: recall his insistence that the meanings of rules, procedures, or language games exist, not in a private world of individual thinkers and agents, but *in the public domain*. Rather than being fragments grasped and followed by individuals one at a time, such procedures are parts of the collective activities in which they are put to work, and help to determine their meanings. Wittgenstein might have found it helpful to study these activities: looking to see how their procedures and meanings are standardized and passed on to new generations, and even how such activities develop historically. Opening that door might finally have led him into a *historicized* practical philosophy, but he never succeeded in walking through it.

How far was Wittgenstein himself aware of the historical precedents of his methods of philosophizing? To the best of my knowledge, he nowhere mentions Pyrrho or Sextus—let alone Montaigne—yet the similarities between his views and those of the Classical Skeptics are too close to ignore. My colleague Richard Schmitt draws attention to the last pages of Sextus Empiricus's treatises *Adversus Logicos* and *Adversus Mathematicos*. The result of Sextus's skeptical argument to "prove that there are no logically valid proofs" is captured in his use of the image of the ladder that the skeptic climbs up, only to kick it away. This passage, of course, parallels the closing paragraphs of Wittgenstein's *Tractatus* so exactly that it is hard to believe that he invented the ladder image for himself. Where, then, did he get it from? Was it an intellectual commonplace in the Vienna of the 1900s? Certainly it is used by Fritz Mauthner, whom Wittgenstein refers to in the *Tractatus*, though some scholars have speculated that Wittgenstein himself may have read Sextus in the current German translation, at the suggestion of the tutors who taught him at home.[8]

Where, then, is analytical philosophy today? In some ways, its initial agenda derived from Aristotle's *Prior and Posterior Analytics*, being built up around the idea of *propositions*, and most of its original problems were in mathematics and inductive logic. Frege, in his *Foundations of Arithmetic*, insisted on the need to "strip away the historical and psychological accretions that veil concepts in their pure form from the eye of the mind"—this final Platonic phrase is in Frege's own words. But later analytical philosophers moved elsewhere: they extracted propositions from their original context in formal logic, and resituated them in the human situations where they are put to practical use. John Searle and J. L. Austin, for instance, both invite us to think of speech as an "act" or "performance": they set aside the idea that propositions and arguments exist in a timeless logical world, in favor of the view that utterances acquire meaning from the situations in which we use them in the same kind of way as all meaningful human actions do. Though neither Austin nor Searle put his point in just these terms, they called on what we might call a "rhetorical" approach to language and knowledge to balance the defects of the geometrical approach.

Even so, a certain rationalism still prevents many analytical philosophers from seeing that Rhetoric is not just a corruption of Rationality, but a serious discipline. They are unhappy to be told, for instance, that the first thing research scientists learn to do—namely, to write up their results in a form acceptable to a reputable scientific journal—is itself an exercise in the Rhetoric of Science! This is why it took until the fall of 1992 for the philosophers of science at the University of Pittsburgh to acknowledge that even Physics is an arena for Rhetoric as well as Reason.

I began going to Wittgenstein's classes more than fifty years ago, and I now have three thoughts about him. First: it is a pity that he did not take a historical attitude to the changes he helped to start in philosophy. His blindness to the significance of history was for me his major lack; in order to make up for it in my own work, I had to hybridize what I got from Wittgenstein with what I found in Collingwood. The questions about the rationality of conceptual change in the natural sciences that preoccupied philosophers of science from 1960 on—questions familiar enough to Collingwood—accordingly fell through the mesh of Wittgenstein's net.

Second, the issues of historical criticism that we find in Ernst Mach's histories of science were not confined to theoretical structures and propositions, as was largely the case with Hertz's *Principles of Mechanics*, which Wittgenstein so much admired. Mach's writings had just as much to do with how the concepts of physics relate to situations *in practice*—including those unspoken relations that Michael Polanyi would later call "tacit." Nor was Mach's argument limited to fields whose purposes are theoretical or explanatory: his historical methods were just as relevant to the medical field, where the central practical purposes are diagnostic and therapeutic.

Finally, as Wittgenstein liked to put it, our imaginations are particularly open to metaphysical yearnings at the point where language "goes on holiday." On occasion, he compared this kind of holiday language to idle wheels that are driven by the cogwheels with which they engage, yet are not equipped to activate other cogwheels. At other times, the rhetorical thrust of his epigram was turned in a different direction. Our yearnings begin at a time when meanings are no longer bounded by the demands of workaday disciplines or responsibilities, and language finds its fulfillment in the High Holy Days. Then we are free to speak in ways that expand outside those boundaries to an unlimited extent: after all, as he put it, *die Sprache ist kein Käfig*—Language is not a Cage.[9]

Even more than Wittgenstein, one twentieth-century writer displayed a concern for the World of Where and When just as sensitive and explicit as that of Michel de Montaigne. Virginia Woolf did her best to pin down on paper the experiences of a person, a place, or a moment as exactly as pen and ink could record. She did this with an eye to colors, to the produce on fruit and vegetable stalls, to the scent and dust of the seasons, as well as to the expressions on the faces of people she passed in the street, the irritations evinced in those encounters, and the anxieties they arouse in the heart of her perfectly rounded character, Clarissa Dalloway.

Those who have read Virginia Woolf's later novel, *The Waves*, might think on a first reading that it involves an excursion into philosophical theory—that its wealth of sensory detail is meant to call to mind the "sense datum" debate among empiricist philosophers of the 1920s and 1930s. But the theoretical analysis of perception by academics, though recognizing physical color, lacks all emotional overtones, while Woolf's writing is always tinged with feelings of joy and anger. Still, there remains something intrinsically "philosophical" in much of her writing. One striking passage in *To the Lighthouse* is the middle section, which depicts the family's seaside house when it is empty during the First World War—the Great War, as we called it in the years before 1939. Only one thing happens in the house during this period of emptiness to mark the passage of time: at one point a scarf falls. In this very moment, the temporal character of our daily experience leaps out from the page.

We should keep in mind that, at the same time, James Strachey's translations of Freud were being printed at the Hogarth Press under the eyes of Leonard and Virginia Woolf, and recognize that *The Waves*—if not specifically about visual perception—has echoes of the "oceanic" experiences that played a part in Freud's later essays. We are left with a series of questions. Is Virginia Woolf's emphasis on feelings, as some would say, a product of her anger? In part, yes. Is she angry only with men, and on behalf of women? Maybe a little. What she commits herself to above all is the "room of her own" where she could write about the minutiae of feeling, taste, and etiquette that women are liable to be more open to—and about—than men: not the abstract fictions of philosophical theory, but the quotidian concerns that I am here referring to as belonging to the World of Where and When.

At least one significant poet who happened to be a male—Wallace Stevens—shared Woolf's preoccupation with these minutiae of feeling. As his *Notes toward a Supreme Fiction* show, this is what separates an academic obsession with formal rationality from everyday life and all its experiences, which—as Hume understood—are charged with all its passions. Thus, the recovery of Reasonableness can restore to the concept of Rationality the richness of which Descartes had deprived the Classical *logos*. By now, the Cartesian heritage is being replaced, even among French philosophers, by the idea that we should think of the activity of philosophizing as being itself "a way of life," as was taught in the Epicurean, Stoic, and other communities of late Greek antiquity. As Wallace Stevens puts it, in the lines I have chosen as an epigraph for this whole book:[10]

> They will get it straight one day at the Sorbonne.
> We shall return at twilight from the lecture,
> Pleased that the irrational is rational.

13

Postscript: Living with Uncertainty

The price of living in the world of the pragmatists and the skeptics is the need to acknowledge that our best-founded beliefs are still uncertain. Neither physics nor psychology can do what the rationalists hoped. Dreamers tempt us with their images, but only as poetry. When the dreams of theory no longer cloud our expectations, we are back in a world of practical hopes and fears.

TO PUT THE STORY TOLD in this book in a nutshell: for the last four hundred years, the ideas of "reasonableness" and "rationality"—closely related in Antiquity—were separated, as an outcome of the emphasis that seventeenth-century natural philosophers placed on formal deductive techniques. This emphasis did an injury to our commonsense ways of thought, and led to confusion about some highly important questions: above all, the relation of the social sciences to the moral and other value-laden problems that arise in the practical professions. This stress on the rationality of formal theories or calculations, and on the need for "value neutrality" in the social sciences, was not universally accepted, but mathematical techniques have had such prestige in our discipline-oriented universities that they continued to entrench themselves well into the twentieth century. They were especially influential in the academic world of the United States, where the need for rational calculations to be complemented by reasonable judgments about their relevance to particular real-life human situations faded, for the time being, into the background.

Only quite recently has the weakness of an exclusive commitment to this kind of mathematical exactitude become generally apparent, along with the need for professionals in clinical medicine, ecological monitoring, and other practical activities to pay attention to moral issues. Even now it takes a sophisticated analysis to convince many behavioral scientists that their theories rest on value assumptions which, if not always explicit, are nonetheless unavoidable. (This is especially hard when the scientists are skilled in such formal, abstract methods of analysis as neoclassical equilibrium theory in economics, and rational choice theory in political science.) Still, at the present time, the tide seems to be turning, and the widespread public attention paid to questions of medical ethics in the press and elsewhere is reflected in a dozen other fields of practice.

Historically, the enthronement of mathematical rationality was just one aspect of a broader intellectual response to the loss of theological consensus following Luther's and Calvin's success in enrolling craftsmen and other members of the newly literate laity into Protestant congregations. Freed by the new availability of printed books to form theological opinions of their own, these congregations resisted Rome's claims to control the teaching of Christian doctrine. After the Council of Trent (as we saw) this ecclesiastical division of loyalties was joined by political rivalries to become a *casus belli* in the Thirty Years' War, from 1618 to 1648.

What the schism in Western Christianity did to undermine general agreement in the human sciences and philosophy was seemingly countered from 1650 on by a commitment to demonstrative philosophy, and the rise of technical disciplines that reached its climax in the twentieth century. Meanwhile, the Westphalian settlement in European politics, the establishment of distinct National Churches, and the general acceptance of a rationalist agenda in philosophy and other sciences, combined to produce an ideological package and a Myth of Stability that was not seriously challenged until after the French Revolution and the First Vatican Council. It was only the loss of one basic element in this package—the supposed "necessity" of Euclid's geometry and Newton's physics—that cast thinkers adrift, and led to the period of intellectual transition that we are still in today. In a World of Complexity, Chaos, and other "non-linear" ways of theorizing, the old alliance of State, Church, and Academy has lost the secure foothold it had kept for so long.

Liberated from the physical determinism that haunted the imaginations of a Tolstoy or a Tennyson, we can also abandon the aim of uniting certainty, necessity, and rationality into a single philosophical package. Uncertainty, disagreement, and respect for the variety of reasonable opinions replace them at the center of our preoccupations, as Montaigne always insisted that they should. If we reconcile ourselves to a skeptical pragmatism that forgets the Myth of Stability, and downplays the centrality of theoretical thinking, we can join Aristotle and Diderot in respecting the manual skills and practical experiences whose right to be the intellectual equals of any system of theory was generally recognized before the seventeenth century.

If René Descartes is a symbolic figure marking the beginning of the Modern Age, we may take Ludwig Wittgenstein as marking its end. The youngest child in the family of an Austrian steel millionaire, Wittgenstein grew up under the wing of his sister, Margaret Stonborough—a strong character, best known nowadays from a portrait by Gustav Klimt. Ludwig was educated at home, outside the public educational system. From the start, he enjoyed mastering both mathematical proofs and practical tasks, such as that of designing a sewing machine that he built with his own hands at the age of ten out of wood, wire, and other materials. Not that the contrast between manual and intellectual skills was of much significance to him: he was encouraged to build the sewing machine by arguments in a popular textbook of practical mechanics that, among other things, suggested a way to circumvent hitherto-unresolved obstacles to producing a machine that imitated this human art.

The fullest expression of Wittgenstein's blend of intellectual and manual skills is seen in the home he designed for Margaret and her husband in the Kundmanngasse, not far from the Danube Canal, a short way downstream from the Schwedenplatz in Vienna. The man whom the Stonboroughs commissioned as their architect was Paul Engelmann, who came to admire Ludwig as a philosopher; when Ludwig—a complete amateur—took over much of the detailed design work, it caused some tension between them. (The house still exists: after threats to it demolish it, and an abortive project to incorporate it into a major hotel, it survives thanks to its present occupants, the Bulgarian Government's Cultural Center.) A combination of intellectual and practical thinking was a feature of Wittgenstein's mind throughout his life, from the jet-driven aerofoils he experimented with at the Metropolitan Vickers factory in Manchester before 1914, to the manometer for measuring blood pressure that he constructed at a World War II burn hospital at East Grinstead, south of London, directed by Gilbert Ryle's brother, John Ryle. He was a man for whom the experience stored in his hands was always as meaningful as that filed away in his head.

At the turn of the twentieth century, the English writer George Meredith exclaimed,

> Ah, what a dusty answer gets the soul
> when hot for certainties in this our life![1]

and so captured the fears, anxieties, and self-doubts that oppressed European intellectuals in the Modern Age. The certainties that John Dewey found philosophers aiming at from 1600 on all took verbal forms, but these verbal "foundations" added no security to our knowledge, as they rested on practical, non-verbal supports. Theoretical axioms stood firm only where their roots went deep into pre-theoretical experience. The World-View of Modernity thus stood knowledge on its head, like a tree painted by Baselitz: verbal superstructure replaced its substantive roots. Nor is this weakness overcome by substituting "post-modernity" for "modernity": all that does is to trade in an unhelpful verbal formula for the insistence that all such formulas are invalid, without exploring the practical foundation of our knowledge. Substituting top growth for roots—formal axioms for substantive experience—must finally give way to a less dogmatic point of view, which leaves the discovery of the preconditions for everyday "certitude"—so different from mathematical "certainty"—to be achieved bit by bit, as we go along.

In any event, the program by which the philosophers of the early Modern period linked Necessity with Rationality and Certainty in a single mathematical package had deeper shortcomings. This was clear when we looked at the goal of *prediction* that has caused problems for the social sciences: substituting uniform forecasting techniques appropriate, at best, to natural phenomena and physical theories for the varied human problems at home in our different enterprises. The things that matter most to us, problems of individual and collective human relations, remain the hardest to forecast; worst of all, a Newtonian view of the human sciences confuses two misleadingly named but entirely different kinds of events—happenings we *expect* in the World of Nature, and actions we *expect of* our fellow humans—and calls both kinds of expectation "predictions" regardless of their differences.

Within limits, weather forecasts, tide tables, and eclipses tell us what to *expect* in the way of rain or shine, planetary motions, or the tides of the sea. What we *expect of* other human beings, however, has little to do with such forecasts: the unpredictability of human conduct is built into the ways in which we think and speak about each other's actions. For now, the gravest physical threats we are subject to as a species may be a collision of the Earth with a wandering asteroid, an unforeseen earthquake, or the eruption of a super-volcano. Nothing could have been said by way of a useful warning to the fifty-odd people who died as a result of the Los Angeles tremor in January 1994, the 6,500 dead at Kobe a year later, or the 20,000 lost in Turkey in August 1999; and even less to the many millions who are vulnerable to a super-Krakatoa. Yet these natural risks are lower on the list of things we can immediately worry about than the stupidity of politicians, the malice of the powerful, the incompetent running of chemical factories, or even the bitter enmity of close relatives.

Human life is where true fragility resides, and it shows the special character of our "expectations of" one another. If published job descriptions specify what is "expected of" candidates for a vacant position, they are understood to say what those candidates *shall* do, not what they *will* do: they are demands, not forecasts. When interviews succeed, again, they awaken hopes; although, at important points in anyone's career, it is impossible to tell with real confidence, in advance, how he or she would in fact perform, if appointed.

This contrast between the ways in which we think about natural phenomena and about human conduct has nothing *unscientific* about it. In both cases, what makes our understanding "scientific" is only marginally an increase in our ability to make successful forecasts. Meteorology is recognized as a "scientific" account of climate and weather, not because television weather forecasts are more or less accurate, but because it sometimes helps us to understand just when—and under just what conditions—the weather is *impossible* to forecast. The birth of hurricanes is one of the kinds of *chocs* that Poincaré foresaw, as precursors of today's "chaotic" phenomena. So, too, human scientists cannot be asked to give accurate forecasts of people's actions: the virtue of the social sciences is again that they sometimes help us understand just why, and under what special conditions, our expectations of people's behavior—either as individuals or as institutions—can reasonably be relied on.

In everyday life, of course, we always live with uncertainties, and one of the tasks of Religion has been to reconcile people to the contingencies of experience, providing either a framework of beliefs about the agencies sustaining the World, or the spiritual exercises by which they can maintain their commitment to life in the absence of such assurances. After the sixteenth- and seventeenth-century Wars of Religion, the need to save Europe from more bloodshed gave this task to a new style of Philosophy, with a "rationalist" program, which kept much of its force up to our own times. Yet for many years all its key documents gave exaggerated accounts of the empirical content of mathematics: geometry in Descartes's *Discourse*, dynamics in Newton's *Principia*, or both in Kant's *Critique of Pure Reason*. The conceptual necessities of these formal schemes of calculation were, thus, misinterpreted as permanent facts, either about the actual Structure of Nature, or about our capacity to impose rational structures on our Experience of the World.

Little of this role as a substitute for theology survives in the natural sciences today. Quite apart from his work on the Three-Body Problem, Henri Poincaré demonstrated that geometrical theorems operate at a remove from all the facts of Nature, so that we are free to choose which of the various "geometries" we can best use to represent spatial or temporal relations. Ludwig Wittgenstein, too, argued in the *Tractatus* that

> it states nothing about the World that it can be described by
> Newtonian mechanics; but [only] that it can be described in
> the way that is the case [as a matter of fact]. It also says some-
> thing about the World that it can be described more simply by
> one mechanics than by another.[2]

The conceptual frame that philosophers from Descartes to Kant found uniquely appropriate to any "rational" system of philosophy thus lost its claims to special authority.

The world as we understand it at present may be the same world as it always was, but we no longer look to physics to underpin the Myth of Stability, and provide the same comforts as before. The claims of contemporary sciences, both natural and human, are a good deal more modest, seeking neither to deny nor to explain away the contingency of things. This greater modesty extends not just to planetary astronomy, as Poincaré showed that it must, but also to evolutionary biology: there, it is ever more strikingly clear that the actual course of organic evolution had no built-in tendency to generate vertebrates, let alone mammals or humans. If the conditions on the Earth at the start of organic evolution were recreated, and set going for the same length of time under the same physical conditions, there is every reason to think that the outcome would be populations of organisms having little or no similarity to those that are in fact found on the Globe as it is at present.[3]

The same "unforecastability" (we saw) is found in the historical events after 1989, and in remarking on this fact Timothy Garton Ash did nothing to set Humanity apart from Nature: uncertainty is a mark of both equally. Some people find this a depressing thought: the anxieties that gave the Myth of Stability its charm do not disappear when Science stops assuaging them. Yet we can equally see the limits to historical prediction as emancipatory. Without the nineteenth-century nightmare of physical determinism or its twentieth-century counterparts in sociology, we can claim again the autonomy (or "free will") that the modern sciences of Nature seemed to discredit. True, beyond a short way ahead, all future events are so shrouded in fog that we have only a severely limited capacity to forecast them. But these limitations also have their compensations: the human "futures" that are most urgent for us are largely the "futuribles" we may succeed in bringing about, not external events that will just "happen to happen."

Much of this was already evident to scholars like Harold Lasswell in the 1930s: seventy years ago, the possibility of using "scenario-building" as a way of estimating the range of futuribles open to us had already been recognized.[4] So if, during the Cold War, scholars in Political Science and International Relations concentrated on the all-embracing theories that (oddly) came to be known as *realism*, this was a step not forward into a more fruitful intellectual future, but backward into older systems of thought. Even cosmologists today have little more than "a crude view of the whole": after the Big Bang—if there was a Big Bang[5]—the evolution of stars and galaxies, quasars and black holes, took a direction no more unique and predetermined than that of organic evolution on our Earth.

A century and a half ago, Alfred Tennyson expressed anxiety at the impermanence of species; and in the 1920s, W. R. Inge, the Dean of St. Paul's, saw the Second Law of Thermodynamics as evidence of long-term decay in Humanity and Nature alike. Grounds for either optimism or pessimism can be quarried from the results of natural science, and will no doubt continue to be. But the determinism that was a feature of physics for so long was, from the beginning, the result of a misunderstanding of the Newtonian Philosophy. So those scientists who work on Chaos and Complexity today develop scenarios applicable not just to international politics or the running of businesses, but to the future of the Earth, the planetary system, and the rest of Nature. Having escaped the compulsions imposed on us by physicalistic ideas in Economics, we no longer have any reason to let our ideas about the Social World be governed by seemingly "ineluctable" influences, whether political, economic, or cultural.

Like Mrs. Dalloway, we can take things as we find them. Without the optimism of the extrapolators who claim to figure out the future from the progress of the Stock Markets or other economic statistics, or the pessimism of those doomsayers who see the effects of Technology as defeating even our best policies, we can map the range of possible futures open to us—either as individuals or as political and social collaborators—and do our best to create conditions that will help us move in better instead of worse directions. At the very least, we can join Aristotle in steering between the rocks that might otherwise stop us from doing the best we could, for ourselves or for our fellows. Once again, that is, we can follow Candide's maxim: rather than worry our heads with Panglossian theories, we can cultivate our gardens.

When all is said and done, then, the best in Philosophy and Natural Science alone can take us only a little way: the World of Actuality is also shaped by our ideals. Our lives are not entirely guided by Rationality and Reasonableness: our dreams also project us into activities that we previously only imagined. "Never doubt that a small group of thoughtful, committed citizens can change the world," Margaret Mead exhorted us; "it is the only thing that ever has."[6] But groups of social agents succeed on the basis of their dreams as much as on their calculations, and the choices we make in working toward productive futures are informed by those ideals.

This tension between the Ideal and the Actual is kept alive by great poets, but their failure to examine carefully enough the relations between these two things carries its own perils. Here, the history of poetry in the Modern period is a source of warnings as well as achievements. The creative sentiments of early nineteenth-century Romantics, for instance, were followed by a reaction: the dreams to which these gave rise proved so impossible to achieve that the pedestrian realities of human life often appeared, by contrast, catastrophic. In *Hyperions Schicksalslied* (later set for chorus and orchestra by Brahms), Hölderlin depicts the lives of the Blessed Spirits—"touched by divine breaths"—as so far out of the reach of human beings that our own lives—"like water flung blindly from cliff to cliff"—are exposed only to fresh injuries every hour.[7]

A similar shadow lies across a poem that has always been one of my favorites, Matthew Arnold's *Dover Beach*. Matthew's father, Thomas Arnold, was far from a pessimist: as Headmaster of Rugby School, he made it the prototypical boarding school, training boys for public service to the British Empire and the Anglican Church. Matthew himself pursued a middle way between two styles of culture, which he called Hebraism and Hellenism—outward conformity to a system of rules, and "sweetness and light"—but his preference for Hellenism ended elegiacally.[8] Listening on a moonlit night to "the grating roar of the pebbles" drawn back by the waves in the Straits of Dover, only to be flung high up the strand, he heard in this repeated sound "the eternal note of sadness":

> Sophocles, long ago, heard it on the Aegean,
> and it brought into his mind the turbid ebb and flow
> of human misery . . .

Where formerly "the sea of faith [had cast] a bright girdle" around the Earth, we no longer have reasons for hope: "the world which seems / To lie before us like a land of dreams / Hath really neither joy, nor love, nor light / Nor certitude, nor peace, nor help from pain,"

> and we are here as on a darkling plain,
> swept with confused alarms of struggle and flight,
> where ignorant armies clash by night.

As rational attitudes, optimism and pessimism cancel each other out. In the end, we can set aside dreams of eternal clarity, return to the World of Where and When, get back in touch with the experience of everyday life, and manage our lives and affairs a day at a time. The activists and practitioners who work with Amnesty International and *Médecins sans Frontières*, manage our water and forests, monitor the practices of political and industrial organizations, and undertake all the other pedestrian tasks of our common affairs—all of these workers live in the present and handle such problems without recourse to shouted slogans or acts of violence: they "cultivate their gardens." These practices begin with intelligent analyses of the factual soil from which our problems spring, but such actions bear fruit only when they are guided by ideals that make rational assessments stepping stones to reasonable decisions. In these terms, a doctor skilled in molecular biochemistry alone is not the kind of professional the future calls for, any more than an engineer who knows only how to compute the size of girders capable of providing a given strength, or an economist who knows only how to calculate the rates of interest needed to maintain a desired return on investments.

So, more and more, emphasis on formal rigor is being supplanted today by a different kind of balance: one between stubborn facts, shared values, and rival interests. The need to keep these varied considerations in harmony may lead in unforeseen directions. Recall Muhammad Yunus's Grameen Bank: its activities broaden every year, and it now builds brick houses for its poor clients to live in, sets up health services—sick borrowers cannot be expected to continue repaying their loans—markets the fabrics made by Bangladeshi women via in-flight catalogues of international airlines, and inspires imitations in every continent.

Nor is it only in technical disciplines like medicine, engineering, and economics that the best practitioners are learning to strike this new balance. Even some philosophers are responding to problems that require the kind of reflective study that leads—like Aristotle's "practical" syllogism—not to opinions but to actions. As a philosopher, Howard Adelman brings his grasp of the history of ideas to bear on the current problems of ethnic violence, by way of his Center for the Study of Refugees, and in doing so acts both as a social agent and as an academic. As a social agent, he focuses attention on the failure of outside governments to handle the conflicts in, for example, Rwanda and Bosnia, sets out to devise early warning procedures for anticipating future civil wars, and plays a part behind the scenes in the Middle Eastern peace process; meanwhile, he writes in academic terms about ethical theories of humanitarian intervention in the affairs of distant peoples. But he would deny that these two kinds of issue are separable. Both of them are concerns for the "practical" philosopher, who sees philosophical theories as relevant to our problems not because they provide formal solutions to abstract queries, but because they confer practical and concrete meaning on the lives of individuals, and families, and political communities.[9]

Thus, the discipline of Philosophy becomes less a *way of life* in Pierre Hadot's sense, like those by which the Stoics and Epicureans in late Antiquity comforted intellectuals in a world in decay, than a *calling* to put reflective analysis to work as an instrument in handling moral, medical, and political issues.[10] Clinical medical ethics is not—in the classic sense—"applied" philosophy, nor in the broad field of public policy need we think of the activity of Amnesty International or *Médecins sans Frontières* as an "application" of rational calculations; rather, they represent the responses of the untutored heart to its perceptions of neglect, indifference, cruelty, and other wickednesses. Not for nothing did Aristotle, in the *Nicomachean Ethics*, present "cruelty" as something we can recognize for what it is, with the same confidence that we identify a triangle; nor does one need to be an Athenian, or even a Hellene, to share in such human perceptions. We recognize these things in our hearts, and only perversity or corruption can blind us to them.

Our first intellectual obligation is to abandon the Myth of Stability that played so large a part in the Modern age: only thus can we heal the wounds inflicted on the Reason by the seventeenth-century obsession with Rationality, and give back to Reasonableness the equal treatment of which it was for so long deprived. The future belongs not so much to the pure thinkers who are content—at best—with optimistic or pessimistic slogans; it is a province, rather, for reflective practitioners who are ready to act on their ideals. Warm hearts allied with cool heads seek a middle way between the extremes of abstract theory and personal impulse. The ideals of practical thinkers are more realistic than the optimistic daydreams of simple-minded calculators, who ignore the complexities of real life, or the pessimistic nightmares of their critics, who find these complexities a source of despair.[11]

Notes

Preface

1. Isaiah Berlin, *The Sense of Reality*, ed. Henry Hardy (New York: Farrar, Straus, Giroux, 1996), pp. 40–41.
2. Ibid., pp. 50–51.

1. Introduction: Rationality and Certainty

1. On this and related translation problems, not just from English to German, but among European languages more generally, see chap. 2, n. 12.
2. Fernand Braudel, *Grammaire de Civilisations* (Paris: Belin, 1963), translated by Richard Mayne as *A History of Civilizations* (London and New York: Penguin Books, 1993), pp. 34–35.
3. A course announcement at the University of Southern California in 1999.
4. Ludwig Wittgenstein, "Logisch-philosophische Abhandlung," *Annalen der Naturphilosophie*, 14 (3/4, 1921), pp. 185–262, translated by C. K. Ogden as *Tractatus Logico-Philosophicus* (London: Routledge and Kegan Paul, 1922, corrected ed., 1933), prop. 2.1. The exact translation of this particular proposition is a matter to which I shall return.
5. Consider, for instance, the very different approaches and terminologies of Otto Neurath, Karl Popper, Rudolph Carnap, and Carl Hempel. For a full history of the changes involved, see Fred Suppe, *The Structure of Scientific Theories* (Urbana: University of Illinois Press, 1977).
6. T. S. Kuhn's *The Structure of Scientific Revolutions* was originally published as the final part of the *International Encyclopedia of Unified Science* (Chicago: University of Chicago Press, 1961), but subsequently ran through two further editions: 2nd ed., 1970; 3rd ed., 1996. In the process, the intellectual content of the book changed more drastically than was generally noticed. In the last edi-

tion, for instance, Kuhn redefined the distinction between "normal" and "revolutionary" science, paradoxically equating it to the traditional logician's contrast between "deductive" and "inductive" reasoning.

Ludvik Fleck's book, *Genesis and Development of a Scientific Fact*, originally in German, was published by the University of Chicago Press in 1979 with a foreword by Kuhn at the suggestion of Edward Shils.

7. R. G. Collingwood, *An Essay on Metaphysics* (Oxford: Clarendon Press, 1940). The resulting argument is discussed at some length in my *Human Understanding* (Oxford: Clarendon Press, 1940, and Princeton, N.J.: Princeton University Press), cf. esp. p. 73. For Collingwood's reflections on the cultural and political situation in Europe in the 1930s, see R. G. Collingwood, *An Autobiography* (London and New York: Oxford University Press, 1939; paperback ed., 1978). After Collingwood's death, his old friend T. S. Knox had his book *The Idea of History* published by the Clarendon Press, with a somewhat apologetic introduction by Knox himself.

8. Gottlob Frege, *Die Grundlage der Arithmetik* (Breslau, 1884), translated by J. L. Austin as *The Foundations of Arithmetic* (Oxford: Blackwell, 1950), p. vii.

9. See the useful collection of papers edited by Martin Hollis and Steven Lukes, *Rationality and Relativism* (Oxford: Blackwell, 1982).

10. Marx W. Wartofksy, "An Intellectual Odyssey," in *Humanities* (Washington, D.C.: National Endowment for the Humanities), 18/2, March/April 1977, pp. 8ff.

11. Ludwig Wittgenstein, *Notebooks, 1914–1916*, ed. G. H. von Wright and G. E. M. Anscombe (Chicago: University of Chicago Press, and Oxford: Blackwell, 1961), 2nd ed., p. 82. This entry is dated September 2, 1916, and reads in the original: "Was geht mich die Geschichte an? Meine Welt ist die erste und einzige."

12. G. E. Moore, *Principia Ethica* (Cambridge: Cambridge University Press, 1903), pp. 66–67.

13. In those years, half a dozen serious books about cosmology attracted popular attention: e.g., those by Max Born, Albert Einstein and Leopold Infeld, and James Jeans.

14. Liddell and Scott, *Greek-English Lexicon*, rev. H. S. Jones and R. McKenzie, p. 984. The use of a single idea, *cosmos,* equally for the marshalling of an army, the Order of Nature, and the arts of personal beauty, was already a feature of Greek Antiquity.

15. John Desmond Bernal's book, *The Social Function of Science,* reprinted by the MIT Press in 1967, was originally published in January 1939.

16. See Michael Ignatieff, *Isaiah Berlin: a Life* (New York: Henry Holt, 1999), esp. p. 176.

17. From this point on, I use "situated" and "desituated" instead of the more familiar "contextual" and "decontextualized": the way in which a lexical item relates to the—largely non-linguistic—situation in which it functions is quite unlike the relation between a shorter text and the longer text of which it is a part. I should have made this change in my earlier book, *Cosmopolis* (New York: The Free Press, 1989).

18. Bent Flyvbjerg, *Rationalitet og magt: Case-baseret studie af planlægning, politik og modernitet* (Copenhagen: Akademisk Forlag, 1991), trans. Steven Sampson (Chicago: University of Chicago Press, 1998).

19. The description of Schoenberg as "a conservative revolutionary" is taken from Willi Reich, *Schönberg oder der konservativ Revolutionär*. For the significance of this description as it relates to the last decades of the Habsburg régime, see Allan Janik and Stephen Toulmin, *Wittgenstein's Vienna* (New York: Simon and Schuster, 1973), chap. 8.

2. How Reason Lost Its Balance

1. See Mary Catherine Bateson, *Composing a Life* (New York: Penguin Books, 1989).

2. See Chap. 1, n. 17, above.

3. A memory of this proof in pure mathematics has stayed with me from my youth, which I have reconstructed from memory, as follows:

> Suppose that the square root of 2 equals the fraction m/n, in its lowest terms. We say *in its lowest terms* because (e.g.) $\sqrt{4} = 4/2$ and $6/3$ as well as $2/1$: the fraction that is *in its lowest terms* is $2/1$, since you cannot keep dividing m and n any further and stay in the realm of whole numbers.
>
> On this supposition, let us now square the equation $\sqrt{2} = m/n$ to get $2 = m^2/n^2$. Next we introduce two more whole numbers, p and q, such that $m = 2p$ and $n = 2q$: p and q, respectively, are smaller than m and n. By definition, $m^2/n^2 = 4p^2/4q^2$, which in turn $= p^2/q^2$.
>
> But we have already shown that $2 = m^2/n^2$, so it also follows that $2 = p^2/q^2$, and (taking square roots) that $\sqrt{2} = p/q$. Since p is smaller than m and q smaller than n, however, this last conclusion contradicts our supposition that m/n is a fraction *in its lowest terms*.
>
> Hence, the opening assumption that $\sqrt{2}$ can be expressed as the fraction m/n, in its lowest terms, leads to a formal contradiction, that the fraction m/n *both is and is not* in its lowest terms. The assumption is, therefore, logically impossible.

This proof is both longer and more complicated than other standard ones. So, on the advice of Ezra Shahn, I follow the example of Courant, Robbins, and

Stewart, *What Is Mathematics?* (Oxford and New York: Oxford University Press, 1941, rev. 1996), or Dirk Struik, *A Concise History of Mathematics* (Dover paperback, p. 48).

The version I include here is not exactly the same as theirs, but draws on exchanges with Hayward Alker, who, as a more experienced mathematician, insisted on making sure that I had covered all the cases.

Alker's personal version reads as follows:

> Assume that the square root of 2 is the ratio of two integers, and express that ratio in lowest terms, factoring out all common denominators > 1, as m/n.
>
> Squaring and redistributing terms, m-squared $= 2$ n-squared.
>
> This implies that m-squared is even; and, because an odd number squared is odd, and an even number squared is even, this means that m itself is even.
>
> So $m = 2p$, for some other integer, p.
>
> Squaring, m-squared $= 4$ p-squared.
>
> Hence 4 p-squared $= 2$ n-squared, and 2 p-squared $= n$-squared.
>
> By the same reasoning, n-squared is even, and therefore n is also even.
>
> This immediately implies a contradiction. For, if both m and n are even, they have a common denominator of 2, contradicting the assumption that they made up a ratio in its lowest terms.
>
> Accordingly, our initial assumption is false, and the square root of 2 cannot be a rational number.

4. For Plato's theory of the shapes of the basic atoms in the *Timaeus*, see Stephen Toulmin and June Goodfield, *The Architecture of Matter* (London: Hutchinson, and New York: Harper and Row, 1962; reprinted by the University of Chicago Press, 2000), pp. 75–82.

5. The most familiar report on Socrates' final days is, of course, that given in Plato's dialogue, the *Phaedo*.

6. Notice that the terms used here—*data, warrants, qualifier*, and so on—are just those introduced in *The Uses of Argument*. As such, they did not have any particular theoretical purpose, but rather followed our pragmatic usage in everyday argumentation.

7. We have two fine English editions of Montaigne's *Complete Essays*, written from different points of view: Donald Frame's Stanford University Press edition (1958) adopts a central humanist's approach, suggesting that Montaigne was something of an agnostic, but M. A. Screech's more conservative Penguin edition (1991) emphasizes Montaigne's religious conformity. Both are well worth consulting: their readings and interpretations complement one another. The key document for understanding this contrast is Montaigne's longest essay, the

"Apologie de Raymond Sebond": see Frame, pp. 318–457, and Screech, pp. 489–683.

To complete the picture, see also the essay on Montaigne by Gore Vidal in *The Times Literary Supplement*, June 26, 1992, reprinted in Gore Vidal, *United States: Essays 1952–1992* (New York: Random House, 1993), pp. 508–519, which takes Screech's translation as its starting point.

8. Recall, for instance, Bombastus von Hohenheim of Basel, better known as Paracelsus, discussed in Toulmin and Goodfield, *The Architecture of Matter*, p. 141.

9. See the destructive critique of the pre-Socratic philosophers in his "Apologie de Raymond Sebond."

10. Léon Brunschvicg, *Descartes et Pascal, Lecteurs de Montaigne* (Paris: Brentano, 1944).

11. The extent of the scorn in which Santayana was eventually held in the Harvard Philosophy Department is illustrated by a story that was told me by Henry Aiken, after he moved from Harvard to Brandeis. In the 1930s (he said) the members of the department had a group portrait painted to hang in their suite of offices; at that time, Santayana was a full member of the department. After the Second World War, the picture was no longer on display, but had been banished to the basement of William James Hall. Where Santayana's figure had earlier been visible, there was now a clumsily patched-in length of bookshelves, dividing the remaining philosophers into two separate groups. Santayana had, quite literally, been "painted out" of the picture.

Gore Vidal visited George Santayana several times in 1948, in his cell at the Convent of the Blue Nuns on the Celian Hill in Rome, where he had spent much of World War II, and gives a delicate account of these visits in his book of memoirs, *Palimpsest* (New York: Random House, 1995; Penguin, 1996), pp. 157–165.

12. My comments on the problem of translating the terms *rational* and *reasonable* into German are based on discussions with Dorothea Wildenburg and Hans van Beinum. A letter from Allan Janik confirms my reading of *Vernunft* as "the rational, or rationalistic, aspects of *Verstand*." He adds, "Practical *Vernunft* is a way of creating that Good Will in the subject which is the only unqualifiedly good thing . . . In Kant, the whole matter is a kind of spiritual exercise; [and] Jews in the mainstream Central European assimilation took it up in just this way."

There is nothing exceptional about the case of *Vernunft* and *Verstand*. One can make a more general point about the limited intertranslatability of the European languages. In Romance languages, such as Italian, philosophical abstractions familiar to English-speaking readers lack any exact parallels. When Ferruccio Rossi-Landi set out to translate into Italian *The Concept of Mind* by Gilbert Ryle, whose way of arguing relies on some highly colloquial distinctions, he found that the very word *mind* had no direct Italian counterpart, and his version finally bore the title *Lo Spirito come Comportamento*.

There is, indeed, a whole field to be explored, which we might call "comparative" philosophy. This would deal with the linguistic differences that make it easier or harder to translate philosophical problems that arise easily in one language into some other language. We might begin by looking at the linguistic issues raised by the claims in Plato's *Theaeteus* about our knowledge of *what is not*. How are we to understand this phrase? The answer, Gilbert Ryle used to argue, is that users of Classical Greek—like users of Black English in the United States today—tended to suppress the "is" in statements like "Socrates is bald": so, "bald Socrates" and "not bald Socrates" were equivalent to our statements "Socrates is bald" and "Socrates is not bald." Citing such cases, Plato presents the question "How do we know *not bald Socrates?*" as entailing the existence of an untrue fact or a non-existent person, in a way that anticipated views about "facts" and "objects" that were later revived by Russell and Wittgenstein. (Not that Wittgenstein overlooked this difficulty: this is clear from his later comments referring to the *Theaeteus* in the *Philosophical Investigations*, props. 46 and 518. See also the discussion of "false knowledge" in Plato's *Cratylus*, 429 D-E.)

Especially tricky questions arise if we contrast the English or German use of the words *self* or *selbst* and the French use of the terms *je* and *moi*. These last questions are only partly overcome by adopting the neologism, *soi*. For a first attempt to deal with these issues, see my paper, "Self-Knowledge and Knowledge of the 'Self,'" in *The Self: Psychological and Philosophical Issues*, ed. Theodore Mischel (Oxford: Blackwell, and Totowa, N.J.: Rownan and Littlefield, 1977), pp. 291–317.

The question of the roles of judgment in geometry, physics, and the other exact sciences will come up again later, particularly in connection with Michael Polanyi's ideas about our reliance on "tacit knowledge" in the actual practice of the exact sciences.

13. Liddell and Scott, *Greek-English Lexicon*, pp. 1057–1059.
14. Ibid., pp. 1569–1570.

3. The Invention of Disciplines

1. C. P. Snow's Rede Lecture was given at Cambridge on May 7, 1959, and led to a worldwide and sometimes confused debate. The latest edition, with a fine introduction by Stefan Collini and C. P. Snow's own afterthoughts, is *The Two Cultures* (Cambridge: Cambridge University Press, 1993).

2. See the *New York Times*, March 22, 1997, p. 14. Pritchett's obituary was written from London by Sarah Lyell, who reported his death at age 96 on Thursday, March 20, and quoted an earlier essay on Pritchett by Eudora Welty in the *New York Times* book review supplement.

3. The best introduction to Galileo's work, from this point of view, is still the survey by Marshall Clagett, *The Science of Mechanics in the Middle Ages* (Madison: University of Wisconsin Press, 1959). In particular, Clagett shows how sixteenth-century mathematicians transformed the methods of the impetus theorists into a foundation for the development of the differential calculus by Newton and Leibniz.

4. This point is more fully made in chapter 2 of my book *Cosmopolis*.

5. See Marshall Hodgson, *Rethinking World History* (Cambridge: Cambridge University Press, 1993), esp. chap. 4, pp. 44–71. Lynn White's *Medieval Technology and Social Change* (Oxford: Clarendon Press, 1962) reminds us of Europe's debt to Asia: the stirrup and the horse collar were the material basis both for the institution of knighthood and for the agricultural prosperity of Northern Europe, whose waterlogged plains could be opened up to farming only with metal plowshares, which called for a force that had to be transferred to the shoulders of the draft animal.

   As for Marshall Hodgson's claim that the East was economically more productive than the West until 1800, this point has been argued in detail, with quantitative data, by Andre Gunder Frank in *Re-Orient* (Berkeley: University of California Press, 1997). The point Hodgson raises about the collective intelligence of Europeans, vis-à-vis Asians, has also (Steve Fuller comments) been stressed by the sociologist Toby Huff, who sees it as responsible for the rise of the medieval university. See also Fuller's own recent book, *Science* (Minneapolis: University of Minnesota Press, 1997), chap. 5.

6. Steven Shapin, *A Social History of Truth* (Chicago: University of Chicago Press, 1994).

7. Compare Aristotle, *Nicomachean Ethics*, VIII. iii, 1156a, 6–7.

8. Contrast, for instance, the story of the ups and downs of the Ottoman armies in Jason Goodwin, *Lords of the Horizons* (New York: Henry Holt, 1998), with the analysis of the situation in Europe in William H. McNeill, *The Pursuit of Power* (Chicago: University of Chicago Press), pp. 128–136, and *Keeping Together in Time* (Cambridge, Mass.: Harvard University Press, 1995), pp. 127–132.

9. A microfilm version of Justus Lipsius, *de Militia Romana*, is available from the University of Kentucky Library. Much of the treatise is, in effect, a scholarly commentary on Polybius, *The Rise of the Roman Empire* (London and New York: Penguin, 1979), book VI, trans. Ian Scott-Kilvert, pp. 318–338. This edi-

tion also has a useful introduction by F. W. Walbank (pp. 9–40) which fills in the background to the relationship between Polybius and Scipio Africanus.

10. Richard Watson, "On the Zeedijk," *Georgia Review* 43, no. 1 (Spring 1989), pp. 19–32.

11. Polybius, *Rise of the Roman Empire*, book VI, chaps. 27–40 (Penguin ed., pp. 324–338). The contrast between Roman and Greek ways of laying out camps is the subject of chap. 40, pp. 338–339.

12. This discussion of cultural differences was the topic of a lecture I gave for the Hortus Botanicus at Leiden in November 1996, and was printed at the University under the title: "Nature, Style and Rationality." Charles l'Écluse, who established the University's Botanic Garden under the name of Clusius, is immortalized in the names of several species of bulbous plants such as *Tulipa clusiana*; l'Écluse was a friend of Lipsius when he was at Leiden.

13. Pierre Duhem, *La théorie physique, son objet, sa structure* (Paris: Rivière, 2nd ed., 1914). I use here the translation by Philip P. Wiener, published as *The Aim and Structure of Physical Theory* (Princeton, N.J.: Princeton University Press, 1954). See in particular chap. 4, pp. 55–104, esp. pp. 63–71.

14. From a vast literature, let me mention just one item for its full "Chronologie de Diderot": namely, Diderot, *Oeuvres Romanesques* (Paris: Garnier, 1962, ed. Henri Bénac), pp. xix–xxxiv.

15. As we shall see in the next chapter, this was one of the main themes of the letters between Gottfried Wilhelm Leibniz and Samuel Clarke, writing for Isaac Newton. See *The Leibniz-Clarke Correspondence*, ed. H. G. Alexander (Manchester: Manchester University Press, 1956).

4. Economics, or the Physics That Never Was

1. The full implications of Poincaré's analysis became finally clear only when his second set of philosophical essays, *Science and Method*, appeared in 1908.

2. For the transition from Copernicus to Newton, over the 144 years from 1543 to 1687, see Thomas Kuhn's book, *The Copernican Revolution* (Cambridge, Mass.: Harvard University Press, 1957). This book is notable for two very different reasons. On the one hand, it gives a detailed account of a fascinating historical episode. On the other, it shows that the transition was no unbridgeable "paradigm shift" between "incommensurable" sets of concepts. Copernicus's revolution thus fails to answer to the definition of "revolutions" that Kuhn gave soon after in the first edition of *The Structure of Scientific Revolutions*.

3. For first-hand evidence of what was at issue here between Leibniz and Newton, refer to *The Leibniz-Clarke Correspondence*, ed. H. G. Alexander (Manchester: Manchester University Press, 1956).

4. Immanuel Kant's *Allgemeine Naturgeschichte und Theorie des Himmels*, first issued in Königsberg in 1755 by a publisher who was on the point of bankruptcy, is still available in an English translation by W. Hastie from Dover paperbacks.

5. Tennyson's *In Memoriam*—written as an elegy for his friend, Arthur Henry Hallam, who died in 1833 at the age of 22—deplored the brevity of human life by pointing to the transience of animal species and geological strata. See A. C. Bradley's *Commentary on Tennyson's In Memoriam* (London: Macmillan, 1951). Charles C. Gillispie has an admirable discussion of the nineteenth-century controversy about the time scale of the universe in his *Genesis and Geology* (Cambridge, Mass.: Harvard University Press, 1951). Cf. Stephen Toulmin and June Goodfield, *The Discovery of Time* (London: Hutchinson, and New York: Harper and Row, 1965, repr. Chicago: University of Chicago Press, 1999).

6. *Acta Mathematica*, vol. 7 (1885–86), pp. i–vi.

7. Ibid., vol. 13 (1889), pp. 1–270.

8. The three volumes on *Méthodes nouvelles de la Mécanique céleste* appeared in 1892, 1893, and 1899; the first set of philosophical essays, *La Science et l'Hypothèse*, came out in 1902.

9. In February 2000, the Near Earth Asteroid Rendezvous spacecraft (NEAR), launched by the U.S. National Aeronautics and Space Administration four years earlier, began orbiting the asteroid 433 Eros, and on Valentine's Day 2000 sent back to Earth photographs that gave the first close view of one of these potentially threatening objects.

10. The most comprehensive accounts of the history of economic theory are Joseph A. Schumpeter's *History of Economic Analysis* (Oxford and New York: Oxford University Press, 1954) and Umberto Meoli's *Lineamenti di storia delle idee economiche* (Turin, 1988). The growth of equilibrium analysis, with reference to Cournot, Marshall, and Walras, is described in Schumpeter's *History*, part IV, chap. 7, pp. 952–963, 990–1026.

   The influence of analogies with physics on the formulation of economic theories has been a subject of much research in the last twenty-five years; two journals publish most of the results of this research: *History of Political Economy* (Duke University Press, from 1976 on) and *Economics and Philosophy* (Cambridge University Press, 1985 on). Philip Mirowski's book, *More Heat than Light* (Cambridge University Press, 1989), is useful, but credits thermodynamics with more influence than I will do here. *The Invisible Hand: Economic Equilibrium in the History of Science* by Bruna Ingrao and Giorgio Israel (Cambridge, Mass.: MIT Press, 1990) is valuable and has a wider scope than its title suggests. Conversely, the influence of economics on the history of physics in the modern era is discussed by Val Dusek in *The Holistic Inspirations of Physics* (Brunswick, N.J.: Rutgers University Press, 1999).

For a survey of market economics in terms of dynamics, see the report by Richard H. Day and Gunnar Eliasson, *The Dynamics of Market Economics* (Amsterdam and New York: North-Holland, 1986), and also H.-J. Wagener and J. W. Drukker (Eds.), *The Economic Law of Motion in Modern Society: A Marx-Keynes-Schumpeter Centennial* (Cambridge University Press, 1986).

11. On Adam Smith, see W. P. D. Wightman's essay, "Adam Smith and the History of Ideas," in *Essays on Adam Smith*, ed. A. S. Skinner and Thomas Wilson (Oxford University Press, 1975). Aside from Smith's best-known works on the *Theory of Moral Sentiments* (1759) and *The Wealth of Nations* (1776), he wrote prolifically about subjects far removed from economics or moral philosophy: for instance, the uses of rhetoric, the history of astronomy, and the origin of languages. For more detailed references, see the Glasgow edition of *The Works and Correspondence of Adam Smith* published by Oxford University Press in the 1970s.

12. Augustin Antoine Cournot was as prolific as Adam Smith, but his published works focused more consistently on cosmology. His doctoral thesis was an analysis of the movement of a rigid body on a fixed plane, and his first appointment was to a chair in applied mathematics at Lyons, but his interests broadened to probability, statistics, and economics, being defined in his *Traité de l'Enchaînement des Idées Fondamentales dans les Sciences et dans l'Histoire* (Paris: 1861, repr. 1922, with an introduction by Lévy-Bruhl) as centered on "rational mechanics" and methodology. Of the 707 pages of this work, only pp. 535–563 deal with Economics.

Cournot's essays in *Matérialisme, Vitalisme et Rationalisme* (1875) also make it clear that he takes Leibniz's side in the dispute with Clarke (cf. chap. 3, n. 15 above).

13. The must useful modern book about Jevons's economics is that by Margaret Schabas, *A World Ruled by Number* (Princeton, N.J.: Princeton University Press, 1990). From the point of view in this chapter, it exaggerates the centrality of Economics in Jevons's thought, but aside from that qualification it has great merits.

14. Like Cournot, Léon Walras was trained in mathematics, but his interests were in economics from the start, as had been those of his father, Auguste Walras, before him. His concern with equilbrium analysis carried further Cournot's ideal of rational mechanics as well as the general spirit of nineteenth-century pure mathematics, as expressed in *Acta Mathematica*. Walras's career from 1851 to 1909 can be followed in the full autobiographical note preserved in the archives of the Centre d'études interdisciplinaires Walras-Pareto, and his letters have been collected by William Jaffé in *Correspondence of Léon Walras and Related Papers* (Amsterdam: North-Holland, 1965). His only direct letters to

Henri Poincaré, in Jaffé's vol. III, nos. 1492 and 1495, are dated in September 1901, but the similarity between economics and mechanics that was the subject of his final paper, *Économique et Mécanique*, in the *Bulletin de la Societé vaudoise des sciences naturelles* (5e série), vol. xlv, no. 166 (June 1909), had preoccupied him as early as the 1840s. In a letter to Deschamps, dated July 5, 1904, he comments: "I knew my father's two basic laws of economics at the age of 14 or 15, as I knew the laws of Kepler and Newton" (*Correspondence*, vol. III, no. 1576).

15. Schumpeter, *History of Economic Analysis*, p. 954, n. 2.

16. For the story of the Bali water temples, read J. Stephen Lansing's book, *Priests and Programmers: Technologies of Power in the Engineered Landscape of Bali* (Princeton, N.J.: Princeton University Press, 1991). See esp. pp. 113–115. A subsequent paper by Lansing and James Kremer, "Emergent Properties of Balinese Water Temple Networks: Coadaptation on a Rugged Fitness Landscape," in *American Anthropologist* 95 (1993), pp. 97–114, analyzes the Water Temples as "a complex adaptive system" of the kind being studied at the Santa Fe Institute. Cf. Lucas Horst (Wageningen Agricultural University), "Intervention in Irrigation Water Division in Bali, Indonesia." His report gives a picture of the mistakes made in the Bali Irrigation Project. As he says, "The Italian and Korean consultants had no or little knowledge of the specific Bali-Subak irrigation": they even described traditional irrigation procedures as making an *arbitrary* allocation of water to the farmers!

17. By now, the story of Muhammad Yunus and the Grameen Bank is familiar, but it is helpful to read Yunus's own account of the experiences that led him to develop his new banking methods, providing small amounts of money with which even the poorest of the poor could finance self-supporting enterprises. See Muhammad Yunus and Alan Jolis, *Banker to the Poor* (London: Aurum Press, 1998); see also Alex Counts, *Give Us Credit* (New York: Random House, 1996), which describes the extension of the Grameen methods to other countries, and David Bornstein, *The Price of a Dream* (New York: Simon and Schuster, 1996), which adds a Canadian point of view.

18. Yunus and Jolis, *Banker to the Poor*, pp. 121–122.

19. Alex Counts, *Give Us Credit*; the best-known example of a Grameen-type operation in the United States is that developed at the South Shore National Bank, Chicago.

20. Yunus and Jolis, *Banker to the Poor*, pp. 68, 81, 235.

5. The Dreams of Rationalism

1. Vienna as the cradle of "modernism" is the subject of Allan Janik and Stephen Toulmin, *Wittgenstein's Vienna* (New York: Simon and Schuster, 1972). See also Carl Schorske's *Fin de siècle Vienna*, especially as regards architecture and

the fine arts. In the last two or three decades, there has grown up a vast literature of "Gay Vienna" books on every level of scholarship.

2. *Tractatus*, prop. 5.5563. Contrast props. 3.323 and 4.002, which imply—Richard Schmitt argues—that "colloquial language can be confusing, or at least less
perspicuous than scientific representation or logically analyzed propositions"
(personal communication).

3. Compare Bertrand Russell's late books, *An Inquiry into Meaning and Truth* (London and Boston: Allen and Unwin, 1940) and *Human Knowledge, Its Scope and
Limits* (London: Allen and Unwin; New York: Simon and Schuster, 1948), with
F. H. Bradley's *Appearance and Reality* (London: Allen and Unwin, 1893), and it
will be clear how lasting was Bradley's influence on Russell's philosophical
thought. Russell was an idealist of Bradley's persuasion in the 1890s, before his
encounters with Frege, Peano, and Whitehead set him on the road to analytical
philosophy; yet he continued to think of Absolute Truth as unattainable for reasons parallel to those that Bradley gave in the case of Absolute Reality, and this
metaphysical position deeply affected his later theories about Language.

   Notice, here as elsewhere, the distinction that Richard Rorty so usefully
marks by contrasting singular, uppercase entities like Reality, Theory, and
Truth with plural, lowercase "real clocks" (i.e., not fakes), "theories" (i.e., rival
ways of framing an argument), and "truths" (i.e., not lies or errors). See the
opening essay in his *Consequences of Pragmatism* (Minneapolis: University of
Minnesota Press, 1982).

4. Plato's *Cratylus* makes great and often humorous play of the idea that the names
of things should be "correct"; and onomatopoeia is used as one example of the
ways in which words can resemble the things or situations they designate.

5. Benjamin deMott, "Comenius and the Real Character in England," *Proceedings
of the Modern Language Association* 70 (1955), pp. 1068–1081.

6. Leibniz's interest in a perfectly exact language dated to his late twenties and
early thirties. Cf. G. W. Leibniz, *Préface à la science générale* (1677); Louis
Couturat, *Opuscules et fragments inédits de Leibniz* (Paris: Alcan, 1903) and *Zur
allgemeinen Characteristik*, in G. W. Leibniz, *Philosophische Werke* (ed. Buchenau
and Cassirer, 1924), vol. I, pp. 30–38. A contemporary commentary on the issues raised by Leibniz's linguistics is to be found in the works of the Pol-
ish-Australian scholar Anna Wierzbicka, who shares many of Leibniz's preoccupations, though not his commitment to a rationalist approach.

7. See my *Cosmopolis*, pp. 101–103.

8. Hanna Fenichel Pitkin, *The Concept of Representation* (Berkeley: University of
California Press, 1967), and Nelson Goodman, *Languages of Art* (Indianapolis:
Hackett, 1976). See also the essays of Marx Wartofsky.

9. See especially Hermann von Helmholtz, *Handbuch der physiologischen Optik*, 3 vols. (Heidelberg: 1856, 1860, and 1867), translated by J. P. C. Southall as *Treatise on Physiological Optics* (Rochester, N.Y.: Optical Society of America, 1924–1925; Dover repr. in 2 vols., 1962).

10. *Tractatus*, props. 4ff., esp. 4.014 and 4.0141; also 2.141 and 4.06.

11. Albert Shalom, *R. G. Collingwood; philosophe et historien* (Paris: Presses Universitaires de France, 1967).

12. The general intellectual background to the debate about a perfect language is set out in Richard Ashcraft's book, *Revolutionary Politics and John Locke's "Two Treatises of Government"* (Princeton, N.J.: Princeton University Press, 1986); see also R. Mousnier, *Les XVIe et XVIIe Siècles* (Paris: Presses Universitaires de France, 1953). A useful survey is the collection *The General Crisis of the Seventeenth Century*, ed. Geoffrey Parker and Leslie M. Smith (London and New York: Routledge, 1978). The immediate reaction to the famous Lisbon earthquake is the subject of Peter Gould's "Lisbon 1755: Enlightenment, Catastrophe, and Communication," in the collection *Geography and Enlightenment*, ed. D. N. Livingstone and C. W. J. Withers (Chicago: University of Chicago Press, 1999), pp. 399–414.

 For present-day parallels, see the essays of Michael Ignatieff in, for instance, *Blood and Belonging* (London: Chatto and Windus; New York: Farrar, Straus and Giroux, 1993).

13. Bertrand Russell, *The ABC of Relativity* (London: Allen and Unwin, 3rd rev. ed., 1960).

14. These matters are treated in depth in the collection of essays edited by Rainer Bauböck, Agnes Heller, and Aristide R. Zolberg, *The Challenge of Diversity* (Aldershot, Eng.: Avebury, and Brookfield, Vt.: Ashgate, 1996).

15. See n. 6, above.

16. Michael Ventris and John Chadwick, *Documents in Mycenaean Greek* (Cambridge: Cambridge University Press, 2nd ed., 1973).

6. Rethinking Method

1. Liddell and Scott, *Greek-English Lexicon*, p. 1091.

2. Feyerabend's autobiography, *Killing Time* (Chicago: University of Chicago Press, 1995), gives a revealing account of his career, which included trying out as an operatic baritone and experimenting with the cinema before he moved sideways, and a bit regretfully, into an academic career.

3. See Björn Gustavsen and Stephen Toulmin, *Beyond Theory* (Amsterdam and Philadelphia: John Benjamins, 1996), pp. 1–4 and 203–225.

4. Claude Bernard, *An Introduction to the Study of Experimental Medicine* (New York: Dover, 1957).

5. In a famous paper written in collaboration with B. Podolsky and N. Rosen, Einstein set out to demonstrate inconsistencies in the new quantum-mechanical approach, but succeeded only in giving rise to a continuing disagreement with Nils Bohr and his colleagues at Copenhagen. See the report *Observation and Interpretation*, ed. S. Körner (New York: Academic Press, 1957), and *Physical Reality*, ed. S. Toulmin (New York: Harper Torchbooks, 1970), pp. 122–142.

6. Cf. Stephen Toulmin and June Goodfield, *The Discovery of Time* (London: Hutchinson, and New York: Harper and Row, 1965, repr. Chicago: University of Chicago Press, 1999), pp. 151–152.

7. Steve Fuller has drawn my attention to Robert Proctor's book, *Value-Free Science?* (Cambridge, Mass.: Harvard University Press, 1991), which is a history of the concepts of "value-freedom" and "objectivity" in the natural sciences: particularly, the link between the Newtonian world view and the idea of a "value-free cosmos," which was later uncritically picked up by the social scientists.

8. Stephen Toulmin, "Concepts and the Explanation of Human Behavior," in *Human Action*, ed. Theodore Mischel (New York: Academic Press, 1969), pp. 71–104.

9. See *Cognition and Categorization*, ed. Eleanor Rosch (Hillsdale, N.J.: Erlbaum, 1978).

10. See Paul Ricoeur, *Hermeneutics and the Human Sciences: Essays on Language, Action, and Interpretation*, edited, translated, and with an introduction by John B. Thomason (Cambridge and New York: Cambridge University Press, 1981). Steve Fuller criticizes what he sees as inconsistent attitudes adopted here to action research and Frankfurt-style social criticism: "Why support one but not the other?" he asks. The answer is that, to the extent that Frankfurt social theorists favor changing institutions, rather than just understanding them, they are on the same side as the action researchers; but a failure to balance suspicion with self-knowledge puts them in other respects in a false position.

11. Richard Gillespie, *Manufacturing Knowledge* (Cambridge: Cambridge University Press, 1991), esp. pp. 182–189.

12. Gustavsen and Toulmin, *Beyond Theory*, p. 203.

13. Christopher Hill, *The World Turned Upside Down* (New York: Viking, 1972); and see my *Cosmopolis*, p. 121:

> Commonwealth sectarians read any proposal to deprive *physical* mass (i.e. Matter) of a spontaneous capacity for action or motion, as going hand in hand with proposals to deprive the human mass (i.e. the "lower orders") of the population of an autonomous capacity for action, and so for social independence.

14. Of all philosophers, John Dewey found the most effective ways of combining abstract thinking with democratic action.

7. Practical Reason and the Clinical Arts

1. Karl Polanyi, *The Great Transformation* (Boston: Beacon Press, 1957; New York: Octagon Books, 1975; first published, 1944). See Frank Knight, *On the History and Method of Economics* (Chicago: University of Chicago Press, 1956–1999), and several of the essays in *Selected Essays by Frank H. Knight*, ed. Ross B. Emmett, vol. I, "'What Is Truth' in Economics?" (Chicago: University of Chicago Press, 1999).

2. The extreme variability of rainfall in the Sahel and other grazing areas of West Africa is discussed in three books: Roy H. Behnke, Jr., Ian Scoones, and Carol Kerven, *Range Ecology at Disequilibrium* (London: Overseas Development Institute, 1993); Chris Reij, Ian Scoones, and Camilla Toulmin, *Sustaining the Soil* (London: Earthscan, 1996); and Ian Scoones, *Living with Uncertainty* (London: Intermediate Technology Publications, 1995). Between them, these books make it clear that the rural economics of the region is rarely, if at all, a matter of "equilibrium": survival depends, rather, on removing all barriers to the free migration of grazing flocks from areas that are hit by drought to those where there is an unusual surplus of water.

3. The quarterly *Economic Development and Cultural Change* was founded at the University of Chicago in 1952 by Bert Hoselitz, with an agenda unlike that most associated with the Chicago Economics Department. It publishes essays covering a broad range of subjects, from Nathan Rosenberg, "The Direction of Technological Change: Inducement Mechanisms and Focusing Devices" (vol. 18, no. 1, part I, October 1969, pp. 1–24), to Howard Spodeck, "The Self-Employed Women's Association (SEWA) in India: Feminist Gandhian Power in Development" (vol. 43, no. 1, October 1994, pp. 193–202). This editorial policy opens its pages to researchers in many fields and academic disciplines, and thus sets an example of what economics can be, when properly situated.

4. Partha Dasgupta, *An Inquiry into Well-Being and Destitution* (Oxford: Clarendon Press, and New York: Oxford University Press, 1983.)

5. The Dasgupta clan has played an major part in the Bengali Brahmin community: Partha Dasgupta's father, A. K. Dasgupta, was a fine economic historian in his own right. See *Epochs of Economic Theory* (repr. Oxford and New York: Blackwell, 1985).

6. Amartya Sen, *Poverty and Famines: An Essay on Entitlement and Deprivation* (Oxford: Clarendon Press, and New York: Oxford University Press, 1981.) Un-

til the day in 1998 when Amartya Sen was awarded the Nobel Prize for Economics, many theorists predicted that he would never get it—especially those who applauded the 1997 winners, Robert Merton and Myron Scholes, whose work was sharply challenged by the near collapse of Long Term Capital Management, whose prime economic advisers they were.

7. See Chapter 6, note 7, above.

8. Schumpeter died four years before the *History* appeared, but the point is in other respects well taken. See W. Brian Arthur, *Increasing Returns and Path Dependence in the Economy* (Ann Arbor: University of Michigan Press, 1994).

9. To borrow an epigram from Imre Lakatos: "For rationalists, Truth flows down from laws or principles to particular cases: for empiricists, it flows up from individual observations to general laws."

10. *Nicomachean Ethics*, II, ii, 3–5.

11. *New York Review of Books*, June 24, 1999, pp. 55–56.

12. Liddell and Scott, *Greek-English Lexicon*, p. 855–856 and 499–500.

13. Robertson Davies, *The Merry Heart* (Toronto: McClelland and Stewart, and Penguin Canada; New York: Viking, 1997), pp. 100–101.

14. See Stephen Toulmin, "Medical Institutions and Their Moral Constraints," in the symposium *Integrity in Health Care Institutions*, ed. Ruth Bulger and Stanley Reiser (Iowa City: University of Iowa Press, 1990) pp. 21–32.

15. See, for instance, Paul Ramsey, *Ethics at the Edges of Life* (New Haven: Yale University Press, 1978).

16. Jeffrey Stout, *The Flight from Authority* (Notre Dame, Ind.: Notre Dame University Press, 1981).

8. Ethical Theory and Moral Practice

1. MacIntyre's position is clearly set out in several of his recent books: notably, *Three Rival Versions of Moral Enquiry* (Notre Dame, Ind.: University of Notre Dame Press, 1990). The core of his position is an account of "traditions": each of us, he claims, is committed—at least, at a given time—to one and only one tradition, which we are either born into or convert to, and accept as an entirety for as long as no further conversion-experience transforms our viewpoint. Those familiar with Kuhn's theory of "scientific revolutions" will recognize in this theory of MacIntyre's a counterpart to Kuhn's theory on the personal level: in particular, there is the same failure on MacIntyre's part to explain how, in one phase of his life—as a Marxist, as a Roman Catholic, or as a "fanatical moderate"—it was rational or reasonable for him to have held a different point of view in an earlier phase.

MacIntyre's theory of traditions has an additional weakness. As Anthony Giddens argues in *The Consequences of Modernity*—writing of our time as being less post-modern than post-traditional—it seriously limits our ways of thinking about our current problems. Giddens does not see our ways of thought as embodied in specific entire traditions: on the contrary, we make up our social and moral activities and perceptions by balancing parts from the various traditions within which our own lives are shaped.

2. "Maxwell's silver typewriter," *The Economist*, June 26, 1999, p. 97.

3. Robertson Davies, *The Merry Heart* (Toronto: McClelland and Stewart, and Penguin Canada; New York: Viking, 1997), p. 185.

4. The importance of the railways to the plots of late-nineteenth-century novels is a topic I was introduced to by Edward Boyle, whose promise as a Conservative politician was matched by his talents as a reader of fine literature.

5. A deeply perceptive (though fictional) account of Virginia Woolf's reactions to life—to her husband Leonard, to their lives together in Richmond and Rodmell, to running the Hogarth Press, but above all to the emotional difficulties of everyday life—can be found in Michael Cunningham's novel *The Hours* (New York: Farrar, Straus and Giroux, 1998). The book's title is a reference to Virginia Woolf's novel *The Years*. Cunningham cites from her *Diaries, 1920–1924*, a letter to Leonard from *Letters, 1936–1941*, and excerpts from the novel *Mrs. Dalloway*, but a great part of the book is a story about people whose lives span the twentieth century from the First World War to the AIDS epidemic, and intersect those of the Woolfs in ways some of which reveal themselves only on the last page.

6. See, for instance, the stories told in James Fadiman and Robert Frager, *Essential Sufism* (San Francisco: HarperCollins, 1997).

7. William Gass, *Fiction and the Figures of Life* (Boston: Godine, 1980), esp. the two essays "Philosophy and the Form of Fiction" (pp. 3–26) and "The Case of the Obliging Stranger" (pp. 225–241).

8. Ibid., pp. 225–241.

9. Ibid., p. 237.

10. Ibid., p. 231.

11. Ibid., p. 235.

12. Davies, *The Merry Heart*, p. 185.

13. See note 1, above.

14. See my essay on the National Commission in the collection of case studies edited by H. T. Engelhardt, Jr., and A. L. Caplan, *Scientific Controversies* (Cambridge: Cambridge University Press, 1985).

15. See Albert R. Jonsen and Stephen Toulmin, *The Abuse of Casuistry* (Berkeley: University of California Press, 1988), chap. 12, pp. 231–249.

16. Here I am using again Rorty's contrast between uppercase abstractions and lowercase particulars discussed in reference to Bradley and Russell in chap. 5, n. 3, above. See, for instance, Rorty, *Consequences of Pragmatism* (Minneapolis: University of Minnesota Press, 1982).

9. The Trouble with Disciplines

1. See chap. 6, note 2, above.
2. Stephen Kern, *The Culture of Time and Space* (Cambridge, Mass.: Harvard University Press, 1983).
3. On Norman Angell and Admiral Mahan, see J. D. B. Miller, *Norman Angell and the Futility of War* (London: Macmillan, 1986), pp. 37–39. For E. H. Carr, the key work is Edward Hallett Carr, *The Twenty Years' Crisis, 1919–1939* (London: Macmillan, 1939; Harper Torchbooks, 1964).
4. Carr, *The Twenty Years' Crisis*, chap. 6, "The Limitations of Realism," pp. 89–94.
5. David Leary, *A Century of Psychology as a Science*, ed. Sigmund Koch and David E. Leary (New York: McGraw-Hill, 1985.)
6. George J. Stigler and Gary S. Becker, "De Gustibus Non Est Disputandum," *American Economic Review* 67 (1977), pp. 76–90.
7. I recall Peter Medawar's drawing this comparison in a conversation, but the same spirit of cautious imaginativeness shines through his books, e.g., *Advice to a Young Scientist* (New York: Harper and Row, 1979).
8. J. B. S. Haldane, "Time in Biology," *Science Progress* 44 (1956), pp. 385–402.
9. On the parallels between organic and cultural evolution, see Robert Boyd and Peter J. Richerson, *Culture and the Evolutionary Process* (Chicago: University of Chicago Press, 1985), and William H. Durham, *Co-evolution* (Stanford, Calif.: Stanford University Press, 1991).
10. See the two books of essays by Samuel Florman, *The Existential Pleasures of Engineering* and *The Introspective Engineer* (New York: St. Martin's Press, 1996): above all the essay "Technology and the Tragic View," in the first of these collections.

    Related issues are dealt with by Michael Davis in *Thinking like an Engineer*, which looks with care at the concept of "professional identity": that is, the personality features that one develops as a result of accepting the commitments of an activity that is both disciplined and socially committed. (For these references, I am particularly grateful to Ton Meijknecht of the Technical University of Delft.)
11. See Ian Mitroff and Elizabeth Denton, *A Spiritual Audit of Corporate America* (San Francisco: Jossey-Bass, 1999).

10. Redressing the Balance

1. Voltaire, *Letters concerning the English Nation* (Oxford and New York: Oxford University Press, 1994), Letter XIV, "On Des Cartes *and Sir* Isaac Newton," pp. 61–66. The original English text of the *Letters* (London: C. Davis and A. Lyon, 1733), as revived by Harcourt Brown in 1967, reads as follows:

> A FRENCHMAN who arrives in *London*, will find Philosophy, like every Thing else, very much chang'd there. He had left the World a *plenum*, and he now finds it a *vacuum*. At *Paris* the Universe is seen, compos'd of Vortices of subtile Matter; but nothing like it is seen in London. . . .
>
> According to your *Cartesians*, every Thing is perform'd by an Impulsion, of which we have very little Notion; and according to Sir *Isaac Newton*, 'tis by an Attraction, the Cause of which is as much unknown to us. . . .
>
> So the irony continues, though Voltaire's eventual allegiance to Newtonianism is clear from the subsequent Letters XV–XVII, pp. 67–86.

2. For the distinction between dissidents and dissenters, see my Jefferson Lecture, "A Dissenter's Tale," reprinted in *Graven Images* (Madison, Wisc., 1998), vol. 5, pp. 1ff.

3. On Richard Chenevix-Trench's manifesto, linking the proposal for *The Oxford English Dictionary* to the British Empire's *mission civilisatrice*, see Simon Winchester, *The Surgeon of Crowthorne* (London and New York: Viking, 1998; Penguin, 1999), esp. chap 5, pp. 91ff. This book also describes the unexpected role in the compilation of the O.E.D. of the collaboration between Dr. James Murray, the director of the project, and William Chester Minor, a veteran physician from the American Civil War, who was at the time living in the Broadmoor Asylum for Criminal Lunatics at Crowthorne, Berkshire, not far from Oxford, as a murderer.

4. Thomas Hobbes, *Leviathan*, chap. XXIX, "*Of those things that Weaken, or tend to the Dissolution of a Common-wealth*"; cf. the critical edition by Richard Flathman and David Johnston (New York: Norton, 1997), p. 169.

5. Stephen Toulmin, "The Role of Transnational NGOs in Global Affairs" (Tokyo: *Occasional Papers* 4, Peace Research Institute, International Christian University, 1997). For a more skeptical view of NGOs, see the *Economist*, January 29, 2000, p. 25.

6. See David Keys's book *Catastrophe* (London: Ballantine Books, 2000), which argues that the consequences of large-scale natural disasters are not just geographical and local, but social and political. He points to the drastic changes in many countries in the years after 535 A.D. and finds documentary evidence of climatic changes in many parts of the world, including spectacular sunsets,

world-wide cloud cover, and unusual rainfall patterns, like those after the 1883 eruption of Krakatoa in the Indonesian archipelago. In the late sixth century, such changes seem to have led to outbreaks of plague, population shifts, and even political and religious changes. Keys speculates that an explosion of Krakatoa in 535 even larger than that of 1883 separated Sumatra and Java, flung dust into the upper atmosphere, and upset both the balance in the ecological environment of rats and also the economic advantages of many countries.

A lesser, but still major, eruption shortly before 1619, whose location is not yet clear, may have produced widespread high-altitude clouds, generated the climatic changes in seventeenth-century Northern Europe that were associated with the loss of agricultural land, and provided—among other things—the setting for the festivals on the frozen Thames described in Virginia Woolf's novel *Orlando*.

7. Timothy Garton Ash, "The Direction of European History," in *The Tanner Lectures on Human Values*, vol. 20 (Salt Lake City: University of Utah Press, 1989), p. 191.

8. Quentin Skinner, *Reason and Rhetoric in the Philosophy of Hobbes* (Cambridge: Cambridge University Press, 1996), esp. p. 253 and pp. 356–357.

9. See John Shotter, *Conversational Realities* (London and Thousand Oaks, Calif.: Sage, 1993).

10. See the symposium "Platonic Insults," in *Common Knowledge*, vol. 2, no. 2 (Fall 1993), pp. 19–80.

11. Benjamin Farrington, *Science and Politics in the Ancient World* (Oxford and New York: Oxford University Press, 1940).

11. The Varieties of Experience

1. The confusions involved in assuming that we could ever talk about a purely private object or sensation were a central theme in Ludwig Wittgenstein's later lectures on the philosophy of psychology, and in his *Philosophical Investigations* (Oxford: Blackwell, 1953).

2. Julian E. Orr, *Talking about Machines: An Ethnography of a Modern Job* (Ph.D. dissertation, Cornell University, 1970; Ithaca, N.Y.: ILR Press, 1977); Julian E. Orr, "Sharing Knowledge, Celebrating Identity: War Stories and Community Memory in a Service Culture," in *Collective Remembering: Memory in Society*, ed. David S. Middleton and Derek Edwards (London: Sage Publications, 1990), pp. 169–189; and Julian E. Orr, "Contested Knowledge," *Anthropology of Work Review* 12 (1991), pp. 12–17.

3. Michael Polanyi, *The Tacit Dimension* (Gloucester, Mass.: Peter Smith, 1983).

4. In her ingeniously titled book, *Knowing Words* (Ithaca, N.Y.: Cornell University Press, 1992), pp. 96–98, Lisa Raphals uses the story of the chef Ding and

his Lord, reported in *Chuang Tzü* (3.31), to illustrate the Chinese counterpart of *metis*, as "a spontaneous perception that can be transmitted but not appropriated, grasped but not seen." On this topic, see also Angus C. Graham's commentary, *Chuang Tzü: The Inner Chapters* (London and Boston: Allen and Unwin, 1981), pp. 62–64, 86.

5. Raphals, *Knowing Words*, pp. 97–98, and Graham, *Chuang Tzü*, pp. 62–64.

6. Gary Klein, *Sources of Power* (Cambridge, Mass.: MIT Press, 1997), esp. chap. 7, pp. 89–110. Klein's report on the experience of this fire chief had a tragic sequel in late 1999, when a very similar catastrophe in Worcester, Massachusetts, widely reported at the time, led to the death of six firemen.

7. Isaiah Berlin, *The Sense of Reality*, ed. Henry Hardy (New York: Farrar, Straus, and Giroux, 1996), pp. 45–46.

8. Marcel Detienne and Jean-Pierre Vernant, *Cunning Intelligence in Greek Culture and Society*, trans. Janet Lloyd (Hassocks, Sussex: Harvester Press, and Atlantic Highlands, N.J.: Humanities Press, 1978), pp. 12–24.

9. *Oxford English Dictionary*, p. 1544.

10. *Nicomachean Ethics*, VI, viii, 9, 1142a.

11. The connection between Nietzsche and Emerson, which comes as a surprise to most American readers, was pointed out to me by Irena Makarushka at Holy Cross College. In recent years, Nietzsche has been rescued from the embrace of the Nazis, and blame for this misleading association is increasingly placed on his sister Elisabeth, who married an extreme nationalist and anti-Semitic politician, Bernhard Förster, and used her brother's writings as a source of propaganda. (The articles in the current *Encyclopedia Britannica* on Friedrich Nietzsche and related topics deserve praise in this respect.)

    Few people today think of Nietzsche as a Kantian, but the links between Kant's moral theory and the more violent twentieth-century political ideologies—though in a form Nietzsche himself did not agree with—are well analyzed in Isaiah Berlin's essay "Kant as an Unfamiliar Source of Nationalism" (*The Sense of Reality*, pp. 232–248). As Berlin adds, in his essay "Marxism and the International in the Nineteenth Century" (*The Sense of Reality*, pp. 117–167), the historical changes of the time gave many nineteenth-century writers ill-assorted bedfellows. Consider Karl Marx's reaction to "the sense of human atomisation"—

    > of the dehumanisation [as Berlin puts it] of which vast impersonal institutions, bureaucracies, factories, armies, political parties were at once a cause and a symptom, with a consequent feeling of mounting suffocation to which Nietzsche, Carlyle and Ibsen, Thoreau and Whitman, Tolstoy, Ruskin and Flaubert had, in their very different ways, given profound poetical expression . . .

Marx (Berlin comments) "translated this horror of anthill life" into "an inevitable phase in human development, possessing its own powerfully creative aspects in the concentration and the rationalisation of human brain-power and energy" (*The Sense of Reality*, pp. 148–149).

12. To see how, in general, *phronesis* contrasts with *metis*, refer to Lisa Raphals, *Knowing Words*, esp. p. 5, n. 14. Nevertheless Martha Nussbaum, a fine reader of Aristotle, sees little difference between *phronesis* and *metis*.

13. *Oxford English Dictionary*, p. 930.

12. The World of Where and When

1. Freda White, *Three Rivers of France* (London: Faber, 1952; illustrated with photographs by Michael Busselle, London: Pavilion Books, 1989). For Michel de Montaigne, see chap. 2, n. 7, above.

2. Jenny Balfour-Paul, *Indigo* (London: British Museum Press, 1998).

3. This reference to the BBC is not just a casual one. In the 1990s, I found it especially rewarding to listen to World Service at any time of the day or night, especially night. After honing their reputation for integrity during the Second World War and later the long years of the Cold War, BBC World Service has become in many ways the representative post-1989 voice. Most of all, the program *Outlook* shows the people of the world to one another, not by talking in theoretical terms about the virtues of diversity, solidarity, or other abstractions, but by presenting slices of life from here or there that speak for themselves. The topics are unpredictably varied—music groups from Ulster or Québec, Karnataka or Gambia; evidence of George Mallory's attempt to climb Mount Everest on the slope of the mountain itself; a Viennese wind band that plays instruments made from vegetables; and a community in the South African desert that fights drought by letting their children play on a carousel built by a local Afrikaans engineer, so that their rotations raise water from an underground aquifer.

4. Wittgenstein's disapproval of the Bloomsbury Circle is described in John Maynard Keynes's book *Essays in Biography* (New York: W. W. Norton, 1951). In the biography *Ludwig Wittgenstein: The Duty of Genius* (London: Cape, and New York: Free Press, 1990), Ray Monk quotes Wittgenstein as remarking that he himself belonged to a culture that ended with the death of Schumann.

5. Friedrich Waismann, *Wittgenstein and the Vienna Circle* (Oxford: Blackwell, and New York: Barnes and Noble, 1979).

6. Philip R. Shields, *Logic and Sin in the Writings of Wittgenstein* (Chicago: University of Chicago Press, 1993).

7. This term is Alvin Weinberg's, coined for Edward Shils's debate on scientific choice originally published in *Minerva,* and reprinted as *Criteria for Scientific Development* (Cambridge, Mass.: MIT Press, 1968).

8. In a paper presented at the Third International Wittgenstein Symposium at Kirchberg-am-Wechsel in 1978, Johann Christian Marek of Graz pointed out the similarity between the image of the ladder that Wittgenstein uses at the end of the *Tractatus* (props. 6.54 and 7) and the arguments that end Sextus Empiricus's *Adversus Mathematicos* and *Adversus Logicos* (Vienna: Hölder-Pichler-Tempsky, 1979), pp. 94–98.

   The question therefore arises: How did Wittgenstein get to know about Sextus and the skeptical tradition in Antiquity? This use of the ladder image—Richard Schmitt argues—is not the only mark of Sextus's influence: the whole idea of the philosopher as having to suspend judgment, and stand by the experience of ordinary life, can also be paralleled there, as Montaigne also knew. Much of this can be found in the *Sprachkritik* of Mauthner, to which Wittgenstein alludes in prop. 4.0031, but he may well have known of Sextus's works—Schmitt adds—from the tutors with whom he studied at home.

9. See Waismann, *Wittgenstein and the Vienna Circle.*

10. Wallace Stevens, *Notes toward a Supreme Fiction,* sec. x., ll. 16–18.

13. Postscript: Living with Uncertainty

1. George Meredith, *Modern Love,* stanza 50.

2. Wittgenstein, *Tractatus,* prop. 6.342: this should be read in the context of the whole passage from 6.341 to 6.346. The present quotation comes from a new translation of the *Tractatus* by Richard Schmitt, which returns to the original German and interprets the far from self-explanatory text in a way that relates it to the ideas of those scientists whom Wittgenstein is known to have read and admired: notably, Heinrich Hertz and Ludwig Boltzmann.

3. Stephen Jay Gould's book, *Wonderful Life: The Burgess Shale and the Nature of History* (New York: W. W. Norton, 1989), reports on the fossils of anomalous animals and plants in a score of extinct phyla from the Cambrian Era, at a time when the precursors of mammals are barely detectable among them. Starting from these strange fossils, he argues that the course of organic evolution is anything but predetermined by "providential" Design.

4. Harold Lasswell, *The Future of Political Science* (New York: Prentice-Hall, 1963; originally published in the 1930s), esp. chap. 5, pp. 95–122.

5. Much popular science today assumes that the "red shift" in the spectra from distant galaxies and other astronomical objects can only be interpreted as evidence

that the present state of the Universe is the outcome of an expansion from an initially compressed state some 10 or 20 thousand million years ago. Yet this interpretation ignores a dozen methodological problems, and rival views have never been ruled out of court. On the methodological difficulties, see Toulmin and Goodfield, *The Discovery of Time*, pp. 250–263. As for alternative views, the Steady State theory—long advanced by Fred Hoyle—is revived in a striking book by Hoyle's colleague Thomas Gold, *The Deep Hot Biosphere* (New York: Springer Verlag, 1999, with a foreword by Freeman Dyson), which points to many phenomena that suggest unorthodox origins for life, and other hypotheses currently as heretical as the theory of Continental Drift was for so long.

6. According to her daughter, Mary Catherine Bateson, this remark was quoted by the *Reader's Digest* after Margaret Mead's death, but its origin remains unclear.

7. Except for choral singers who know Brahms's *The Song of Destiny*, few English-speaking readers may be familiar with Hölderlin's *Hyperions Schicksalslied*. This poem catches strikingly the tensions between the ideals of a dreamer and the realities of everyday life (the following translation is my own): "You wander overhead in the light, / softly pillowed, ye blessed Spirits! / glittering Godly breaths / lightly move you, / as an artist's finger / her holy harp-strings. / Free from Fate, like the sleeping / infant, breathe the heavenly ones. / Chastely retained / in a modest bud, / blooms for ever / your Soul, / and your blessed eyes / gaze on calm / eternal clarity. / But to us is granted / no place to rest in: / shrinking and falling, / suffering humans / blindfold from one / hour to another, / like water flung / from cliff to cliff, / year long down into the Unknown."

8. See, e.g., A. Dwight Culler, *Poetry and Criticism of Matthew Arnold* (Boston: Houghton Mifflin, 1961), pp. 161–162, 562–564.

9. Howard Adelman and Astri Suhrke, *The Path of a Genocide* (London and New Brunswick, N.J.: Transaction Publishers, 1999).

10. Pierre Hadot, *Qu'est-ce que la philosophie antique?* (Paris: Gallimard, 1995).

11. In her poem for President Clinton's inauguration, Maya Angelou spoke to those who cherish the needs of the world—those of human beings, young and old, strangers and brothers, and all living beings equally:

> History, despite its wrenching pain,
> cannot be unlived, but if faced
> with courage, need not be lived again.
> Lift up your eyes
> upon this day breaking for you.
> Give birth again
> to the dream.

Index